INSIGHT GUIDES

The world's largest collection of visual travel guides

MONTREAL

Edited by Stephen Scharper and Hilary Cunningham
Update Editor: Joanna Ebbutt
Principal Photography: Carl and Ann Purcell

Editorial Director: Brian Bell

APA PUBLICATIONS
Part of the Langenscheidt Publishing Group

INSIGHT GUIDES
Montreal

CONTACTING THE EDITORS: Although every effort
is made to provide accurate information in this
publication, we live in a fast-changing world and would
appreciate it if readers would call our attention to any
errors or outdated information that may occur by
writing to us at Apa Publications,
P.O. Box 7910, London SE1 1WE, England.
Fax: (44) 171-403-0290.
e-mail: insight@apaguide.demon.co.uk.

First Edition 1991
Second Edition (updated) 1999

Distributed in the United States by
Langenscheidt Publishers Inc.
46–35 54th Road, Maspeth, NY 11378
Fax: (718) 784 -0640

Distributed in Canada by
Prologue Inc.
1650 Lionel Bertrand Blvd., Boisbriand
Québec, Canada J7H 1N7
Tel: (450) 434-0306. Fax: (450) 434-2627

Distributed in the UK & Ireland by
GeoCenter International Ltd
The Viables Centre, Harrow Way
Basingstoke, Hampshire RG22 4BJ
Fax: (44) 1256-817988

Distributed in Australia & New Zealand by
Hema Maps Pty. Ltd
24 Allgas Street, Slacks Creek 4127
Brisbane, Australia
Tel: (61) 7 3290 0322. Fax: (61) 7 3290 0478

Worldwide distribution enquiries:
APA Publications GmbH & Co. Verlag KG
(Singapore branch)
38 Joo Koon Road, Singapore 628990
Tel: 65-8651600. Fax: 65-8616438

Printed in Singapore by
Insight Print Services (Pte) Ltd
38 Joo Koon Road, Singapore 628990
Fax: 65-8616438

Discovery CHANNEL®

This guidebook combines the interests
and enthusiasms of two of the
world's best known information pro-
viders: Insight Guides, whose range of titles
has set the standard for visual travel guides
since 1970, and Discovery Channel, the
world's premier source of nonfiction television programming.

The editors of Insight Guides provide both
practical advice and general understanding
about a destination's history, culture, institutions and people. Discovery Channel and
its Web site, www.discovery.com, help millions of viewers explore their world from the
comfort of their own home and also encourage them to explore it firsthand.

As project editors of this book, Insight
Guides appointed a team, **Stephen
Scharper** and **Hilary Cunningham**,
who also happen to be husband and wife.
Scharper, at the time an editor of Orbis Books
and Twenty-Third Publications, has contributed articles to numerous religious and secular publications. He has since abandoned
a comfortable home and job to accompany
his wife on her field research in Arizona, Mex-
ico, and Guatemala, and has followed that
with a doctoral program in religious studies
at McGill University in Montreal. Cunningham,
project editor of the first edition of *Insight
Guide: Canada,* brought to bear her training
as an urban anthropologist; she served as
Insight's consulting editor while pursuing her
PhD in cultural anthropology at Yale.

For this book, the couple assembled a
team of writers and photographers who set
about capturing "the two solitudes" of this
bilingual city.

Lysiane Gagnon, who wrote the introduc-
tory chapter, is a native of Montreal and a
journalist with over 20 years' experience. She
has long been a political columnist for *La
Presse,* Canada's major French-speaking daily
and is a frequent contributor to magazines,
radio, and television. She has won two National Newspaper Awards and written several
books, including *Chroniques Politiques,* a
collection of columns on national politics.

Scharper

Cunningham

Gagnon

Legault

Foran

Ladky

Sher

Lyon

Mark Kingwell, a distinguished journalist whose contributions range from history to ice hockey, is a former member of the Rusty Staub "*Grande Orange*" fan club of the Montreal Expos. He holds degrees from the Universities of Toronto and Edinburgh, and has taken a doctorate in political philosophy at Yale University. He continues to hold in creative tension his enthusiasm for sports and his academic career.

Charles Foran and **Mary Ladky**, another married team, were major contributors, writing several of the Places chapters as well as features. Foran, a widely-published fiction writer, holds a BA degree from the University of Toronto, and both he and Ladky hold masters degrees in literature from University College, Dublin. Foran's incisive reviews and commentaries inform the pages of the *Montreal Gazette*, *Canadian Forum*, the *Globe and Mail*, *Saturday Night*, and *Insight Guide: Canada*. Ladky, who has taught in the US, and, with Foran, in China.

Matthew Parfitt, a Montreal aficionado with a moderate interest in baseball, writes authoritatively about gardens, parks, stadiums and bohemian mores. His vibrant writing appears in *Insight Guide: Canada*, as well as numerous periodicals and journals.

Emil Sher writes with insight and first-hand experience of Jewish life in his native Montreal. His essays have been published in the *Globe and Mail*, *Compass* and numerous other journals, and his work has been broadcast on the Canadian Broadcasting Company.

Nancy Lyon, some of whose photography enlivens this volume, also plied her literary skills in the Day Trips chapter. A Montreal resident, Lyon has had considerable success in her career as a travel writer. As a travel columnist for the *Montreal Gazette*, she has rafted down the rapids of the Rouge and Batiscan rivers, biked through the mountains of Estrie, Quebec, and explored the culturally rich streets of Quebec City. She describes herself as "an American, born in Nashville, raised in Indianapolis, schooled in Virginia, but an exile at heart." Lyon also updated an edition of *Insight Pocket Guide: Montreal*.

Louise Legault, another Montreal resident and distinguished travel writer, channels her self-described "fanaticism" for Montreal into her article on festivals and her piece on shopping in the Travel Tips section. A translator and former editor of a Montreal travel magazine, Legault is co-author of *Montreal, the International City*, and has been working on a tour guide to Quebec.

Katherine Snyder, the diligent compiler of the fact-packed Travel Tips section, has a remarkable talent for being "imaginatively efficient." An expert on café culture, she has put together a comprehensive guide to Montreal's best offerings.

This edition of *Insight Guide: Montreal* has been throughly updated by **Joanna Ebbutt**, a writer and editor specializing in travel who has previously worked for Insight as the author of *Insight Pocket Guide: Toronto*. As well as updating the color section of the book, Joanna has completely overhauled Travel Tips to keep pace with the many new hotels, restaurants and facilities in this dynamic city.

Like all Insight Guides, this book owes an enormous amount to its pictures. The images represented here are mostly the work of **Carl** and **Ann Purcell**, an internationally known photographic and writing team based in the Washington DC area. They have written and illustrated two books, *The Traveling Photographer* (Amphoto) and *A Guide to Travel Writing and Photography* (Writer's Digest Books), and have also photographed *Insight Guide: Bermuda*. They fell in love with the diverse visual excitement of Montreal and delighted in discovering "the hidden nooks and crannies in a truly multicultural city."

The editors of this book would like to give a special thanks to **Archives Canada**, to the **Canadian Hockey Hall of Fame**, to **Gilles Bengle** of the Greater Montreal Convention and Tourism Bureau, and to **Diane Di Tomasso** of the Quebec Government Office in London. They also want to thank the people of Montreal, whose convivial spirit shines through in this book.

CONTENTS

History

Montreal: A Tale of Two Solitudes
by *Lysiane Gagnon* 23

Decisive Dates
by *Hilary Cunningham* 32

Beginnings: The River and the Mountain
by *Mark Kingwell* 35

Religious Roots
by *Hilary Cunningham* 44

The Coming of the British
by *Mark Kingwell* 49

A Woman's Lot
by *Hilary Cunningham* 52

The Habitants
by *Hilary Cunningham* 56

Conflict and Confederation
by *Mark Kingwell* 60

Games for Idle Hours
by *Hilary Cunningham* 67

Modern Montreal
by *Mark Kingwell* 71

The Quiet Revolution
by *Mark Kingwell* 76

Features

The Montrealer
by *Charles Foran* 81

The Jews of Montreal
by *Emil Sher* 87

Politics, Language and Identity
by *Charles Foran* 95

Intellectuals versus Streetfighters
by *Mark Kingwell* 101

The Life and Times of Pierre Trudeau
by *Mark Kingwell* 102

Why Ice Hockey Matters
by *Mark Kingwell* 107

Preceding pages: French motif; decorated window.

Places

Introduction
by Stephen Scharper **121**

Old Montreal
by Charles Foran **125**

A Living Language
by Charles Foran **132**

Festival City
by Louise Legault **147**

Downtown
by Mary Ladky **151**

**The Grande Dame of
Sherbrooke Street**
by Mary Ladky **156**

Bohemian Montreal
by Matthew Parfitt **173**

The Jazz Scene
by Matthew Parfitt **179**

Westmount and Outremont
by Mary Ladky **183**

Park Mount Royal
by Hilary Cunningham **186**

Outremont Cafés
by Mary Ladky **191**

St Joseph's Oratory
by Hilary Cunningham **192**

Stadiums and Gardens
by Matthew Parfitt **199**

Day Trips
by Nancy Lyon **209**

Maps

Montreal **122**
Old Montreal **126**
Downtown **152**
Olympic Park and
Botanical Garden **200**

TRAVEL TIPS

Getting Acquainted
The Place 226
Climate 226
Economy & Government 226
Time Zones 226

Planning the Trip
What to Wear 226
Entry Regulations 226
Health 227
Money Matters 227
Public Holidays 227
Getting There 227
Traveling with Children 228
Disabled Visitors 228
Tourist Information 228

Practical Tips
Security & Crime 229
Medical Services 229
Extension of Stay 229
Business Hours 229
Tipping 229
Media 229
Postal Services 229
Telecoms 230
Consulates 230

Getting Around
On Arrival 230
Public Transport 230
Taxis 230
Car Rentals 230
On Foot 230
Bicycle Rental 231

Where to Stay
Hotels 231
Longer-Term Residences 233
Bed & Breakfast 233
Residences/Student Housing . 233

Eating Out
Where to Eat 234
Drinking Notes 236

Attractions
Things to Do 237
Areas of Interest 237
Churches 237
Parks 238
Tours & Cruises 238

Culture
Museums 239
Art Galleries 240
Concerts & Opera 240
Theaters & Movies 240
Nightlife 240
Jazz 240

Festivals
Calendar of Events 241

Shopping
General 242
Shopping Areas 243
Department Stores 243

Sports
Participant 243
Spectator 244

Language
General 245
Words & Phrases 245

Further Reading
General 250
Other Insight Guides 250

Art/Photo Credits 251
Index 252

MONTREAL: A TALE OF TWO SOLITUDES

Viewed from the south, Montreal reads like an open book. The left-hand page, spreading to the west, is in English. The right-hand page, opening to the east, is in French. But ethnic groups from all over the world populate the twin pages. Close the book, and the cover is in French. Yet the text is bilingual, with strong cosmopolitan accents.

Simple? Not really. Montreal is a city of obvious charm. It offers a gentle way of life exceptional in North America, and it is one of those rare cities with a lively downtown where an evening walk is perfectly safe. But Montreal is nonetheless a city of tensions – not racial but linguistic. They are resolved, day after day, in a lifestyle developed over the years by a population that has long since mastered the art of compromise.

Montreal is the second largest French city in the world (after Paris), where the sidewalk cafés and the breakfast croissants are not considered at all exotic. It was built by Scottish merchants, whose Victorian homes remind you of London and Edinburgh. It is the city where, with French the official language, you can pass your whole life speaking nothing but English.

Montreal is also an Italian, Greek, Vietnamese, Haitian, or Lebanese city; a city of the Ashkenazi Jews and the Sephardic Jews. You never have far to walk to find lemon grass and grape leaves, falafels or sea urchins, kiwis and raw-milk paste, fresh pasta and Paris-style baguettes – not to mention the world's best bagels. (No, not in Manhattan, nor Brooklyn, will you find bagels more golden on the outside and more tender on the inside than those you buy in Montreal, fresh out of the old wood-stoked ovens of Fairmount and St-Viateur streets, whose recipe emanates from the *stetls* of Romania.)

In Montreal you can see French and European films while they're playing in Paris, and American films while they're playing in New York. This is a city where the newsstands bend under their stacks of dailies in French and English – from Montreal, from Paris, the *Times* of New York and the *Times* of London.

Here the TV offers two public channels in French and two in English, two commercial channels in French and one in English, plus

the big US networks and a channel that rebroadcasts the best TV programs of France, Belgium and Switzerland.

Beginnings: The origins of Montreal lie in the St Lawrence River, from whose waters, in 1642, appeared the founders of the humble little French town christened Ville-Marie. The vestiges of Ville-Marie are still to be seen, not far from the docks, in the beautiful stone buildings, humble chapels, and narrow paving-stone streets of "Old Montreal."

French Canadians are not a "minority" here as are the Puerto Ricans of New York, the Cubans of Miami, or the Asians of Los

Preceding pages: Jacques Cartier Bridge; Raymond Mason's "Illuminated Crowd" sculpture on McGill College Avenue; view from the port; tourist carriages; sleighing to the ski slopes. Left, café society: bring your own dog. Above, boy at a Christ Church wedding.

Angeles. The forebears of the *Montréalais* were the first European settlers in North America – in 1534, they founded a sedentary society organized on a Western model. Nor are French Canadians simply exiled French Europeans: from as early as the 17th century, they established a society that was distinct from that of their European ancestors.

The city of Quebec, the only city in America to be surrounded by ramparts like the fortified cities of Europe, was founded in 1608, when North America was a continent known only to the Amerindians and Inuits. This little cluster of colonists, trappers, and adventurers dispatched the great *voyageurs*

who discovered the Mississippi and the Rocky Mountains to the west, and who founded the first colonies from which would issue the great cities of the northeastern US.

In the US, only Louisiana has retained some of the traits of the far-off days of French rule, through the Cajun culture and a Civil Code inherited from the Napoleonic era. In Canada, however, the descendants of the first French colonists have multiplied to form a mighty minority who live, learn, and work in French – 6 million people (nearly a quarter of all Canadians), of whom 5 million are in the province of Quebec.

Unique status: With over seven million inhabitants, Quebec is the second largest province in Canada after Ontario, which numbers 9½ million. Canada is a federation, dividing its political power between the central government and the 10 provinces. Each province has its own parliament and relatively extensive powers, especially in education, health, and social affairs, as well as a goodly share of the economic ones.

Because the province of Quebec is the main home of the French Canadians and the only territory where they comprise the majority of the electorate, its successive governments have gradually acquired additional special powers, following upon accords with the federal government. Quebec is the only province that collects its own taxes, for example, and it maintains a network of delegations abroad functioning somewhat after the fashion of consulates.

Quebec is likewise the only province whose official language is French, although the large English-speaking minority reaps the ongoing benefits of a complete network of schools, universities, and hospitals, entirely at public expense, and functioning in English. It is in the Montreal vicinity that immigrants make their homes – turning this region into a cosmopolitan, bilingual islet.

In 1760 the British conquest changed the face of the continent. French Canadians, suddenly deprived of their elite, who returned to France, turned inward upon their own little community, under the protective wing of the only institution left to them, the Catholic church, whose precepts they observed by reproducing at a rate historians find nowhere outside of China.

Long undereducated, and thought of only as cheap labor, the French-speaking Québécois today make up one of the most sophisticated populations of the continent. In just a few years, beginning with the close of the 1950s, the Québécois decided to make up for lost time. They modernized their educational system, took on more public responsibility, and shook off the tutelage of the church. Once the "City of a Hundred Belfreys," Montreal became the cutting edge of this quiet revolution – appropriately named, since it was accomplished without civil violence.

Today the city's monasteries, convents, and seminaries are condominiums, and its churches serve as recreation centers.

This period of intense intellectual and cultural ferment inevitably engendered a strong independence movement, which continues to this day. In 1980, a popular referendum came out 60 percent against a secessionist project proposed by the sovereignty government of René Lévesque. However, aspirations for autonomy, always within the limits of a parliamentary democracy, remain lively. Despite the adoption of language laws by various provincial governments – such as the controversial Bill 101 in 1977 – requiring

vive the Commission de Protection de la Langue Française.

Under the French regime, Montreal played second fiddle to the city of Quebec. It was only with the English conquest and the arrival of the Scottish merchants that Montreal "took off" to become the great metropolis of Canada – a position it retained until the 1950s, when Toronto supplanted it as Canada's center of commerce and finance.

The proud memory of this period remains in the beautiful Victorian buildings of the Golden Square Mile, that 19th-century fief of the first great Canadian businesses, and in the campus of McGill, the first university of

commercial signs to be written entirely in French, many francophones are still haunted by the fear of assimilation, and all the more so now that demography is no longer on their side. The pendulum has swung to the other extreme, and the Québécois birth rate is among the lowest in the world.

In the summer of 1996, the provincial government introduced a series of amendments to the province's 19-year-old French Language Charter, one of which was to re-

Left, Christ Church's reflected glory. <u>Above</u>, Montreal Trust Building.

Canada, on Rue Sherbrooke. A great part of the architectural legacy of Montreal is of British inspiration. Indeed, Montrealers visiting London experience a sense of having been there before: a thousand-and-one details – in the architecture, the street map, and the statuary – remind them of their own city.

Anglophones and francophones: In Montreal, the two great founding peoples of Canada live side by side. Of the 3 million inhabitants of the metropolitan area, some 70 percent are French-speaking, 15 percent use English as their native tongue, and the remainder are more or less recent immigrants who, with the passing of the years, have been integrated into either of the two great linguistic groups – often to the anglophone, so potent is the global sway of the English language.

Coexistence has almost always been peaceful. But the francophone and anglophone communities – the "two solitudes," as Canadian novelist Hugh MacLennan described them – have developed into two parallel, homogeneous societies. They have emerged side by side without ever melding, each with its own schools, colleges and universities, hospitals, newspapers, novels, theaters, business communities, and insurance companies. Each community has its own proletariat

While most Montrealers are bilingual, rarely does their network of friends and activities encompass both communities to any significant extent. Francophones and anglophones meet at work, in business, or at Le Centre Molson, where they cheer with equal enthusiasm "their" hockey team, the Montreal Canadiens. But Montreal resolutely remains the city of two solitudes. There have been a number of intermarriages over the years, but one language finally prevails in most partnerships, and the family is acculturated to one of the two language groups.

This division obviously undermines the cultural potential of Montreal, and the mis-

and bourgeoisie – the anglophone bourgeoisie is in Westmount, on the southwest slope of Mont Royal, while the francophone bourgeoisie is located in Outremont, on the northeast side of the same mountain.

Even the night crawlers of Montreal have parallel habits. The centers of anglophone night life are the pubs and discos of Crescent and Bishop streets; francophone night life is in the sidewalk cafés and bistros of Rue St-Denis. But these are not ghettos, and many Montrealers like an occasional stroll on the "other side," becoming temporary tourists in their home town.

understandings engendered by mutual ignorance sharpen the linguistic tensions. French, long considered to be the tongue of "peasants," has been the dominant language since the early 1970s, even in large private business. Francophones, who once found themselves relegated to second-class jobs, have vigorously asserted themselves in the business area, and now control a great proportion of Montreal's erstwhile anglophone institutions. Not all anglophones welcome this development, and not all francophones have forgotten the old vexations. And both communities still battle, deploying the weapons of law and administrative measures, to attract new immigrants.

The basic problem is that each of the two communities perceives itself as a vulnerable minority. The anglophones, a majority in Canada but a minority in Quebec, see their numbers dwindling, and fear for the survival of their institutions. The francophones, in the majority in Quebec but in the minority in Canada, have the feeling of speaking an ever-threatened language. All of this sparks endless political battles – battles which fortunately have remained verbal.

Montreal is not Belfast. In daily living (let the politicians go on clashing) Montrealers have developed the art of good-humored coexistence. On Saint Patrick's Day, thousands of francophones don the green and descend to Ste Catherine's Street for the parade, celebrating with their anglophone fellow-citizens and cheering the floats that depict the history of the large Irish minority of Montreal, who have been a fixture here since the mid-19th century.

Québéoois French: The French spoken in Montreal is shot through with English expressions, and Quebec English is laced with gallicisms. An anglophone Montrealer will speak of a *manifestation* instead of a demonstration, a *cocktail* for a cocktail party, a *convention* for a contract, and a *dépanneur* for a convenience store.

While Montreal has two languages, it also has a throng of ethnic and cultural communities. The two most populous – Italian and Jewish – are also the oldest. The immigration of southern Italians and European Jews goes back to the 19th century, continuing through the first decades of the 20th century. Their respective contributions have melded into the city as a whole, like a powerful, fecund graft. Italian and Yiddish are scarcely ever spoken any more, and these two communities, where the rate of French-English bilingualism is remarkably high, have long been integrated into the common life of Montreal.

Their family closeness, however, has enabled them to retain more of their own characteristics than other European immigrants.

Left and above, Montreal's love of festivals takes creativity onto the streets.

Germans, Hungarians, Slavs and Scandinavians, for example, have, in fewer than two generations, melted into the anglophone community. True, the motivation for this separatism is no longer economic, but there are still Italian quarters in the northeastern corner of the isle of Montreal, where Montrealers of Sicilian origin make a living from prosperous construction businesses, and from open-air markets.

There are also municipalities with a large Jewish majority, such as Côte-St-Luc and Hampstead. The Ashkenazi community of Montreal is especially noteworthy in that, of all the Diaspora communities, it is home to

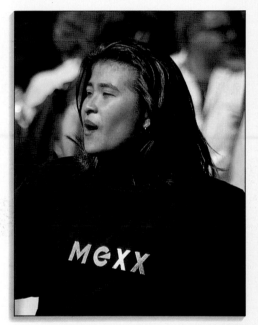

the largest proportion of survivors from Nazi Germany. This makes the community very sensitive to Quebec nationalism, even in peaceful form. Characterized by an extremely high level of education, the Jewish community is distinguished in all domains, especially medicine, and it has left a deep mark on the intellectual life of Montreal.

The European immigration, which formed so many successive layers in so many quarters of Montreal, has given way in recent years to mighty waves of immigrants from Asia, the Antilles, and the Near East. These new groups have transformed the face of the city. Haitians work the taxis, Chinese and Greeks the fast-food restaurants, and Moroccan Jews the garment district. Tomorrow their children will be physicians, professors, and – why not? – prime ministers.

New communities: Rue St-Laurent is the best place to find the traces of these new communities. Running from the St Lawrence River all the way to the River of the Prairies, it divides the isle of Montreal in two – the francophone part to the east, the anglophone to the west. This street was the traditional path of the immigrants as they got off their boats and gradually made their way "up" to the quarters of the lower middle class in the

postmodern restaurants, it is now the place to go if you want to find youth of every extraction, in an exciting mix of colors and tongues. Moreover, every year the city is host to an impressive series of popular festivals: a film festival, a jazz festival, a winter festival, an international theater festival, and more.

French lifestyle: The Protestant work ethic once fueled Montreal's economic expansion; but it is the French influence that has especially marked its lifestyle. Although Toronto recently extended its bar opening hours to 2am, Montreal drinks to 3am and allows diners to bring their own bottles of wine into many of its restaurants.

northern end of the city. They then streamed toward the middle-class neighborhoods, eastward or westward, depending on the language of their adoption.

To the south you will still find Chinese grocery shops, little Jewish stalls, Portuguese fish stands, Greek tavernas, and creole bars, with each new layer of immigrants covering the last and pushing northward. The most recent wave has been the yuppies. The old garment factories are "lofts" now, and the old thoroughfare, Rue St-Laurent, is under accelerated gentrification. Sprinkled with avant-garde fashion shops and

Montreal women have the reputation of being the most elegant and stylish in all of North America. The most modest secretary will not go out without her makeup, and her skirt, shoes and blouse will be in the latest style. All the polls indicate that the Francophones – men and women – spend more on clothes, as well as on home furnishings, than any other community on the continent. As a case in point, Montreal has as many, if not more, importers of Milanese furniture than New York.

Montreal is the only city in America where French cuisine is not reserved for a special outing but is part of everyday life. When Montrealers entertain, the five-course dinner will always be enhanced with wine, generally imported from France. A Montrealer rarely considers drinking a Canadian wine, despite their much improved quality!

Cosmopolitan character: It is characteristic of small countries to be less ethnocentric and more open to foreign contributions than the great, self-sufficient powers. Because Canadian culture is too limited as a sole reference point, the Montreal elite, even before the appearance of Marshall McLuhan's "global village," have always been among the most cosmopolitan in the world. They read *Le*

Richler and the lyricism of a Réjean Ducharme; with its provocative avant-garde theater and its vibrant motion picture industry that invariably pulls down the Canadian cinema prizes, Montreal can boast that it offers the most creative and most diversified cultural life in Canada.

This is partly because the francophones, isolated by language yet too North American to import everything from France, had to develop their own cultural products. They have also been unwilling, unlike their compatriots in other Canadian provinces, to settle for US imports. And so Montreal is one of the rare cities of the world where, in the 1980s,

Nouvel Observateur and the *New Yorker*, Marguerite Yourcenar and Milan Kundera or Tom Wolfe, and they explore the universe with the open mind that comes from the practice of two languages and a long habit of life in a heterogeneous milieu.

With four universities (two French and two English), three French dailies and one English, one French weekly and two English; with a rich, challenging literature, serving up both the biting prose of a Mordecai

Left, mural with a message. **Above**, life on Rue Denis.

Dallas was not perched near the top of the TV ratings. Nor were other globally-popular programs such as *Coronation Street* or *Yes Minister*. The most-watched "soaps" are produced in Montreal.

Welcome to Montreal, then. But be careful crossing the street: Montrealers are always a little anarchic, and a stop light doesn't mean a thing. Montrealers have raised jaywalking to a high art, and they flaunt it. Drivers participate in this artistic display by slowing down only at the last second. If you survive this first contact with Montreal's "street" scene, the rest will be easy.

1535: On his second trip to North America, the French navigator Jacques Cartier visits an Iroquois village, Hochelaga, later to become the site of Montreal. He names the mountain there *Mont Réal.*

1608: Samuel de Champlain, the French explorer, establishes Quebec City, the first permanent settlement in Canada.

1611: Samuel de Champlain explores Montreal and builds a wall, the island's first European construction, near the St-Pierre River.

1615: First Catholic mass in North America is celebrated on the island of Montreal.

1642: The first colonists arrive, establish a tiny colony and name it Ville-Marie.

1643: After severe flooding, the commander of Ville-Marie, Paul de Chomedy de Maisonneuve, erects a wooden cross on Mont Royal.

1648: On November 24 Barbe Meusnier is born – the first European born in Ville-Marie.

1658: Montreal's first teacher, Marguerite Bourgeoys, begins teaching in a stable located in Ville-Marie.

1672: The first streets are laid out and named by Dollier de Casson: among them is Notre-Dame, in honor of the Virgin Mary, the patron saint of the colony.

1716: The French decide to build a wall around Montreal to fortify it.

1754-63: The French Indian War (called the Seven Years' War in Canada and Europe). French and British tensions (the latter joined by the Iroquois) escalate in North America. The French build a series of new forts and refuse to withdraw as the British protest. The French beat Washington's troops at Fort Necessity in the first battle of the war.

1759: General James Wolfe attacks French forces near Quebec City and, after three months, defeats them on the Plains of Abraham. Montreal is captured by general Jeffery Amherst in 1760. The surrender of New France is signed in Montreal and British troops take over the town, which has 60,000 inhabitants.

1763: Under the Treaty of Paris, the French give most of their land in Canada to the British. They keep two tiny islands south of Newfoundland: St-Pierre and Miquelon.

1774: The Quebec Act is enacted: it extends Quebec's borders and guarantees the use of French language and freedom of religion.

1775: As the American revolution begins, United Empire Loyalists come north.

1776: Benjamin Franklin, Samuel Chase and the Jesuit Charles Caroll visit Montreal in an attempt to convince French Canadians to join the American revolutionary cause against England. English troops arrive in June and the Americans withdraw.

1778: The first issue of *Gazette du Commerce et litéraire pour la ville et le district de Montréal* is printed. It later becomes *The Gazette.*

1792: Montreal is divided into two sections, east and west, with Saint-Laurent Street as the dividing line.

1801–20: The walls around Montreal are demolished.

1809: Canada's first steamboat, *The Accommodation*, sails the St Lawrence River from Montreal to Quebec City.

1812–14: The Americans attempt to invade Canada but are eventually repelled. The Treaty of Ghent ends the war.

1832: Montreal is incorporated as a city. From 1844 to 1849 it serves as the capital of the Province of Canada.

1833: Jacques Viger is elected the first mayor of Montreal. On July 19, the city adopts the coat of arms and the motto *Concordia Salus.*

1837–38: French Canadians lead a rebellion against the Château Clique; one leader, Louis Joseph Papineau, is exiled.

1843: The first classes are held at McGill University.

1852: The Great Fire in Montreal: 9,000 people are left homeless.

1860: The Crystal Palace, designed by J.W. Hopkins, is constructed.

1867: Canada and the Atlantic Provinces of Nova Scotia and New Brunswick become the Dominion of Canada.

1885: The Canadian Pacific Railway, based in Montreal, completes Canada's first continental railroad.

1886: Canada's first transcontinental railway train leaves Montreal for Vancouver.

1889: First automobile arrives in Montreal.
1914: World War I army conscription divides French and English Canadians.
1924: Cross on Mont Royal is illuminated.
1928: 22,000 people attend the opening of Montreal Stadium.
1929: Stock market crashes and the Great Depression ravages city's finances. The bridge across the St Lawrence River is completed. It is named after Jacques Cartier in 1934.
1940: Montreal Mayor Camillien Houde urges

French Canadians to defy a government plan for conscription during World War II. Most French Canadians oppose the military draft. Federal authorities put Houde in a prison camp until 1944.
1954: Jean Drapeau is elected mayor for the first time.
1959: Britain's Queen Elizabeth II and the president of the United States, Dwight D. Eisenhower, open the St Lawrence Seaway.
1963: The terrorist Front de Libération de Québec (FLQ) joins the Quebec separatist movement. Between 1963 and 1968, the FLQ claims responsibility for hundreds of bombings and armed robberies in the Montreal area.
1967: Opening of the World's Fair, Expo '67, in Montreal. Over 50 million people attend.
1970: In October the FLQ kidnap British Trade Commissioner James R. Cross and Quebec Labor Minister Pierre Laporte. Prime Minister Pierre Trudeau sends federal troops to Montreal. Laporte is murdered. Cross is released after the government guarantees his kidnappers safe passage to Cuba.
1976: The Parti Québécois wins the provincial election; Olympic Games are held in Montreal.
1980: Voters defeat a proposal to give provincial leaders the right to negotiate Quebec's political independence from Canada.
1982: Marguerite Bourgeoys is canonized.
1985: The Liberals gain control of the provincial legislature and Robert Bourassa becomes premier of Quebec.
1988: Meech Lake Constitutional Accord acknowledges the importance of Quebec's "separate and distinct culture."
1990: Amid threats of Quebec's separation from Canada, the Meech Lake Accord fails to be ratified.
1992: The 350th anniversary of Montreal's founding is celebrated.
1993: The separatist Bloc Québécois become the Official Opposition party in Canada's federal parliament, led by Lucien Bouchard.
1994: Robert Bourassa hands over the Liberal party reins to Daniel Johnston, who leads the party to an electoral defeat. Jacques Parizeau's Parti Québécois party wins a resounding victory.
1995: Federally-minded voters in Quebec narrowly defeat a referendum proposal in favor of Quebec's independence. Parizeau resigns.
1996: Lucien Bouchard takes over leadership of the PQ.
1998: Quebecer Jean Charest, leader of the federal Progressive Conservative party, is persuaded to switch allegiance and take over as leader of Quebec's demoralized Liberal party. In November Bouchard calls a snap election. Although the PQ won, it was not the forecasted wipeout of the Liberals, who won 43.7 percent of the popular vote compared to the PQ's 42.7 percent.

BEGINNINGS: THE RIVER AND THE MOUNTAIN

Each in its way symbolizes the influences which have shaped the city. The mountain, ancient symbol of man's spiritual journey, dramatizes the missionary faith which founded the first European settlement here. The river, flowing past the island on which the city stands, created the highway which made Montreal such a natural center for trade and commerce.

—Aline Gubbay, urban historian

Begin with the obvious. The fortunes of Montreal have been varied and spectacular – sketchy Indian settlement, French missionary outpost and trading center, throbbing industrial pile, tourist destination. Through all this, two facts have remained constant: the broad flow of a river and the upward thrust of a mountain.

In Montreal, understanding history begins with understanding geology. For here, in a time before history, hot lava from beneath the earth's crust forced its way to the surface and created the volcanic mountain whose burnt-out remains Jacques Cartier was to claim, millennia later, for King Francis I of France. At 760 ft (230 meters) Cartier's "Mount Royal" (Mont Réal) is hardly in the class of the Rockies, but its hardened cone of volcanic basalt nevertheless withstood the glacial ice that scoured the rest of this region more than 10,000 years ago.

Those same glaciers, receding sheets of ice two or three miles thick, forged the complex waterways and thousands of islands that mark the fertile St Lawrence River Valley. The island now known as Montreal is situated near the confluence of two powerful rivers, the St Lawrence and the Ottawa, whose waters meet in violent confrontation before heading east to the Atlantic. With its flat, fertile expanse and single conspicuous peak, the island is a peaceful contrast to the turbulent rapids that surround it.

Preceding pages: Montreal's maritime past. Left, Lake of Two Mountains. Above, Samuel de Champlain, the city's first developer, in 1611.

The river and the mountain serve to frame the city's unique history. Montreal's early mixture of contradictory impulses – the first French settlers traded as assiduously for furs as they did for souls – has characterized the city through the centuries. It is a place where opposites not only attract, but marry. French and English, wealthy and destitute, radical and conservative, federalist and separatist – all have found a place, sometimes an uneasy one, in this rich human settlement.

The history of Montreal is therefore a narrative in two dimensions, a history that mirrors its fortuitous location. Horizontally, it is one of arduous co-existence, conquest, uneasy reconciliation and assimilation. That story continues today as Montrealers struggle to maintain a common life when their cultural and linguistic differences threaten to pull them apart.

Vertically, the story of Montreal is a story of individual visions – political, commercial and religious – that drive men and women to these shores to carve out ideal cities that appear in their dreams. But other dreams have always persisted, and Montreal can neither boast nor mourn any single vision of itself. It is no city on a hill, no new Jerusalem. Instead it has been, and is, *many* cities, a place where successive generations of dreamers have come to try and turn their dreams into reality.

Early Montreal: The earliest settlers of the island now known as Montreal were, of course, Indians, mainly of the Huron, Algonquin and Montagnais tribes. There is no way of telling how long these people had been residing on the island when the first European, Jacques Cartier, set foot here on October 2, 1535. His account speaks of an

island already criss-crossed with Indian trails and possessing one apparently permanent settlement, Hochelaga ("at the place of the beaver dam"). This was a circular, palisaded village inhabited by Algonquin and Hurons living in communal long houses. The site is probably close to where McGill University now stands.

Though the inhabitants appeared filthy and ignorant to Cartier, they enjoyed the benefits of a disease-free, complex society. It was governed by a closely guarded oral history, sophisticated natural pantheism, and a consensual form of rule in which senior

men of the settlement would meet to agree on policy, war measures, and division of labor. The tribes existed as loose associations of many far-flung settlements and roving bands. Together, the Algonquin, Huron, Iroquois and Montagnais nations occupied most of the St Lawrence River Valley, the Great Lakes, and what is now New England.

Among the Indians, meat was not consumed every day, and in addition to the fruits of the hunt, many Indians subsisted on a paste of cold cornmeal and animal fat that later became known to the French as *sagamité*. The Hurons turned their efforts to cultivating the land. Beans, squash and corn were their staples and were mashed into pastes or boiled to make soups. This semi-agricultural way of life made for settlements more permanent than those of the Algonquin or the Iroquois, and it was probably Hochelaga Hurons whom Cartier encountered in the early months of 1535.

Jacques Cartier was a professional sailor from the town of St-Malo, a proud Frenchman in an age whose most accomplished naval men were Italian and Iberian. His king, Francis I, had charged him with a simple task: "To discover islands and countries where they say there is a lot of gold." King Francis was a man of limited imagination but boundless ambition, and the voyage on which he sent Cartier was only the first of many undertaken at his behest.

In these early days of the Age of Discovery, France's influence in North America became unparalleled, driven by the cupidity and religious aspirations of French monarchs, and realized by the unusual versatility and capabilities of their subjects. Cartier was one of these men, a brilliant navigator and a surprisingly deft diplomat.

As a geographer, he was unfortunately limited by the ignorance of his times. Like everyone else, Cartier thought that North America was Asia, and that the rumored mountains of gold and unlimited supplies of spice and silk were within his grasp. He sailed his convoy of three ships, led by the flagship *Grande Hermine*, as far as he could up the St Lawrence until, near the north shore of an island, his progress was stopped by impassable rapids. It was here that the fateful encounter between European and Indian, the beginnings of Montreal, took place.

Cartier dressed himself "gorgeously" for his first formal call on Hochelaga, and upon entering the village saw the horseshoe-shaped stockade that was typical of a Huron village. The Hurons were friendly to Cartier, and being impressed by his "floating island" and his strange dress, they took him to be a traveling minor deity. He was shown their settlement and taken to meet Agouhanna, the chief of Hochelaga.

Agouhanna, wary of the strange visitor, decided to show him the local sights. Cartier was conveyed to the summit of the island's

supplied him with some rock samples and Cartier hurried back to his ship. After a brutal winter's sailing, he reached France to report to King Francis and have the samples of "gold" and "diamonds" analyzed. They turned out to be iron pyrite (fool's gold) and quartz crystal.

But Cartier had also brought with him another gift from Agouhanna, a different kind of treasure, and one that was to fuel much of the exploration and colonization of Montreal – and Canada. It was the pelt of the Canadian beaver, an intelligent herbivore native to North America and possessed of a rich warm coat.

small mountain, and from this vantage he could see the river winding its way east for hundreds of miles. Here was the route to the Orient! He planted a cross, claimed the site for King Francis as the Hurons looked on baffled and pronounced the site Mont Réal – a name that did not come into general usage until a century later.

He also asked Agouhanna if he knew where to find the "shining rocks" he had heard were to be found in the area. The chief cheerfully

Left, an early Québécois winter. **Above**, spring cleaning, pioneer-style.

Over the next two centuries, European demand for the pelts, which could be made into fashionable hats and garments, would explode. During this same period, many of the Indians, who found the pelts could be traded for weapons and implements, came to view the beaver as a powerful animal deity whose merits they had failed to recognize. Their desire for the products of European technology – pots, guns, alcohol – allowed profit-driven Europeans to exploit their canoeing and trapping skills. The value of goods traded for pelts was far below the price they would bring in Europe.

Cartier revisited Montreal in 1541, but did not linger long, and the general settlement of New France was now centered on what were to become the Canadian provinces of Nova Scotia and New Brunswick. By 1604, the new French king, Henry IV, a devout Huguenot (Protestant), had granted to his Huguenot friend, the Sieur de Monte, a monopoly on all the furs in New France.

Without manpower, such a monopoly was worthless, but one of Monte's closest friends was a tireless figure who possessed the drive and imagination needed to settle New France and allow the fur trade to flourish. His name was Samuel de Champlain, a man of unusual

HEMING.
COUREUR DE BOIS

resourcefulness who would become known as "the Father of New France." Champlain, an accomplished soldier and scholar, made several journeys to New France in the early years of the 17th century, and he founded settlements in Acadia (part of what is now Nova Scotia) and Quebec.

In 1611 he visited the island of Montreal and found that the Hochelaga settlement mentioned in Cartier's account had disappeared. He ordered his men to clear an area by the river bank and called it "Place Royale," a name the area possesses to this day. Champlain also took a fancy to the small

island offshore from Montreal and used the dowry of his teenage wife, Hélène Boulé, to buy it. Like many Montreal place names, it was informally canonized when Champlain's wife was long dead: it is known today as Ile Ste-Hélène, and is part of the permanent park erected when the World's Fair, Expo '67, was held in Montreal.

Champlain's main settlement was in Quebec City, which he founded on July 3, 1603. But he visited Montreal again in 1615, this time on the north shore of the island, and here happened to meet two priests of the Récollet (Franciscan Minor) Order, Denis Janet and Joseph le Caron, both arrived from France.

Together with Champlain's men, these two performed the first Catholic Mass in North America on June 24, 1615. The setting was not auspicious for this momentous event, nothing more than a clearing and some rough wooden tables, but Champlain knelt with the two tough little priests. Many, many more masses would be said in New France.

Champlain, known to the Indians as Agnonha, was a colonial governor who was devout and warlike by turns. He had earned the enduring enmity of the Iroquois by killing more than 300 of them at Ticonderoga, matching European technology – primitive firearms known as arquebuses – against bow and arrow. His allies, the Hurons and Algonquins, also feared and hated him. Yet they bowed to his attempts at regulating the fur trade. He was not a man lightly crossed.

While Champlain was consolidating his power in Quebec City, the energetic Récollet priests were doing their best to consolidate God's power further upstream. Not surprisingly, the Indians proved unwilling converts. The continuing aggression of the Iroquois against Port Royale created many early Christian martyrs among the Récollets and the Jesuits, known to the Indians as Black Robes. The priests were sometimes befriended by the Hurons or Algonquins, but were more often despised and feared as bizarre sorcerers who refused to have sex, share their belongings, or live communally.

Conversions were recorded, especially by the Jesuits, but they were of dubious theological validity and cost a high price in French lives. Jesuit priests were tortured and then gruesomely killed by the Indians, who believed that signs of weakness in conquered enemies made the conquerors stronger.

The *Relations* of these events, which were graphic tales written and circulated by the Jesuits in France, inspired a general religious zeal. The name "Mont Réal" became synonymous with a forlorn heathen place in need of salvation. In 1627, the prime minister of France was the Machiavellian figure Armand Jean du Plessis, better known as Cardinal Richelieu, who, seeking tirelessly to make France the preeminent power in the world, controlled the court of Louis XIII with a mixture of guile and terror.

Anjou. Olier and Dauversière had met by chance in Paris, discovered a common missionary passion for converting "heathen" Indians, and determined to start a permanent mission at Montreal.

They could not help viewing their meeting as providential. Pooling their resources, they set off in 1641 with a group of 50 missionary members of their newly created "Société de Notre Dame de Montréal" under the leadership of Paul de Chomedey, Sieur de Maisonneuve. The new mission was to be established for the sole purpose of converting Indian souls to Catholicism, and Olier specified that the Notre Dame settlers "should

At Richelieu's urging, Louis granted title to all land in New France to a group of shrewd French businessmen known as the Company of One Hundred Associates. Unable to exploit all the territory themselves, the Associates granted subleases to likely settlers. The title to the island of Montreal was granted by the Associates to two fervent believers, Jean-Jacques Olier, later founder of the Order of St Sulpice, and Jerome de la Royer de la Dauversière, a tax collector from

Left, fur trappers ravaged Quebec's beaver population. **Above**, 19th-century campfire supper.

have nothing to do with the fur trade." There would be difficulty enough, they cautioned Maisonneuve, in "planting the banner of Christ in an abode of desolation and a haunt of demons."

Maisonneuve, a tough ex-soldier and Knight of Malta now driven by religious fervor, founded his colony, "Ville Marie," on Champlain's Place Royale site after a hard Atlantic crossing. On reaching the shore, he fell on his knees and gave thanks. A rough palisade was quickly erected, and the first Mass of the new settlement was said on August 18, 1642.

The consecrated host was displayed all day on the altar to show that this place had been claimed for Christ; at nightfall the altar was lit by firefly lanterns. Father Vimont, Superior of the Jesuits at Montreal, told his small congregation, with unusual prescience: "You are a grain of mustard seed that shall grow till its branches overshadow the earth. You are few, but this work is the Word of God. His smile is on you, and your children shall fill the land."

Life was extraordinarily hazardous and arduous for the newly arrived settlers. Attacks by Indians were a constant danger, their crops refused to take in the soil, and the

The Iroquois raids were a more constant and nagging danger and, until his men learned canoeing skills sufficient to meet the Indians on the water, Maisonneuve was forced to adopt a defensive posture. Nevertheless, Iroquois ambushes, often of workers returning to the palisades after a day in the fields, killed more than 50 people between 1643 and 1650 – this in a community that numbered fewer than 150.

To guard against ambushes, the settlers employed guard dogs who warned the French of stalking Iroquois warriors and prevented many deaths. Most famous of these was Maisonneuve's dog, Pilote, whose keen nose

melting snow caused disastrous annual floods. In December 1642, the confluence of the St Lawrence and St Peter rivers rose violently, lapping at the edges of the fledgling settlement. Maisonneuve, in great fear, planted a cross on the threatened bank and vowed that he would erect another on Mont Royal if the waters receded – which indeed they did, on Christmas Day. On the feast of Epiphany (in early January) a procession, with a grateful Maisonneuve himself at the rear bearing a heavy wooden cross, scaled the hill and planted this token of thanks for God's mercy.

frequently detected the approaching Indian warriors before they were visible. The dog was immortalized along with Maisonneuve in a statue located in old Montreal.

The first baptism of an Algonquin child occurred at Ville Marie in 1642, and this was a great victory for the embattled missionaries. After all, conversion of the pagans was their reason for enduring the hardships of life in New France. But as they gathered around the rough baptismal, their thoughts might have turned to the great cost of salvation. How many more would have to die so that a few Indian souls could be saved? So many of the Indians did not want them there at all, and many others simply did not find the prospect of eternal life with God a joyful one.

Would this first native Christian child find itself an outcast, or an apostate, in later life? The devout could banish such doubts, but not all of the Ville Marie company were as stout in their faith as the ascetic Récollet priests and the grim Maisonneuve himself.

In 1644, fed up with the continual Indian harassment of the settlement, Maisonneuve walked out like a Western gunslinger to meet the leader of the Iroquois in single combat. It wasn't by any means a fair fight, Maisonneuve having armed himself with

population came the need for new services. In 1644 the young nurse Jeanne Mance opened Montreal's first hospital, l'Hôtel Dieu, which was also the first building outside the palisades. Mance, who had almost died on the voyage from France, regained her strength to tend to those less fortunate.

The schoolmistress Marguerite Bourgeoys, another deceptively frail Frenchwoman, founded the settlement's first chapel, Notre-Dame-de-Bonsecours – still standing, after several rebuildings, on its original site in Old Montreal. This "Sailors' Church" welcomed generation after generation of weary river-goers to the safety of God's house.

two pistols), but he succeeded in killing the chief at what is now known as Place d'Armes, and a statue of this dedicated founder of Montreal stands there today.

Despite the religious fervor of some at Ville Marie, the settlement flourished more as a French outpost than a center of conversion. The quick wealth of the fur trade brought more people, including the so-called *filles du roi*, young Frenchwomen brought to Montreal to marry the male settlers. With a larger

Bourgeoys's order of nuns, Le Congrégation de Notre-Dame-de-Bonsecours, was authorized by Louis XIV in 1671, the first native Canadian religious order. The Notre-Dame Congregation was, until well into the 20th century, one of North America's most influential institutions for the education of Catholic women, and Bourgeoys was raised to sainthood in 1982 by Pope John Paul II.

Montreal was now North America's premier Roman Catholic city and remained so for almost two centuries. Dominated in the early days by Franciscans and Jesuits, the city later welcomed Jean-Jacques Olier's St

Left, tranquillity in 1791. **Above**, Paul de Chomedey de Maisonneuve lays down the law.

Sulpice fathers, and the so-called Gray Sisters (more formally known as Les Soeurs de la Charité de l'Hôpital Général de Montréal), who tended to the poor and derelict. The Oblates, Christian Brothers, and Sacred Heart Sisters also found their way to the city.

All the schools of Montreal and many of its most impressive buildings are the result of the church's great hold on Montrealers. When the Notre Dame Cathedral of Montreal was built in 1829, it drew visitors from across Canada and the United States; it was then the largest church in North America and remained so until St Patrick's Cathedral was built in New York in 1879.

In 1874 there were 74 churches of all denominations in Montreal – one for every 2,000 inhabitants. Even at this date they were still largely Catholic, but with several tasteful additions from the Church of Scotland and the Anglican Church. Harriet Beecher Stowe, author of *Uncle Tom's Cabin*, wrote in 1860 that "Montreal is a mountain of churches," while Mark Twain took a more jaundiced view: "This is the first time I was ever in a city," he wrote in 1881, "where you could not throw a brick without breaking a church window."

Muscular Christianity: During the 1660s, the governing spirit of Ville Marie was the energetic Superior of the Sulpicians and keen amateur historian François Dollier de Cassons (1632–1702). He was a strapping, 6' 5" (2.2-meter) ex-soldier who, with his cassock tucked up for greater freedom of movement, surveyed the town's first street plan, planned a canal to bypass the Lachine rapids, and built the first parish church and a seminary for the Sulpicians, the order that was still the official owner of the island.

In 1663, however, Louis XIV took formal possession of all the land and trade of New France, and land parcels and trading licences henceforth were granted only by the Crown and its representatives at Quebec. The island of Montreal was divided into land packets known as *seigneuries*; the owners, or *seigneurs*, subdividing their land into long and narrow tenant parcels known as *rangs*, which were farmed by *habitants*. For a nominal rent – "half a sou plus a pint of wheat per acre" in 1667 – the *habitant* was given the land to work, on which he built a dwelling for himself and maintained a road. He was also bound to grind his grain at the *seigneur's* mill, for a fee of course.

Seigneuries were typically divided up into long strips rather than chunks in order that every *habitant* could have some river access. This division is still evident in Quebec estates. The *habitant*, with his dyed wool cap (*toque bleu*), blanket-cloth coat and tasseled sash, remains a ubiquitous, if somewhat clichéd, symbol of rural Quebec. Bonhomme, the snowman symbol of Quebec City's annual winter festival, also wears the toque and sash of the *habitant*.

The landowners themselves built grand stone houses on estates away from the riverbank. Named after their owners, some of these châteaux are still standing: Château de Ramezay, one of the first, served later as the seat of Montreal's government; De La Salle House can be found in the suburb of Lachine (named rather hopefully as a stage on the road to China, *La Chine*). But while Ville-Marie seemed to be gaining a foothold on the island, the Indian threat did not lessen. On August 4, 1689, the worst Iroquois raid yet left 200 people of Lachine dead. Another 100 were captured and never returned.

There followed 10 years of sustained fighting with the Iroquois, which effectively halted the fur trade on which Montreal's prosperity depended. The early Montrealers entered the 18th century on a pensive note, but the diplomatic new Governor-General of Montreal, Hector de Callières, managed to negotiate a peace treaty with the Indians. In 1701 more than 1,300 Indians, representatives of 40 different nations, were persuaded to come to Montreal and camp outside the city's walls for peace talks. De Callières, skilled in smoothing over old grievances, circulated among the assembled chiefs and hammered out a deal all could accept. Surveying the hundreds of tents, camp fires and milling Indians and Frenchmen, de Callières cried: "*Voici la paix. Oublions le passé.*"

Peace had come, yes. But it was not destined to last for long.

Right, ruthless Iroquois raids were common until the mid-1600s.

RELIGIOUS ROOTS

I
f faith can move mountains, it can also settle them, as the establishment of Montreal shows. In 1642, approximately 50 members of the *Associés de Notre-Dame pour la conversion des sauvages de la Nouvelle France en l'île de Montréal* crossed a capricious ocean to found the Ville-Marie mission near the "royal mountain" looming over Montreal's landscape. (Unfortunately, they didn't receive a formal invitation from the Iroquois, the *sauvages* who were their object of conversion.)

The religious fervor of 17th-century France, which was marked by the creation of numerous religious orders and lay evangelizing groups, spilled over into New France, which rapidly became populated by both old and new religious congregations.

As history painfully shows, however, colonies do not live by faith alone. In Montreal, Catholicism combined with fur and the *fleur-de-lis* to form the defining triptych of the city's early history, and this medley led to an ecclesiastical power and control unprecedented in North America, a power that remained relatively undiminished until the "Quiet Revolution" deep in the 20th century.

Ever since Sieur de Maisonneuve planted a towering crucifix in thanksgiving for Ville-Marie's survival of a flood in 1643, Montreal's visage has been Janus-faced, characterized by both political and religious profiles.

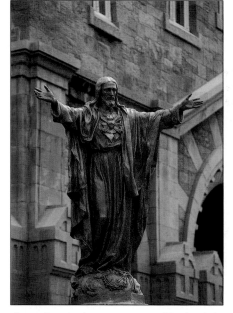

New France was envisioned as both a source of wealth for France and as a North American beachhead for the Counter (or Catholic) Reformation – an attempt by the Roman Catholic church to respond to the rapid and lasting emergence of the Protestant reformers.

The Jesuits were among the first missionary orders to brave the frigid but fertile colony of New France. Their missions in South America, Ethiopia, Russia, India, and China were well-known, largely through the publication of their exploits in *Relations*. Their fame led not only to a steady flow of vocations, but also to handsome donations from well-endowed patrons.

Called "Black Robes" by the Native Americans, the Jesuits sought converts among the aggressive Iroquois and more pacific Huron peoples. For many of these missionaries, their vocations ended in martyrdom. During the 1650s, the Iroquois attacked Quebec City, Trois-Rivières, and Montreal, the three centers of the French fur trade along the St Lawrence River. Montreal, which was a natural "command center" for the fur trade, was saved from being virtually wiped out by the efforts of Adam Dollard and 16 companions, who perished in a stand against several Iroquois war parties on Ottawa River.

Upon learning of these attacks, Louis XIV, the "Sun King," bestowed his radiance upon his valuable but besieged colony. In 1661, he declared the small community of under 2,000 settlers a royal province, and dispatched 1,000 troops to protect the colony.

All public appointments were from then on handled by the crown, and the governor, the "intendant" (who maintained the royal authority and oversaw economic development), joined with the Roman Catholic bishop to form a sort of triumvirate called the Sovereign Council. In New France, therefore, unlike the British colonies, cross and sword united to block inchoate democratic initiatives.

Bishop Laval was quite happy to pick up the political mantel that was proffered him by the king. As chief prelate from 1649 to 1688, this ascetic cleric secured vast lands for the church. He also established a seminary (the forerunner of Quebec's Laval University) and controlled education in the colony. (The separation of church and state was as heretical an idea as predestination in New France.)

A major figure in the ecclesiastical educational system of Montreal was Marguerite Bourgeoys (1620–1700), who was to become Canada's first female saint. A dramatic amalgam of courage, compassion, and conviction, Marguerite set sail for Montreal in 1657 with M. de Maisonneuve, 100 men, and a handful of girls and women. During the undulating passage, she served as both nurse, prelate, and mortician, nursing the eight men who died of plague during the voyage and preparing them for watery graves.

Marguerite, who eventually founded the Congrégation de Notre-Dame, counselled, catechized, and cared for many of the 1,000 *filles du roi* who streamed to New France between 1665 and 1673. In a French colonial version of "Here Come the Brides," King Louis XIV sponsored the migration of young girls to the colony, "entirely free from any natural blemish or anything personally repulsive," to help populate New France.

In a further effort to increase the number of (French) mammals on its few snowy acres, the crown granted baby bonuses, penalized bachelors, and provided handsome pensions for fecund parents. Parents were also required by law to have their sons married by the age of 18 or 19, and their daughters had to be betrothed by 14 or 15.

In many ways, the church was attempting to build a more *Catholic* France in North America, a new "city on the hill" that would somehow be more pristine than its European counterpart. Marguerite Bourgeoys was the "trump card" played by the church in this enterprise.

Dubbed "mother of the colony," Marguerite, in addition to chaperoning the *filles du roi*, recruited French and Canadian girls as teachers, organized a boarding school, established a school for Indian girls on the Sulpician reserve of *La Montagne*, as well as a domestic arts school. As a guardian of virgins, Marguerite was well aware of the dangers of the opposite sex. While travelling to Nantes, en route to the New World, Marguerite was accosted by scores of aggressive men. She recounted in her diary, "I could not leave the coach... all these men said many insulting things to me... I closed the door and barricaded it with everything I could."

Marguerite's survival skills would serve her and her charges well in a colony where women were a scarce and precious resource. Although Bishop Laval refused to allow her and her co-workers to take religious vows, they were eventually permitted in 1698 to become a non-cloistered religious community. Although she was widely considered by her peers to be a saint when she died in 1670, Marguerite was not officially canonized by the church until October 1982.

Today you can see where Marguerite welcomed the King's wards at Maison Saint-Gabrielle (on Favard Street). Built in 1688, this served a farm center, elementary school, and, finally, the first school of domestic arts for young women in New France. Part of the present-day structure dates back to 1698.

Perhaps no one more epitomized the strength of the missionary church than Abbé Dollier de Casson, Superior of the Sulpicians in Montreal. A towering figure, he could apparently lift two men simultaneously, one in each hand.

While praying on his knees one evening by the Bay of Quinté, it is said, Dollier de Casson was harangued by a young Indian, who mocked him with obscenities. Without getting up, the forceful cleric shot out his right arm and sent the brave sprawling. He finished his prayers uninterrupted.

Abbé Dollier de Casson built the Sulpician Seminary at Place d'Armes. Begun in 1680, this is the oldest building in Montreal and one of North America's oldest. It is now a retirement home for the religious community

The work of religion, in education at every level, and in ministry for the sick, the impoverished, orphans, and elderly has been of central importance to Montreal's history. Throughout the city, religious schools, hospitals and seminaries are among the oldest, most enduring institutions.

The tenacious grip of medieval Christendom on Montreal began to relax, however, after 1950. Government intervention in the areas of health and education brought radical changes to the complexion of Catholicism in Montreal and the province of Quebec in general.

The "Quiet Revolution," followed quickly by the Second Vatican Council (1962–65), led to a major exodus of many of the Quebec church's vowed members. It also led to a substantial loss of its power and authority. Between 1967 and 1983, the ranks of religious congregations in Quebec dropped by 40 percent.

Perhaps more than any other North American city, Montreal exudes the ambience of a community where church and state were long and enduring bedfellows. As you pass by Montreal's numerous churches, centuries-old hospitals and houses for various religious communities, pause for a moment just to recall the lives affected by the faith and fervor of 17th-century Catholicism. ∎

Left, Jesus lives in St-Denis. Above, Tiffany window in Erskine and American Church.

THE COMING OF THE BRITISH

After the peace of 1701 between the French and the Indians, Montreal rebuilt itself, dropped the name of Ville-Marie, and concentrated on becoming the trading center its location seemed always to promise. The pursuit of the beaver pelts was furious, sometimes unscrupulous, and almost always at the expense of Indians on the lookout for European liquor, guns, and utensils. Traders typically exchanged goods for pelts at far below market price, reserving the massive profits for themselves and exploiting the Indian trappers who had risked life and limb to bring in the pelts.

The lure of quick wealth was too much for most early Montrealers to resist, and "everyone turns trader" a contemporary traveller noted. The aging Dollier de Casson wrote of the fur trade gloomily, describing "the diabolical attractions" of quick wealth and the resulting *"perdition générale"* of Montreal. Even Montreal's clergymen ventured out to the trading stalls beyond the city gates to barter their utensils and equipment for furs that would bring massive profits in Europe.

The Indians, however, were not the only ones to pursue the beavers into their habitat. Toughened *coureurs de bois* – French woodsmen skilled in the arts of paddling and trapping – steered fur-heavy canoes into Montreal harbor and looked for a good price. Some of these hardy souls had "gone native" and barely appeared French to the civilized denizens of Montreal. Their supplies sold off, they and the Indians would proceed to get roaring drunk on cheap liquor, collapsing in dirty heaps or copulating, fighting, and drinking until dawn.

In 1721, the town fortifications were improved with 18-foot stone walls, bastions, a citadel, and more cannon. The wooden buildings inside the walls, always at risk of fire,

were replaced in accordance with building regulations that called for stone walls and roofs of slate, tile, or tin. "The town has suffered by fire very materially at different times," the traveller Isaac Weld wrote some time later, "and the inhabitants have such a dread of it, that all who can afford it cover the roofs of their houses with tin-plates instead of shingles. By law they are obliged to have one or more ladders, in proportion to the house, always ready on the roofs."

Drama and dancing: For almost five decades the little town boomed, its *seigneurs* and traders gradually becoming wealthier as the demand for beaver furs grew in Europe. In the long winter months, leisure time was unlimited and the Ramezays, Vaudreuils, and other prosperous families of Montreal enjoyed amateur theatricals, dancing, and sugaring-off picnics in which a festive party sledded out to the maple stands to collect sap for maple syrup.

The more prosaic *habitants*, at least as protrayed by sentimental artists such as Cornelius Krieghoff (1812–72), loved to

Preceding pages: Queen Victoria, ever watchful of her rebellious French subjects. **Left**, after Wolfe's defeat and death in 1759, British troops took decisive control of the town. **Above**, the exiled Québécois leader Louis Joseph Papineau.

dance, play cards (a pursuit officially banned by the church), and drink heavily. Krieghoff is perhaps the best known of the artists who chronicled the scenes of daily life in early Quebec. His paintings are seen frequently on posters, postcards and, memorably, the label of a brand of Canadian whisky.

It was 1756 when the Seven Years' War brought an end to the prosperous peace. Armed conflict, this time between French and English, once more ruptured Montreal. The English, long eager to get a foothold on North America and the riches it promised, ran up against the well-oiled imperial designs first proposed by Richelieu. Neither

colonies. Richelieu's influence was long gone, and the desire for imperial might was waning in a France wracked by internal difficulties and facing battles with English and Prussian soldiers on its own land. (The satirist Voltaire conveyed one prominent attitude to France's colonial adventure when, in *Candide*, he famously dismissed New France as "a few acres of snow.")

The English and French forces met in a decisive battle in Quebec City in 1760. The French commander, Montcalm, defending a stout fort, did not reckon on a flanking maneuver. The English went upriver past the city, scaled the cliffs, and surprised the French

side had any illusions about their colonial ambitions, despite the rhetoric of religious conversion habitually used by the French.

The English, after several abortive attempts to oust the French, massed their efforts in the middle of the 1750s, attacking first at Ticonderoga. Louis Joseph, Marquis de Montcalm, ruled the French forces from his headquarters in Montreal and scored an impressive short-handed victory at this first battle site.

The English forces were superior, however, and they were not hampered by the political machinations that prevented an all-out effort on the part of France to keep its

forces from the rear. Montcalm was defeated and killed on the Plains of Abraham by the British general, James Wolfe, who was also killed. In September 1760, the British general Lord Jeffrey Amherst entered Montreal through the Récollet gate and was met by Vaudreuil, the governor of New France, who formally surrendered. The British flag flew over Montreal for the first time on September 9, 1760. In 1763, under the Treaty of Paris, France ceded its territories to Britain, ending the era of French control in Montreal.

Despite this enormous change in political direction, daily life did not alter much for the average Montreal inhabitant. The British Governors were sensitive to the fact that several generations of Frenchmen were responsible for whatever European civilization, trade and development the colony enjoyed. No land was stripped from the *seigneurs*, and the Quebec Act of 1774 accepted the French language and Roman Catholic religion as essential parts of Quebec culture.

A cosmopolitan mix: But by this time one could hear a broad Scottish burr on the streets of Montreal, or the haughty bleat of English nobility. The demographics of the city changed radically during the next genera-

(a "brick") was fixed at eight coppers; bakers could not charge more than 10 coppers for the heavier brown loaf, usually of six pounds. Slavery was also a prevailing concern, and the governors thought it best to distance themselves officially from the buying and selling of humans so widely practiced in parts of the republic to the south. It was decreed that "no tavern, alehouse or innkeeper do receive, harbor, or entertain any bond or servant slave or slaves, drinking, gaming or loitering in their houses, under a penalty of £5."

From this time on, and especially in the decades immediately before the American

tion, and the population exploded with an exuberant commercial eagerness. Montreal was still a boom town, on whose streets leather-clad *coureurs de bois* (woodsmen), fresh from the river portages and Indian camps, rubbed shoulders with Scottish merchants, English soldiers, and aristocratic French *seigneurs*.

New civil regulations also marked the influence of English bureaucrats on Montreal. In 1765, the price of a four-pound white loaf

Trade rapidly became brisk in ice blocks (left) and timber (above).

Civil War, Montreal was a frequent destination of slaves trekking toward freedom on the so-called Underground Railway.

The strategic position of Montreal – Dollier de Casson had called it "the dyke of Canada" – made it a desirable military target, and during the American Revolution (1775–83) the city once again came under attack. The first American overture was a failure. In 1775 the garrison at Montreal heard that Ethan Allen and his famous "Green Mountain Boys" were marching along the Longue Pointe road, just east of the city. A small force of English and French soldiers ad-

A WOMAN'S LOT

The law making marriage a co-partnership, and creating *communitié de bien*, is sanctioned by the code of French law, called *Coutûme de Paris* which indeed is the text book of the Canadian lawyer; the wife being by marriage invested with a right to half the husband's property; and, being rendered independent of him, is perhaps the remote cause that the fair sex have such influence in France; and in Canada, it is well known, that a great deal of consequence, and even an air of superiority, is assumed by them...

—*A British View of French Canada, 1807*

Many 18th-century male observers of women in New France were struck (not always favorably) by the taken-for-granted independence women enjoyed and the potent influence they exerted in the colony, no matter what their cultural background.

Although 18th-century French attitudes toward women were more flexible than those of the British, they were far from being, in modern terms, "progressive." Under French laws, wives were expected to follow their husbands, even if that meant traveling to an entirely new country. So French culture alone can't take credit for this remarkable phenomenon.

A look at the female immigrants themselves offers better answers. The two main types to emigrate to the colony were the *dévotées*, dedicated religious women or nuns, and the *filles du roi*, government-sponsored immigrants. Most of these women were highly educated and, significantly, were self-motivated in their decision to try out life in New France.

The *dévotées* rapidly developed badly needed hospitals and schools. As a result, they secured for themselves an important place in the social structure of the colony. Moreover, they permanently established the education of girls as a part of colonial culture, hence passing on to these women two extremely important assets for an independent lifestyle: an education and a trade.

Most of the *filles du roi* were originally urban dwellers and were trained in a wide variety of skills.

Many of these women also brought dowries with them that, though they would have been modest in France, were small fortunes in the New World. Since wives were a scarce resource among the men of the colony, those women who owned property were highly coveted.

The inhabitants of New France seem to have been distinctly unhindered by the Puritanical attitudes toward sex that established such a firm foothold in New England. These more "open" colonial attitudes stemmed from a parent culture that viewed human sexuality both with tolerance and interest. Marriage ceremonies tended to be more public than private, and kinfolk as well as the larger community had a penetrating voice in deciding who could marry whom. In French Canada, marriage contracts were often signed by not only the bride and groom's extended families, but also by *all* the people who attended the wedding.

The involvement of this wider community in the marriage reflects the family effort to protect a bride's property. As a result, many a wedding resembled a business deal rather than a sacrament. The European medieval tradition of *charivari* (wedding night riot) was also transplanted in New France. If the community disapproved of a marriage, they staged a *charivari*, a noisy boycott of the couple's home, an event which could endure for several days.

Family life among the *habitants* and *habitantes* of colonial Lower Canada was distinguished by one significant feature: the home and the place of work were not regarded as separate realms. Women worked as bonesetters, bookbinders, woolfillers, laundresses, wigmakers, pedlars, greengrocers, moneylenders, auctioneers, educators, and nurses. They toiled in the fields next to their menfolk, and some were active in less expected areas such as arduous bricklaying and back-breaking stonework. In addition, many of the children were sent out of the home at an early age either to a nursemaid or to learn a trade, a tradition that freed many mothers from the exhausting and time-consuming task of raising families.

The combination, then, of a French cultural heritage and the unique roles they played in New France, provided many women with an unusual degree of independence. ∎

vanced to challenge the invaders, and Allen was easily defeated and captured.

The garrison commandant, an old soldier called Prescott, threatened to cane the arrogant Allen, and he had to be dragged off by his men. Allen was imprisoned on board the ship *Gaspé*, moored in harbor, and Montrealers rejoiced at having "caged the great New Hampshire incendiary."

However, the jubilation was short-lived, for in the autumn of 1775 General Richard Montgomery advanced toward the city with a much larger force, and the governor, Sir Guy Carleton (later Lord Dorchester), was compelled to surrender without resistance.

liberty "monstrously ill-digested" and soon regarded the Montrealers as "rascals and enemies" and even "dam'd Tories."

Peace breaks out: Benjamin Franklin arrived in June 1776 to smooth over these rough spots, but his overtures were rejected. The Americans left in 1783 when Britain massed a large army near Montreal, and a peace treaty was signed with the new United States republic the same year.

Perhaps the only palpable benefit of the American occupation was that one of Franklin's associates, a propagandist called Fleury de Mesplet, decided to stay on and ply his printing trade in Montreal. In a shop on

The attitude of the Americans was then, as it is now, that the occupied people should be overjoyed to be freed from the shackles of colonial rule. Montrealers were invited to "seize the opportunity presented to you by Providence itself" and join the not-quite-Continental Congress. But the Americans failed to reckon with other ideas of freedom; Montrealers were happy and prosperous under the British and mocked the American deliverance and its agents. The Americans, on the other hand, found Canadian notions of

Above, sawing ice on the St Lawrence Seaway.

Rue de la Capital, a narrow lane off Rue St François-Xavier, he began printing Canada's first newspaper, *La Gazette du Commerce et Littéraire*. In 1788 the paper was produced in English as well as French, a concrete indication that English had arrived in the city.

You can still pick up a copy of the *Gazette* today – it is now Montreal's major English daily – and find some of those "monstrously ill-digested ideas" that so offended American sensibilities.

Many other commercial enterprises began in these decades to serve the needs of the wealthy fur traders and their employees, and at the same time the influx of United Empire Loyalists fleeing the anti-monarchist revolution to the south swelled Montreal's population. The focus of the town shifted away from the harbor settlement and toward what is now downtown Montreal.

The city's new aristocracy was largely Scottish in origin, and it included many enterprising rogues who had taken advantage of the wide-open colonial life to make their vast fortunes in fur trading. Simon McTavish, Joseph Frobisher, William McGillivray, James McGill, and Simon Fraser were the stars in Montreal's social and commercial firmament in this era. Their names also dot

bequeathed by Edinburgh University graduate James McGill, who wanted the colony to have "an English college on a liberal scale." With $10,000 and the 46 acres of land known as Burnside, the university was begun. When classes began in September 1843, the college site was still countryside, and its 20 hardy students tramped across fields full of crops and grazing cattle to reach the fount of wisdom. They had to dress "in plain, decent and comely clothes, without superfluous ornament" and wear gowns to their lectures on medicine, classics and mathematics.

Beaver Hall Hill, site of Canada's first men's club, also owes it name to the Nor-

the rivers and regions of western Canada which they were the first to explore.

In 1783 a group of them founded the North-West Company, a fur-trading cooperative begun in order to challenge the hegemony of England's Hudson's Bay Company. The Nor-Westers were absorbed by the Hudson's Bay Company in 1821, but for decades it raced them to the fur trade in the west and north of Canada.

Just as their names filled in the maps there, the Nor-Westers left their mark on their home base of Montreal. The city's main English-speaking university is built on land

Westers. Membership in the Beaver Club was limited to those who had wintered in Canada's wilderness, *le pays d'en haut*, and during the long Montreal winters the adventurers would gather here to tell tall stories, drink whisky, and sing the canoeing songs of the old *voyageurs*, paddling away for all they were worth with their walking sticks, fire tongs, or dress swords. The minutes of one dinner meeting, for February 28, 1809, record that the 24 attending members drank 38 bottles of wine as well as 26 bottles of beer in what must surely have been an extremely rowdy evening.

The grand houses of the new fur lords, dwarfing the châteaux of the early *seigneurs*, were sited away from the town in the elevated environs of Westmount and Mount Royal itself. The name Westmount is still synonymous with privilege and old money in Montreal's society lexicon.

While these Scottish "lords of lake and forest," the "hyperborean nabobs" of the fur trade (as Washington Irving had enthusiastically called them), spoke English among themselves, most were bilingual, the result of necessary traffic with their *voyageur* paddlers and, in some cases, of Scotland's Auld Alliance with France against the English.

In the same year, 1786, the Englishman John Molson opened his brewery on the banks of the St Lawrence. He also established a small shipping line that was to expand quickly over the next 50 years. Molson, who was a great favorite among the French *habitants* along the river, is an appropriate emblem for this golden age of commercial Montreal. Starting out with almost nothing in the new colony, he made his vast fortune by working hard to meet the simple needs of its inhabitants. He is reputed to have said that "An honest brew makes its own friends" – a slogan found on his family's beer bottles to this day.

Many of these Scots, including McTavish, McGill and Frobisher, also married French Canadians. They were models of biculturalism in action, happy in a city still essentially French. It was not until the spring of 1786 that an English play, Goldsmith's *She Stoops to Conquer*, was performed in Montreal by a professional troupe from Albany, New York. No other play is mentioned in the history of Montreal for almost 13 years, so presumably drama did not agree with the tastes of these northern hearties.

Left, and above, Notre-Dame Cathedral.

When Molson's brewery opened, a bottle of strong beer cost nine cents, mild ale went for seven cents, and small or table beer cost five cents. Molson also built Montreal's first hotel and its first commercial theatre, the Théâtre Royale.

Molson's brewery was the first to be built in North America and, while the steamship line that used to run his two ships – the *Accommodation* and the *Swiftsure* – between Quebec and Montreal is long gone, you can still enjoy Molson's lager or ale in any Canadian tavern. The Molson family continues to play a prominent role in today's Montreal.

THE HABITANTS

There are some who love good food,
Beans with pork, and small green peas;
Or plenty of pork also with beans,
There are some who eat, others who don't.
The spoiled gherkins in the salad,
There are some who eat them and make
themselves sick.
But to eat pea soup
The Canadiens are always ready!
Ah! ah! the Canadiens are always ready!
　　　　　　　—French Canadian Folk Song

Imagine yourself a very long way from home, so far away that the prospect of returning is next to impossible. You are in a strange land, known for its fierce winters and covered by a tenacious, seemingly impenetrable forest. You will be the first to settle the new colony – you will plan your settlement without really knowing much about the country, taking risks, experimenting, and desperately hoping that all will turn out well.

You will give birth to your children on the kitchen table, perhaps with the help of a midwife or perhaps not, and each day you will toil to provide the necessities of life: preparing meals, making soap

and candles, mending and washing clothes. At the end of your days your face will betray the marks of a rough life outdoors and of bearing too many children, and your hands will show the scars of many harvests. But you will have lived an honest life, even a prosperous life – the life of a French Canadian *habitant* or *habitante*.

"To be always ready," as the above folksong proclaims, seems more appropriate for the Boy Scouts of America than for fledgling colonists, yet it is an apt shibboleth for the first European inhabitants of Canada.

No one could possibly envy the hardships the first French Canadians faced in their new land – the bitter and lonely winters, unpredictable crops, and the relentless necessity of becoming self-reliant. These are all things that every Canadian pioneer confronted. But the French managed to settle along

the St Lawrence in a unique fashion and, in so doing, founded a truly distinct society.

New France's first permanent homesteads (evidence of which can still be seen today), were uniquely linked to the available and oh-so-crucial water sources. The original plots were very long, narrow strips of land with one terminus facing the St Lawrence River. In the original settlements, water frontage was usually 600–750-ft (200–250-meters) wide and had a depth of several miles. Following a French feudal model, colonization in French Canada used *seigneurs* – usually merchants, soldiers, priests and gentlemen farmers – as principal real estate agents for frontier properties. Usually a large tract was granted to a *seigneur* who had to promise the French crown that he would settle the land. Once *habitants* (farmers) were found, they were given tenancy on the land and had the responsibility to build a house, harvest crops each year, pay rent (*cens*) and fringe benefits (usually a yearly ham or a tub of butter) to the *seigneur*, and agree to the *corvée* (a feudal service) that most often involved construction and road work. In return, the *seigneur* erected a mill and oven, handled disputes, and tried to nurture an environment of bucolic prosperity.

A typical stretch of farmland was usually divided into several tiers: close to the house (and therefore the water) was a vegetable garden, a broad band of cultivated land followed, then meadows and pasture lands, and finally a timber reserve or wooded area used for fuel, tools and building material.

In the 18th century when New France's population expanded dramatically, a second row of backlots (and eventually a third) were joined to the first band. Each cluster of these lots, referred to as a *rang*, had its own council house, school, chapel, butter and cheese dairies, and frequently included a rural women's circle. The poor people in each community were cared for by means of *guignolées* (collections), and communal working projects were organized for building, moving, woodcutting, harvesting and land clearing.

The narrow plots along the river became the fundamental social unit of early French Canadian culture, and they profoundly influenced the way in which New France emerged. The linear settlement pattern with houses clustered along the waterfront established a compelling solidarity among the *habitants*. Few other colonies in Canada developed this kind of built-in interdependency. As one historian has noted, the uniformity of these narrow lots created a "peculiar social equality among households" with mutual assistance playing a key role in the community. As a result, French Canada never suffered from the rise of the large estate and the divisive social stratification associated with it.

One institution reflecting the importance of neighbors was the *premier voisin* (first cousin), usually the head of the next-door family. Invited to most family functions and included in all important decisions, the *premier voisin* helped out with any major project and was called upon for help when any emergency arose. In return, his family always received a loaf of bread on baking day or a slab of meat during the slaughtering season.

The life of the farmer in France was, in many ways, remarkably suited to Canada. Both France and the St Lawrence region were good dairy countries with few milk-souring heat waves and possessed soils suitable for growing *légumes*, root crops, hay, and fruits rather than cereals. The core diet of the *habitants* strongly echoed the typical fare of a French peasant, with a few changes: peas and pork became central ingredients in many dishes, particularly in the form of a daily staple: pea soup.

One 18th-century trader recorded the recipe for this now famous French Canadian dish: "The tin kettle in which they [a group of fur traders] cook their food would hold eight to ten gallons. It was hung over the fire, nearly full of water, then nine quarts of peas – one quart per person, the daily allowance – were put in; and when they were well bursted, two or three pounds of pork, cut into strips, for seasoning, were added, and allowed to boil or simmer until daylight when the cook added four biscuits, broken up, to the mess, and invited all hands to breakfast. The swelling of the peas and biscuits had now filled the kettle to the brim, so thick that a stick would stand upright in it... The men now squatted in a circle, the kettle to the mouth, with almost electric speed, soon filled every cavity." (From Edith Fowke's *Folklore of Canada*).

In New France, the *habitants* could supplement their diet with game, particularly wild hare and venison, as well as an abundant supply of fish from the St Lawrence River. Eels, which were considered a delicacy in France, were more readily available and were eaten raw, smoked, dried and stewed.

The folklorist Edith Fowke notes that the *habitants,* following an old French recipe, would simmer the molluscs in cream along with cider, salted pork and onions. British colonists to the south imported this recipe, where it was to become New England clam chowder.

In the new colony, milk became a core part of the French peasant's diet and was used in the preparation of almost every meal. In one popular dish, milk was boiled; then chunks of bread were thrown into it along with great quantities of maple sugar. The soggy mixture was spooned out into bowls and eaten as a kind of bread pudding in the evening. These game and milk dishes were rounded out by wild berries, garden vegetables, especially carrots, onions, cabbage, turnips and eventually potatoes. Cabbage dishes were also popular because, according to French folk medicine, cabbage cured venereal diseases, increased a mother's milk, and prevented hair from falling out.

The *habitants'* daily menu consisted of a breakfast of pancakes, bread, salted pork, and cider (until replaced by coffee and tea). A noontime lunch of pea soup with fried potatoes and a garden vegetable followed. At around 4 o'clock in the afternoon, leftovers from lunch would be consumed along with a cucumber salad and bread smeared with either pork fat or butter.

The final meal of the day was eaten at eight or nine o'clock in the evening, when a bowl of bread cooked in milk and sugar would be served along with cider.

Although today's French Canadian diet has changed drastically from that of the *habitants*, many of the old foods associated with holidays are still remarkably popular: *tortières*, meatball stew, sausages, onion sauce, maple sugar candies and donuts among them. Even by today's health-conscious standards, Canada's first European settlers had a healthy diet that was well balanced in calories and protein and, with few exceptions, pleasing to the average palate. ∎

With the bumptious Americans to the south, peace was unlikely to endure. War came once more in October 1813, when 5,000 troops under Major-General Hampton advanced on Montreal from the west. A decisive battle was fought at Chateauguay, where fewer than 1,000 Canadians commanded by Lieutenant-Colonel Charles de Salaberry defeated the Americans.

Although Montreal was the first city of Canada, both commercially and strategically,

timorous Montrealers lived in daily fear of having their throats cut by savage Irishmen. One of their marching songs gives a better idea of their motives, and mien:

We are the Fenian brotherhood, skilled in
the arts of war
And we're going to fight for Ireland, the
land that we adore,
Many battles we have won, along with the
boys in blue
And now we're going to conquer Canada –

the main battles of the War of 1812 were fought in Ontario. But Montreal did feel the effects, if only psychological ones, of the unrest in the threat of "Fenian raids."

The Fenians, Irish Americans whose name comes from the Irish motto *Sinn Fein* (which translates to "ourselves alone" and is today the name of the Irish Republican Army's political wing), harassed settlers all along Canada's southern border during the 1812 war and after America's bloody Civil War (1861–65).

The sallies of the Fenians never amounted to anything like an invasion, even though

because we ain't got nothing else to do.

But the Fenians did have some bite, as Canadians learned in the early morning of April 7, 1868. Thomas d'Arcy McGee, one of the Fathers of Confederation, was returning from an all-night meeting when he was shot and killed outside his home in Ottawa by agents who claimed to be connected with the Fenian cause. This has the dubious distinction of being the first political assassination in Canadian history. When news of the death travelled, a huge crowd of mourners gathered to wait for D'Arcy McGee's body at Montreal's Bonaventure Station.

A salutary effect of the War of 1812 was that its threat to Canada's economy hastened the founding of the colony's first bank, the Bank of Montreal, which was chartered in 1817. The war had also indicated the very real danger of moving men and supplies past the Lachine Rapids when time was of the essence; nobody had successfully navigated the rapids that had stopped Cartier, and they remained extremely arduous. In 1821, with money "panhandled" from the provincial and British governments, the Lachine Canal was completed – almost 200 years after a canal had first been suggested by the far-sighted Dollier de Cassons.

completed a grand term in office, performing Montreal's first census and donating the land for Viger Square, Montreal's most popular park, between the 1860s and 1890s.

Montreal's first mayor also coined the city motto, *Concordia Salus* (Health lies in Concord), giving it the distinctive coat of arms that conjoins the national symbols of France, England, Scotland and Ireland. The Societies of St Jean-Baptiste, St Andrew, St Patrick and St George were all founded at this time. "Concordia Salus," certainly, but old ties still die hard.

The prosperity and optimism of the 1820s were shattered by events that shook Montreal

Improvements were also evident on the city streets, lit from 1815 onward with gas lamps. The purpose of this innovation appeared to be mostly social – a decree said the lamps were installed so "that ladies might be induced to visit their friends much more frequently."

Also in this period (1825), the City of Montreal was incorporated, and its first mayor, Jacques Viger, was elected. Viger

Preceding pages: fashion was as important in 1897 as it is now. Left, and above, Cornelius Kreighoff's portraits of French-Canadian life.

in the 1830s. The 1837 rebellions in Toronto and Montreal indicated that not everyone was satisfied with the colonial government and its wide-open opportunities for the rich to get richer.

In Montreal, a group of reformers known as *les Patriotes* and led by, among others, Louis Joseph Papineau demanded the reform of a system that was to a large extent controlled by a clique of family interests. Representative government was a radical notion in these times, of course, and the majority of people found the demands of the *Patriotes* unpalatable.

Britain refused to acknowledge the 92 resolutions drawn up by Papineau and his associates which demanded, among other things, the dissolution of the appointed governing Council of Lower Canada, known as the *Château Clique* (the reference is to Château St-Louis, Quebec's Government House). Papineau called for a council of elected representatives to replace the inbred and self-serving clique, which, like the Family Compacts controlling Upper Canada, doled out privilege and contracts with the arrogant disdain of absolute monarchs.

The atmosphere in Montreal was ripe for violence: cholera epidemics in 1832 and 1834 had ravaged the population, and political clubs and duelling societies fomented the unrest by meeting publicly to argue and fight. On November 6, 1837, a fierce riot broke out on peaceful St James Street and spilled into Place d'Armes. After dark, the house of Papineau and the offices of the *Vindicator*, a newspaper supporting him, were wrecked. Two weeks of uneasy silence were broken by the imposition of martial law when Sir John Colborne, the commander-in-chief, set up his headquarters in the Château Ramezay and dispatched troops to hunt down the *Patriotes*. Many, including Papineau, fled to the United States.

Others were not so resourceful. Twelve captured *Patriotes*, most of them young men who had worn, with a jaunty tilt, the white "O'Connell" top hat, a recognized badge of the radical, were publicly hanged by the authorities. Sixty or 70 more were banished, and Montreal's last sight of the Rebellion was a chain gang of forlorn prisoners being marched down to the Bonsecours landing stage, there to embark on their long journey to New South Wales or Tasmania.

The sentences may seem harsh, but despite its new metropolitan status, Montreal was still a frontier town, and magistrates felt obliged to judge stiffly. In 1817, the crimes of sacrilege and shoplifting were still punishable by execution, as was the even more serious crime of horse-stealing. Petty crimes were typically punished with humiliation in

Right, the men's snowshoe club turned essential winter footwear into an excuse for social activity.

the stocks or the pillory, but judges were also in the habit of having small-time criminals branded on the palm of the hand with a heated iron. The brand, in the shape of a crown, was held to the flesh for as long as it took the convicted criminal to repeat "*Vive le roi!*" three times. It was more likely to be "God save the King!" however, since the session lists from these times show that the vast majority of tried criminals in Montreal were British or itinerant Loyalist Americans, and not francophone Québécois.

Britain's reaction to the trouble in the colonies was to dispatch the Earl of Durham to survey the state of public affairs there.

Lord Durham's famous *Report on the Affairs of British North America* was the first document to isolate French-English tensions as a source of political worry in Canada. In 1841, partly as a result of Durham's suggestions, the provinces of Upper and Lower Canada (today Ontario and Quebec) were joined in an Act of Union that was the beginning of modern Canada. In 1843 Montreal was made capital of the new united Province of Canada, but it enjoyed that honor for all too short a time: only five years.

In 1848, while revolution was sweeping Europe, the reactionary element of Montreal

sacked the Parliament Building and burned it to the ground after the legislators approved a bill to compensate *Patriotes* punished in 1837. The members of the house fled, leaving the building to be destroyed. The vandals, carrying the Speaker's ceremonial mace, ran through the streets and attacked the residences of the parliamentarians, including that of the governor-general, Lord Elgin.

After this debacle, the Canadian parliament was moved to Toronto and alternated between there and Quebec until a permanent site was chosen in Ottawa, on the banks of the Ottawa River. A Boston newspaper gave a gloomy picture of the city in the 1840s: "Montreal wears a dismal aspect... the removal of the seat of government caused some 4,000 inhabitants to leave... every third store seems to want an occupant and empty houses groan for tenants."

If that weren't enough, typhus brought to the city's harbor in 1847 killed more than 6,000 people; the Great Fire of 1852 – only the worst in a long series – lasted for 26 days, destroying 1,200 buildings and leaving 9,000 people homeless.

Despite these setbacks, Montreal was well on its way to becoming what one contemporary called "the first city in magnitude and commercial importance in British America." Although the fur trade was waning, the enterprising rich of Montreal had diversified their investments and Molson's steamship line was doing a good trade between Montreal and Quebec City.

A guidebook of the time also recommended the city's brisk weather. "The climate," it said, "though severe in winter, is exceedingly conducive to health and longevity and the average mortality is much less than many other cities in North America."

The old harbor had been renovated by a number of energetic young builders, including Englishman John Ostwell, who at the tender age of 19 was given the job of designing the new Customs House. The new Bank of Montreal building was erected in Place d'Armes by the Scot David Rhind, who based it on Edinburgh's grand Bank of Scotland building.

The railways came to Montreal in 1853 when the Grand Trunk Railway Co. began running a service to Portland, Maine, following it with a line to the still provincial city of Toronto in 1856.

A final event symbolizes this era of expansion and commercial vigor, when Montreal was the New York of Canada, its St James Street as important as Wall Street. In 1860, Albert, the 19-year-old Prince of Wales (later King Edward VII), opened the magnificent Victoria Bridge.

The stage was now set for Montreal to assume primacy of place in the new confederated Canada. In the 1860s, as suggested earlier, the American Civil War and Fenian aggression reached the minds of Montrealers.

hearing of the conference to which they had not been invited, decided to crash the party and plead their own case. At the head of this group was John A. Macdonald, the wily, alcoholic Scotsman destined to be Canada's first prime minister, whose slightly irresolute portrait now adorns Canada's $10 bill.

Macdonald and his cohorts chartered the *Queen Victoria* in Quebec City, loaded her with $13,000 worth of champagne, and steamed down the St Lawrence to Prince Edward Island. Despite a very modest reception – a single oyster boat – Macdonald was able, with the aid of his precious cargo, to persuade the Atlantic colonists that Canada

Blacks fleeing slavery were now to be seen on the city streets, and a defeated Jefferson Davis sheltered for a time in a house on Mountain Street. Fear of growing American influence made confederation a popular notion among Montrealers.

In 1867, representatives of the Atlantic colonies decided to meet in Charlottetown, capital of Prince Edward Island, to discuss the prospects for a united Atlantic Colony. The leaders of Upper and Lower Canada,

Left, watching the ice break up on the St Lawrence. **Above**, the leisured classes soon created parks.

should be part of any union. The rough terms for confederation were agreed upon at what one disgusted New Brunswick editorialist described as "the great intercolonial drunk." They were later ratified at a conference in Quebec, and on July 1, 1867, the British North America Act created modern Canada by joining Nova Scotia, New Brunswick, Ontario and Quebec.

The new country was embroiled in scandal almost from the beginning. MacDonald quickly became involved in the Métis Rebellion scandal, an uprising that occurred when the government purchased Rupert's Land out west but neglected to take into account the indigenous population living there. The Métis were a mixture of French and Amerindian, and their leader, Louis Riel, won the sympathy of many Montrealers. When MacDonald decided to have Riel hanged, he was quoted as saying: "He shall hang though every dog in Quebec should bark in his favor." Riel's death only served to entrench French-English hatred.

In addition, to hasten a railway link to western Canada and the Pacific, Macdonald and his colleague from Lower Canada, Georges-Etienne Cartier, had accepted party contributions from a group of Montreal busi-

With the CPR deal cut if not dried, Macdonald's ailing campaign was bolstered by "anonymous" gifts of money, first $60,000 and then $35,000. With his campaign in its final days, Macdonald foolishly wired Sir Hugh for more: "I must have another ten thousand. Will be the last time of calling. Do not fail me."

Sir Hugh considered the political financing simple tactics in good business, but the public did not see it that way. The office of Sir Hugh's solicitor in Montreal was ransacked late one night by a confidential clerk, and as a result the incriminating telegram appeared on the front page of Montreal's

nessmen who wanted the contract to build it. The Canadian Pacific Railway (CPR) Bill was passed by Parliament in 1870 but the backroom dealing reached public attention soon after. Focus of the scandal was Sir Hugh Allan, a prosperous Montreal shipper frequently to be seen walking the streets in a tartan waistcoat, his bushy beard well-groomed, or surveying the grounds of his massive estate, Ravenscrag. The estate's mansion, a self-congratulatory tribute to Canada's then richest man, is still standing. Today it houses the Neurological Institute of the Royal Victoria Hospital.

newspapers. Macdonald and Cartier had to resign, and a despairing Cartier died the following year. Macdonald, a more accomplished political survivor, outlasted the public's short memory for wrongdoing and was back in office in 1878.

The railway was delayed, but not stopped. On June 28, 1886, with bands playing, the first passenger train steamed out of Montreal's old Dalhousie Station, bound for Port Moody, British Columbia.

St Jean-Baptiste Day celebrations. June 24 has always embodied a marked French nationalism.

GAMES FOR IDLE HOURS

Most people today, faced with so many leisure pursuits, can scarcely imagine a time when no organized recreation existed. Yet such was the case for the first French Canadians who, especially during the long winter months, had, to put it plainly, time on their hands. They talked away the evenings, of course, played cards, and sometimes held dances; but a common amusement, which has now all but died out in North America and Europe, consisted of parlor games.

Folklorist Maurice Tremblay has recorded several Québécois parlor games, descendants of colonial French Canada's indoor recreation. He divides these games into two categories: games that test strength and skill; and games that fool or mystify one of the players.

Because the games stem from the experiences of a predominantly Catholic and agricultural society, they can tell us much about early Québécois rural life. Many of the games draw on physical endurance, emphasize a battle of wills, and incorporate the imagery of farming. Others (such as "The Last Judgement") poke fun at the church and are a kind of risqué satirizing of popular religious myths. While some of the games are moderately indecent and others are downright crude (such as "Breaking Wind"), all combine a sense of mischievous fun and high spirits.

The games probably also functioned as important social tools since they taught a kind of practical folk-wisdom to each participant: recognition of one's limitations, humility, a sense of humor, determination, endurance, and good-natured competitiveness. As Tremblay writes of these intriguing parlor games, just as "peasant wisdom encourages ambition and appreciates real worth, it endeavors on the other hand to teach humility in success, a knowledge of one's shortcomings, and the acceptance, with equanimity, of the vexations as well as the joys of life."

Below is a sampling of how many of Montreal's first *habitants* "bided their time" through indoor frolics. Most of the games listed are men's activities, although some (like "Asking Favors of the Holy Virgin") have special roles for women.

Games of Strength and Skill

Smacking Bottoms: Two players sit on the floor, the feet of one between the legs of another, each holding a towel in his right hand. While one rolls on his back the other slaps him on the buttocks with the towel. The players take turns until one cries out for mercy.

Kissing the Thumb: A player hangs himself by the arm to a pipe in the ceiling or beam; he then must raise his body to kiss his thumb.

Loading the Sheep: A player lying on the floor makes himself go limp as if dead; a second player tries to lift him onto his shoulder.

Threading a Needle Sitting on a Bottle: A bottle is laid on its side and a player sits on it cross-legged. The player must then thread a needle while trying to keep the bottle from rolling.

Duelling Forks: The feet of two players are tied together; then their hands are tied together under their thighs. Both hold forks between their hands and try to prick each other's buttocks. This goes on until one gives up.

Pulling the Stick: Two players, sitting facing each other on the floor with the soles of their feet together, grasp a broom horizontally. Each pulls the broom towards him until the stronger pulls the weaker up off the floor.

Games of Mystification

Asking for Favors from the Holy Virgin: A woman puts a veil over her hair and sits on a chair, playing the role of the Holy Virgin. Other players bring her someone who wants to ask her for a favor. After listening to the request, the Holy Virgin makes the applicant come close to her and sprays him or her with water, previously held in her mouth.

The Last Judgement: A table is set in the middle of a room and covered with a large rug, one corner of which falls to the floor. Another rug is placed on the floor facing the Judge, but with one end of it extending under the table. One player is the judge and sits on a chair behind the table. Another player hides beneath the table, and so is hidden from view. The people to be judged are in another room, unaware of the man under the table. They are brought in one by one. After being questioned, each one is condemned to hell and the player hiding underneath the table pulls the rug from under the condemned. Surprised (and hopefully frightened), the condemned person falls to the ground.

Nursing the Sick: The person playing the doctor is sent out of the room. He is then called in to nurse a sick child but is given a spoon whose handle has been previously heated.

Weighing the Bacon: The player to be weighed has a blanket put over his head. While two other players pretend to weigh him by lifting him under the arms, a fourth player places a basin under the one being weighed and they let him fall into it.

Breaking Wind: Two men lie down with the head of one near the feet of another. One man places his seat against the other who tries to break wind if he can. The game goes on in turns.

Shooting the Rapids: Several people sit astride a long bench. The first player grips the ends of the bench while the others cross their hands over the eyes of the person in front. The game is supposed to consist of the first player not losing his grip as the others pull him backwards but, unbeknownst to him, the player covering his eyes has had his hands covered with soot which is smeared all over the first player's face. ∎

Montreal faced heady times. It was now indisputably the center of the unified Canada, a Canada optimistic about its coast-to-coast railroad and its imminent entry into the 20th century. It was also arguably the most beautiful city in the country.

In 1868 an American visitor marvelled at the fine architecture of the town. "I am much struck," he said, "by the continued rapid growth of this now great northern city... The buildings everywhere in course of erection would dignify any city. There are none in the United States which present finer specimens of street architecture than are found, not isolated here and there, but in long blocks and throughout the city." This excellent aspect was visible in the newly developed harbor, with a terrace of new buildings in the then popular neoclassical style. Wealthy merchants from the old town moved their premises to larger lots on Ste-Catherine and Sherbrooke Streets. In 1891 Henry Morgan opened Canada's first department store, the Colonial House, later taken over by the Hudson's Bay Company.

But the glow of these golden years was dimmed by social inequity and industrial hardship. Montreal had several desperate, disease-ridden slums of which Point St Charles was the largest, a jumble of shacks housing the workers from Robert Griffin's soap factory and so known locally as Griffintown, a name it retained well into the 20th century.

Immigration was, from the late 19th century on, both blessing and curse. The cheap source of labor the immigrants provided for booming industry (now including huge grain elevators on the waterfront and heavier shipping) was welcome; but the population explosion posed serious difficulties for Montreal's housing and sanitation resources. In 1825 the population of Montreal was 26,000; by 1850 it had doubled. By 1865, it had doubled again and the city passed the 100,000 mark. By 1910, Montreal's population was more than 500,000 and growing fast. The lot of many people was unremittingly hard: back-breaking factory work, tiny shacks to live in, and the threat of epidemics.

The new Montrealers came from everywhere: Ireland fleeing famine, from eastern Europe, from China, from Greece, Italy and Portugal. And they followed the pattern being established in cities all over North America. While the older inhabitants moved farther from harbor and train station – in the case of Montreal, farther up the hill – the new

Montrealers put down their battered suitcases wherever, and as soon as, they could.

Today one can walk up Boulevard St Laurent, the fabled "Main" of Montreal, and map the ethnic neighborhoods with ease: a kind of striatic record of Montreal's immigration waves, with the Chinese on La Gauchetière, the European Jews near St-Urbain, the Greeks along Avenue du Park. Here, along with some of the city's best restaurants, you can find people sitting on their terraces and balconies, retaining traditions from the turn of the century.

With this new diversification in Montreal, the old moneyed families began increasingly

Preceding pages: the 20th century brought a building boom. **Left,** the ultra-modern BNP building. **Above,** the Olympic Park Tower.

to shut their doors. In the 1890s Montreal was known as "the city of merchant princes," but the princes were haughty. No longer did the aristocrats of Montreal walk the streets like James McGill, or even the garrulous Sir Hugh Allan. Instead they stayed in their Westmount estates, found others like themselves in exclusive new men's clubs like the Canadian and the Mount Royal, and moved around Canada's business counters from inside buildings that rose away from the downtown streets.

Few bothered to learn French as their grandfathers had, and the gap between rich and poor, English and French, widened. The French still played the dominant role in Montreal's daily

Québécois perceived themselves as once more bullied by imperial aggression overseas. The premier, Maurice Duplessis, spoke for many when he argued that the federal government did not speak for French Canadians.

There was no easy solution. Jailing objectors was one option, but it risked creating martyrs. The federal government's inability to meet this crisis with effective measures became a sign of its ongoing problem with the separatist sentiments among the Québécois.

The early English governors of Lower Canada had not faced the French fact squarely; now the easy mix of French and English that marked Montreal's early history was no longer

life, but the English minority controlled a disproportionate slice of the city economy. The animosity between French and English Montreal was exacerbated by the conscription controversy of World War I.

The Québécois men of Montreal had no quarrel with Britain's enemies, and many objected to being forcibly enlisted in the war effort. These so-called "zombies" became the scourge of Canada. They were vilified in the national press and publicly declared cowards.

The same issue arose during World War II. Whereas the war seemed to offer many English Canadians relief – and a job – the

available. Economic disparity, the sense that control rested with a few privileged Westmount families, and the reality of Canada's growing anglophone population all contributed to the feeling among French-speaking Canadians that they were second-class citizens, a nuisance, and in danger of being assimilated forever.

Moreover, by the 1950s, Montreal was no longer riding the strong wave of industrial and commercial success that marked its entry into the new century. Canada's focus was shifting away from the river ports and toward the Great Lakes, especially Toronto. The strong axis that had existed between Montreal and New

York – since John Jacob Astor had entered the fur trade in the 1820s by wooing ambitious Montrealers away from the Hudson's Bay and North-West companies – began to shift too.

No longer did the wealthy of Montreal hire New York's celebrated architects to construct their massive monuments to themselves. Montreal was still a desirable place for a New Yorker to visit, but now for pleasure rather than business. The sidewalk cafés and brasseries of Paris could be found here now, populated by black-clad existentialists puffing on Gitanes and looking as though the weight of angst was just too, too much. But if the high-rollers from New York wanted to talk turkey,

The church, no longer able to exert daily control, retreated in sulky seclusion. The descendants of Quebec's *habitants* were radicalized. Montreal and Quebec City, site of the provincial government, became hotbeds of intellectual activity as the thinkers of Quebec society tried to find their footing in the shifting international terrain. Separatism fomented in the seminar rooms of Université Laval and Université de Montréal, and then in the cafés of Grand Allée and Rue Ste-Catherine. The prevailing feeling was that Quebec was culturally French, and always had been. Why were the people of Quebec enduring a federalist government policy that failed to protect the

they headed for dour, provincial Toronto and the gleaming towers of Bay Street.

So, like all Quebec, Montreal was in some disarray in the post-war period. In the 1950s and '60s the so-called "Quiet Revolution" (*see page 76*) transformed the rural province from an almost feudal Catholic society into a 20th-century democracy. Change, once slow to arrive, now worked its double-edged magic.

Left, Prime Minister MacKenzie King, center, with wartime leaders Franklin D. Roosevelt and Sir Winston Churchill. Above, Pierre Trudeau (left in picture) brought style to government.

uniqueness of that culture and forced them, in effect, to become English?

Ottawa was conciliatory and threatening by turns, but matters did not come to a head until October 5, 1970, when the *Front de Libération du Québec* (FLQ) captured the British trade commissioner, James Cross. Five days later the FLQ kidnapped the Quebec labor minister, Pierre Laporte, whose body was found two weeks later. These acts of terrorism followed an extensive FLQ letter-bombing campaign, and frequent calls for "Independence or Death!"

The Prime Minister, Pierre Trudeau, himself a Québécois and product of Laval's radical law faculty, invoked the War Measures Act (Canada's equivalent of martial law) for the first time during peace in this "October Crisis." The revolution, expected daily by the students on Montreal's streets, never came. Instead came the soldiers – 10,000 of them – ordered into Montreal on October 16.

But separatism was not quelled. The Parti Québécois (PQ), formed in 1968 by the dynamic René Lévesque, gained power in Quebec on November 15, 1976 and worked to bring the matter to a vote. The PQ's 1979 referendum on "sovereignty-association" failed with the voters, but succeeded in driving many of the strong English minority from

Montreal, where they had clustered for 300 years. Businesses quietly left Montreal during the 1970s and '80s, setting up shop in Toronto instead, thus sealing Montreal's commercial fate. Between 1976 and 1981, an estimated 100 head offices left Montreal, taking about 14,000 jobs with them. If Montreal business had been sputtering in the '50s and '60s, it was now in a tailspin.

The separatism issue brought Montreal and Quebec generally to the attention of the world. When, in 1967, General Charles de Gaulle stood on the steps of Montreal's City Hall and cried *"Vive le Québec libre!"* it was a slogan heard not only from coast to coast in Canada, but around the globe.

Yet other less polemic features of the city have also achieved world fame. In 1967, to coincide with Canada's centennial celebration, the World's Fair was held in Montreal. Expo '67 brought millions of visitors, foreign and domestic, to Canada's most culturally diverse (if no longer most powerful) city. Aggressive politicking on the part of Montreal's legendary mayor, Jean Drapeau brought the city the 1976 Summer Olympics.

After the disaster of Munich in 1972, when terrorists slaughtered members of the Israeli team, the Montreal Games were a massive success. And most of the Olympic visitors cared little that the city had overspent vastly on the facilities, or that the Olympic Stadium is still unfinished according to the original plans (though now modified and home to Montreal's major-league baseball franchise, the Expos).

With the defeat of the Parti Québécois in the 1980s, Quebec's political focus shifted away from strong separatism to a more demanding participation in Canadian confederation. The 1988 Meech Lake constitutional accord guaranteed Quebec's right to "a separate and distinct culture" – its failure to be ratified in 1990 revived hostility between French and English Canadians. Under Quebec's restrictive language laws, Bill 101, merchants were not allowed to display English signs in their windows. Unilingual donut bags were seized, Harris tweed imports were stopped until a French translation was supplied, and windows displaying "Wet Paint" signs were smashed.

Slowly, the elements of a new deal emerged. For the west, the appointed Senate would be replaced with an elected body designed to enhance the power of regions over the national government. For Québec, a modified version of its five Meech Lake demands would be included. Rights of immigrant Canadians and women would be explicitly reconfirmed, and the issue of self-government for natives would be tackled. This ambitious project culminated in a second Accord, in August 1992 at Charlottetown, PEI. The Accord was submitted to a national referendum in October, requiring majority support in all provinces to pass. Six provinces passed it by narrow margins. Four, including Québec, rejected it soundly. In the wake of the defeat, all talk of constitutional amendment was abandoned, and Prime Minister Brian Mulroney resigned soon afterwards. His successor, Kim Campbell, led the party into a disastrous general election which left it with just two seats instead of 153. The Liberals, under Jean Chrétien, took over the reins of power, with the separatist Bloc Québécois the second largest party.

This shock result boosted the fortunes of Lucien Bouchard, formerly a Progressive Conservative environment minister who had quit over the failure of Meech Lake and founded the Bloc Québécois. The son of a

defeated by a wafer-thin margin of 1.12 percent. Québec's separatist premier, Jacques Parizeau, resigned, but there was little for the "winners" to celebrate. The high turnout of 93 percent of voters proved the strength of feeling on both sides, and the government in Ottawa had to face the fact that half of Québec was seriously discontented. How long before the next referendum – and what would the result be? The answer from Lucien Bouchard was unequivocal: "Keep hope," he told a dejected rally, "because the next time will be ours."

Politics in Quebec is not so simple, however. In April 1998 Daniel Johston resigned

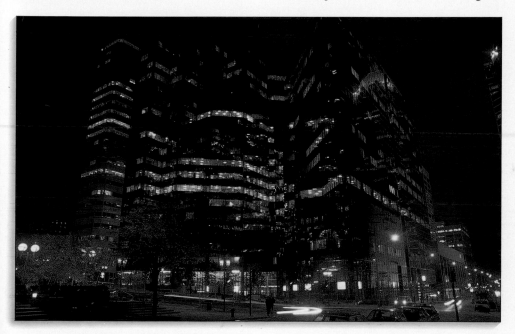

truck driver from the northern forestlands of Lac St-Jean, he became the most charismatic Canadian politician since Pierre Trudeau. The amputation of his left leg after he was attacked by a flesh-eating bacterium only served to enhance his charisma.

Although himself a Quebecer, Jean Chrétien underestimated the strength of the separatist movement and was given a rude shock when, in a 1995 referendum, the proposal to grant Québec independence was

Left, the old-style Windsor Station. **Above**, the new-style Mercantile Bank Building.

as leader of the province's Liberal party and Jean Charest was persuaded to switch from leader of the federal Progressive Conservatives to leader of Quebec's Liberals. In November Bouchard called a snap election. The Liberals' performance was less than inspiring and pollsters unanimously predicted a massive defeat for the party. Although the PQ won 75 seats compared to the Liberals' 48, the Liberals won the popular vote. Going into the millennium, Quebecers are prepared to give the PQ government another chance, but their enthusiasm for another referendum has markedly declined.

THE QUIET REVOLUTION

Despite its many historic sites, Montreal will strike the visitor of today as a quintessentially modern place, a city of glass towers, busy streets, and cosmopolitan population. It was not always so. In the years immediately following World War II, when most of North America was chugging happily towards the Space Age, the province of Quebec still resembled something like a medieval society. Montreal, its urban jewel, was run like an isolated city-state. Church interests dictated public policy from backrooms, political corruption was rife, and the people lived in ignorance of a wider world.

The series of events that changed the face of modern Quebec, and made Montreal's reputation as Canada's most interesting city, are called in Canada "the Quiet Revolution" – an appropriate label in a country with little history of civil violence. Quebec's revolution *was* quiet, but it changed the province in profound ways. If in today's Montreal you notice keen political debate in the newspapers and cafés, people taking advantage of the city's cultural opportunities, remember that it was not always possible. If you notice, less charmingly perhaps, fewer black cassocks on the streets and more churches sinking into disrepair – this, too, is the legacy of Quebec's social revolution.

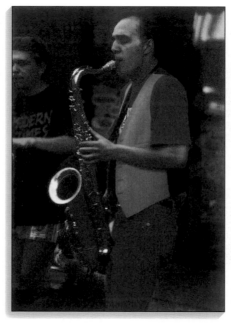

Change, when it came, was swift. Quebec moved wholesale into the 20th century in just a few years (roughly 1960–65), with a handful of journalists, intellectuals and disaffected workers challenging the stagnation of the *ancien régime* with articles, debates and labor action. And what was the focus of these quiet revolutionaries of Quebec? The answer is not surprising. Reformist feeling on the streets of Montreal, as on the streets of Paris two centuries earlier, focused on two targets: the church and the state.

The Roman Catholic church, long a powerful force among Montreal's French Canadians and Irish, had found new strength in the mid-century influx of eastern European immigrants. It continued to play a role in Quebec life not significantly different from the days in the 18th century, when prelates banned card playing and sacrilege was punishable by death. Rural and small-town inhabitants of Quebec lived in grinding poverty, deferring to the wisdom of parish priests and corrupt politicians, looking on Montreal and Quebec City as though they were foreign capitals instead of their own cities.

The Church did little in those post-war years to dispel the ignorance and backwardness that held most of Quebec in thrall. The province's parish priests controlled most aspects of daily life, ruling rural Québécois with a combination of moral terrorism and personal authority.

Rebellious parishioners, even schoolchildren remiss in their catechism, were likely to be isolated and accused during Sunday sermons. Also, many of the province's most corrupt politicians learned their politics, as well as their theology, at the hands of Catholic educators, and were schooled early in the practice of annexing the moral high ground in debates on social policy.

Until the 1960s, political control of Quebec was lodged firmly in the hands of premier Maurice Duplessis (1890–1959) and his Union Nationale party. With a stranglehold on the provincial parliament – known as the National Assembly – Duplessis and his cronies were able to barter public works for votes, sell liquor and building licenses for huge profits, and stretch their political tenure into a graft-ridden 16-year dynasty.

Duplessis had first been elected in 1937 and had guided disgruntled Québécois through the conscription crisis of World War II, articulating very well the isolationist stance most Québécois found persuasive. But from 1944 to 1960 the Union Nationale enjoyed absolute power in Quebec, and as a result allowed themselves the luxury of absolute corruption.

A royal commission investigating the Union Nationale in 1961 estimated that more than $100 million worth of graft had been paid out by companies doing business with the provincial government in these years. The going rate for Montreal liquor licenses (later to be had for about $100) was $30,000. Duplessis, a hysterical anti-communist, busted strikes with glee, enjoyed publicly humiliating his own ministers, and taunted his hapless opponents who could not promise the roads and hospitals he traded for votes.

Through all this, Quebec's powerful English minority remained unmoved; it was the journalist André Laurendeau who first suggested that they were actually supporting Duplessis as the province's *roi nègre*. The complicity of the English economic czars of Montreal suggested to Laurendeau, and to many others since, that Duplessis was a puppet – a "black king" allowed to rule a profitable colony by imperial interests jealous of their investments. While Duplessis was denouncing English businessmen in public, his tyrannical government was providing them with a very stable investment environment.

meshed with new liberal feeling that found the moral totalitarianism of the Church outmoded and offensive. And the casual nexus between church and state was one of the first targets of the newly radicalized thinking, ending an era in which the parish priest would inform his parishioners of the "morally right choice" – the Union Nationale candidate – in provincial elections. Economic changes were also underway, and as Quebec's abundant natural resources (hydro-electric power, uranium and timber) became more valuable than ever in world markets the Québécois began to experience fledging fortune.

The nation, too, was changing. In 1965, to signal that the country had broken its firm ties with the British Empire tradition, the old Canadian flag,

Still, the voters of Quebec have their own complicity to answer for; Duplessis did not stay in power because of the tacit approval of a few dozen powerful Montreal anglos. René Lévesque, who served in the Liberal government that finally overthrew the Union Nationale after Duplessis's death, called his reign *la grande noirceur* (the great darkness) and said Quebec had been "cursed" and "damned" by the dictatorial premier's tenure.

Duplessis's death in 1959 proved a catalyst to change beyond the walls of the provincial parliament. Rural Québécois discovered that ignorance and poverty were not divinely-ordained conditions. The resentment building against the Duplessis government, in the universities and elsewhere,

modeled on the Union Jack, was replaced by the Maple Leaf Flag.

By the late 1960s, the new political feeling had gelled into strong Quebec separatism, the Church was either retreating into sullen isolationism or embracing the reforms of Vatican II, and the people of Quebec were enjoying a level of economic prosperity unimaginable a decade before. As befits a *quiet* revolution – there were no barricades, no storming of prisons, no guillotine – Montreal today shows few signs of massive social change. But, seen in religious, political and economic terms, the revolution in Quebec's daily life was real enough: *le roi nègre* was dead. The *joi de vivre* that many Montrealers experience and express today has its roots in this "quiet" death of a quasi-theocracy that had dominated their culture for close to three centuries. ∎

Left, jazz in St-Denis. **Above**, Human Steps typify the modern dance style.

Who lives in Montreal? Well, the city has more than its fair share of luminaries. Anybody who's anybody in French Canadian politics and culture can be found here. Not, perhaps, in the phone book, but at theaters and cinemas, the chic St-Denis eateries and late-night cafés.

Pierre Trudeau sightings have been a popular topic of conversation for decades. The former prime minister is one of the most famous downtown residents, although the death of his son in a 1999 skiing accident has, at least temporarily, made his outings less frequent. The streets of Outremont, an exclusive inner-city neighborhood, are packed with present and past political figures whom most Canadians would recognize, if not necessarily put a name to.

The French Canadian entertainment industry is also firmly ensconced in Montreal. Television and film stars frequent the restaurants around the Canadian Broadcasting Corporation (CBC) headquarters in the east end, while the more famous, such as comedian Michel Coté and director Denys Arcand, choose cafés nearer their residences. Rock stars Misou Misou and Robert Charlebois, athletes Maurice "Rocket" Richard and Jean Beliveau, plus the central figures in the Quebec literary scene, Michel Tremblay, Yves Beauchemin and Réjean Ducharme call Montreal home. Those well-known French Canadians who *don't* live in the city are, more often than not, residents of the "other" center of French culture – Paris, France.

The English community, though much smaller, also boasts a few notables. Poet and songwriter Leonard Cohen is associated indelibly with the "Plateau" neighborhood, while novelist Mordecai Richler has immortalized the former Jewish area along Rue St-Urbain. The tycoon business family the Bronfmans, also live here. Other minority communities in the city, including Caribbean, African, European and Asian, all claim

Preceding pages: young Montreal. Left, a ride at La Ronde. Above, taking it easy.

their own rich and famous, all have their venues in which to see and be seen, their newspapers and magazines where stars rise and fall. Montreal is not only a large center but a cosmopolitan one. Diversity is its principal wealth.

Clichés and generalizations only serve to drain vitality from the group being portrayed. In fact, the city is so diverse that finding the "ordinary" Montrealer could be difficult. It is not always possible to say where he or she

eats, or even shops. The "average" Montrealer doesn't exist, because this is a city of 3 million exceptions. Nevertheless, one can venture a few observations about the urban resident. People, after all, *are* Montreal. Buildings and landmarks merely express the will and personality of a population.

French-style: Our fictional but typical French Montrealer is named Madeline. She lives with her husband in a condominium one street east of Outremont. The apartment is a second-storey walk-up with the standard exterior staircase. The building, located so near the classy neighborhood, was recently renovated; prices went up, poorer people moved out, and Madeline moved in. Buying a condominium makes sense in Montreal, a city where nearly 40 percent of the population live in apartments. Buying an apartment "almost" in Outremont makes dollars and sense; resale value is helped by location. The apartment is, by any standard, spacious – long corridors, high ceilings, with a balcony overlooking the street. The couple, both in their early thirties, are childless. They have space in abundance.

Madeline's husband works near the airport, she in a government office in Old Montreal. He takes the car; she rides the

entertainment listings. There are literally hundreds of things to do – music, theater, night clubs – but she ends up making a reservation at a restaurant that is favorably reviewed. It is the end of the week. Her husband will be tired, and she too wouldn't mind a quiet meal. The restaurant is moderately priced and allows customers to bring their own wine. That is more economical. With the mortgage, taxes, payments on the car…

Because it is Friday – pay day – Madeline and two colleagues have lunch in a restaurant. The waiter, who is an anglophone, addresses them in French, but Madeline often answers in English, or English *and* French,

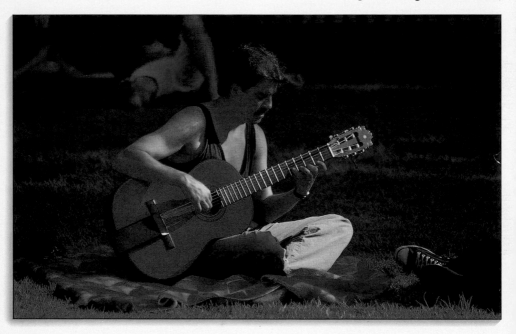

number 80 bus down to Rue St-Antoine. Leaving at eight o'clock, she barely manages a cup of herbal tea and a piece of fruit. While waiting for the bus Madeline buys *La Presse* newspaper, for lighter reading during the ride, but hopes her husband will pick up the more serious *Le Devoir*. In her heart, though, she suspects he will opt for the tabloid *Le Journal de Montréal* – there was a Canadiens hockey game last night and *Le Journal* has the best sports coverage.

At work, where she supervises a department, Madeline spends a 15-minute break eating a muffin and reading the newspaper's

just as she and her friends, one of whom is Italian, switch easily from language to language amongst themselves. She orders a salad. What do they talk about? Work. Husbands. The figure skating competitions on television. One colleague, who is reading a Michel Tremblay novel, offers to get tickets for his new play, opening in Montreal next week. They agree in principle to attend a Sunday performance. All three women smoke and order decaffinated coffee.

Later in the afternoon Madeline gets off the bus at Rue Laurier to shop. She spends 15 minutes in a bookstore admiring Milan

Kundera's new novel and a collection of Québécois fiction, but decides to just pick up a few magazines for the weekend. Besides, she has work from the office in her briefcase: who has time to read? At the bakery she buys croissants for breakfast and delectable cakes for a late-night snack. At the *Société des Alcools* she lingers over the wines, finally selecting a three-year-old Chablis for dinner. A bit of window shopping follows. But it is still too cold, even in April, and she walks quickly home. The car is nowhere to be seen along the street.

Her husband returns shortly afterwards with a copy of *Le Journal* rolled under his

sip cognac while watching the last 20 minutes of the CBC news. Then they go to bed, too tired to watch the video.

English-style: Our English Montrealer is named John. He is a bachelor who lives in NDG (Notre Dame de Grâce), a predominantly English-speaking neighborhood north of Westmount. His apartment is a "3½," meaning one bedroom with a kitchen and living room, and is rent-controlled – the only reason he still lives there. John drives a five-year-old Honda that he finally paid off six months ago, exactly two weeks before a garage bill left him $600 poorer. Commuting from NDG to the Sherbrooke architectural

arm. Traffic on the Metropolitan was even worse than usual, he complains, and he stopped to rent a video – *Batman*, dubbed into French – for midnight viewing. After changing, chatting with Madeline's mother on the phone – her parents live in Chicoutimi, where she grew up – the couple slip the wine into a paper bag and look again at the address of the restaurant. Her husband, on learning that the cuisine is a mix of Thai and Chinese, hopes it won't be too spicy.

Later that evening they eat the cakes and

Left, playing in the park. **Above**, two's company...

firm where he works usually takes 15 minutes, traffic permitting. This morning the traffic does not permit, however, and he arrives at the office a little late.

The firm is composed of French and English speakers. Fifteen years ago, when John first started working there, most business was conducted in English. Today, French predominates. John, who was raised in Westmount and NDG, is fluent, though some of the older anglophone employees speak French only haltingly.

At lunch John hops onto a subway and rides to Place des Arts. He hopes to buy

tickets for that night's concert at The Spectrum, but he arrives to find that it is sold out. Instead he picks up *The Gazette* and spends his hour in the record shops along Rue Ste-Catherine. He buys two compact discs for his system and a cassette for the car stereo. Montreal is a great city for music. Listings for the weekend alone include classical concerts, jazz in bars, lots of rock bands, a Senegalese singer at Concordia University, and a group of Pakistani musicians in a converted church in Côte-St-Luc. The previous December the Rolling Stones played at Olympic Stadium.

Back at the office he returns a phone call from his friend Marc, a francophone friend from his McGill University days nearly 20 years before. Most of his friends are anglophones. Though a few have left Montreal – including his parents, who were relocated to Toronto in 1978 – most continue to live in Westmount, NDG, or Pointe Claire, and continue to work for downtown firms and companies. At parties his friends often talk about the political situation and about moving away, but only rarely do they turn their words into action and uproot themselves. Montreal is, after all, their home.

Marc has great news: tickets for the Canadiens game the next night. It is April, and April in Montreal means hockey playoffs. Tickets for playoff games are impossible to get without connections. How did Marc manage it? John doesn't ask.

To celebrate he invites his friend to dinner. They meet at seven o'clock to enjoy a fiery Indian meal at a tiny restaurant off Rue Queen-Mary. The restaurant owner conducts business in English, which Marc speaks flawlessly. Afterwards the two men go for a few beers in an old college haunt near U de M (Université de Montréal). John orders and begins to tell his friend about work, a woman friend, his plans to buy a fancy new car. The band, a horn-driven R&B ensemble, is from Toronto. They both agree the band is well worth the cover-charge.

Different worlds? Hardly. Same city? Clearly. The city can be "home" to anyone. Anyone can, likewise, call it home.

Left, acquiring the right image.

It's difficult to find a level shelf in Nat Levine's grocery shop on Rue St-Viateur. Cans lean at odd angles, boxes waver and teeter. But if you're looking for a second-hand kettle or a pair of old boots, Nat's the person to see. Walk past the old-fashioned scale, past the bins of vegetables and fruits. Worn paperbacks and salvaged toasters jostle for shelf space in a dusty, cluttered corner. Paintings hang on the wall, crooked and unframed, and very affordable.

At one time, Nat's shop was down the street, on the corner of Jeanne Mance, just east of Avenue du Parc, across from the bagel shop warmed by the wood-burning oven and from the kosher butcher where Hassidic Jews carefully eye cuts of meat. A popular Greek restaurant expanded, and Nat was forced to move. But he still provides home delivery – free of charge – to long-time customers such as the elderly woman on Hutchison Street who phones in her order, being too frail to make the trip.

When Levine's grocery first opened for business almost 50 years ago, most of Montreal's Jews could have strolled to the shop in minutes. They lived around the Main, or Boulevard St-Laurent, a Yiddish-speaking world framed by French street names like Cadieux, Esplanade, and Marie-Anne.

Multilingual mix: Today, the city's Jewish community is no longer shaped by the alleys and winding staircases of one neighborhood but by the textures of many. Yiddish swirls along the streets of French-speaking Outremont as Hassidim prepare for Friday night services. Elderly Jews shuffle through the streets of Côte-des-Neiges and Snowdon, stopping to catch their breath or exchange gossip. Their bilingual grandchildren (they speak both English and *French*, not Yiddish) play in distant, grassy suburbs like Dollard des Ormeaux.

And still they come back to the old neighborhood, the Main, the children of parents

from Poland, Hungary and Lithuania. Their children, too, make a modern-day pilgrimage to the street described as "the funnel through which repeated waves of Jewish immigrants entered Montreal." Tucked between the fashionable boutiques and trendy cafés on the Main are bits and pieces of the old community, scattered fragments along St-Laurent.

The old community is there as you step onto the wooden floor at Schreter's dry goods store: walls clothed with suits and sweatshirts, shorts and shoes. Once there, it's only a few blocks south to Schwartz's deli: open the door and walk through a curtain of smoked meat that local gourmets claim is second to none. ("When I die," a framed tribute proclaims, "I want to go to Schwartz's.") And catering to those Jews who prefer a slice of heaven is Berson's monuments just across the street. Granite tombstones, polished and blank, rest waiting to be carved.

Migrations and exodus: An epigraph for Montreal's Jewish community would be premature. At 96,000, the community is alive and well, rooted in a history committed to survival. By standing on the corner of Rues Notre-Dame and St-Jacques, you can hear the echoes of the city's – and the country's – first synagogue, which was built in 1777 by the Sephardic community, descendents of the Jews expelled during the Spanish Inquisition.

Geography and history unravel in an inseparable knot. Distant countries have shaped the city's Jewish community. Tensions in Russia altered the face of Montreal, particularly when the assassination of Czar Alexander II in 1881 sparked a series of pogroms, the Russian word for devastation, a synonym for organized massacres. Jews were the targeted scapegoats and Canada was regarded as a hand filled with promise, Montreal being its palm.

The Russian pogroms triggered the first large wave of Yiddish-speaking immigrants. Until then, Montreal's Jewish community was small. In 1847, when Jews numbered less than 200, the first Jewish society was organized to provide relief to the community's poor and needy, particularly the newer immigrants. In the last two decades of the 19th century, some 13,000 Jews arrived in Canada. Owing to the circumstances which forced them to flee, they were aware of the very sense of Jewishness that had cost lives in Russia. Customs and a way of life that existed in the *shtetls* (small Jewish towns) of old Europe were adapted to the streets of Montreal.

Docks to sweatshops: Through the funnel of the Main the wanderers streamed. Poor and displaced, they relied on mutual aid societies

such as the first Hebrew Sick Benefit Society, founded in 1892. The need for financial help and medical benefits was acute. For some, it was a short trip from the docks to the sweatshop. They worked under deplorable conditions in the garment industry, toiling in cramped sweatshops wedged into old buildings, with little air or light. Days were long, wages were low.

One testimony from the period recounts the following anecdote: "One cloakmaker turned his four rooms into a shop and supposedly kept the other three as a home for his wife and seven children. But the shop was all

over the place... A woman was making bread on a table, upon which there was a baby's stocking, scraps of cloth, several old tin cans and a small pile of unfinished garments. In the next room was an old woman with a diseased face, walking the floor with a crying child in her arms. Such conditions were typical in all garment centers."

The poor working conditions proved to be fertile turf for Jews in a labor movement committed to social change. Ideologies developed in eastern Europe by such groups as the Bund, a Jewish socialist party founded in Russia in 1897, were renewed in cities like Montreal with the drive to educate and unionize exploited workers. The Workmen's Circle saw itself not simply as a mutual benefit society but also as part of the larger labor movement, which was struggling to end capitalist exploitation.

Sidewalks became stages for social change. Corner stores turned into political arenas. Bookshops were transformed into debating dens. "Elstein's bookshop on Ontario Street was more than a store," reported one account. "It was virtually a club where anyone who read books would meet to argue politics and orientations."

The expanding community: Politics stretched far beyond the Main itself in Montreal. Three-quarters of the federal riding of Montreal-Cartier, centered around the Main, was Jewish. In August 1943 they made history by electing the first communist, Fred Rose, to the House of Commons.

Amidst the dust of the depression, small cottages sprouted into prayer houses. Hebrew resounded through forgotten lofts and spare rooms in industrial buildings. By 1940, 40 of Montreal's 50 synagogues were located within a mile of each other. Rue St-Urbain alone – immortalized in the novels of Mordecai Richler – had six.

Richler writes of the Jewish district, it was "an all but self-contained world made up of five streets; Clark, St-Urbain, Waverley, Esplanade and Jeanne-Mance, bounded by the Main on one side, and Park Avenue on the other... On each corner a cigar store, a grocery, and a fruit man. Outside staircases everywhere. Winding ones, wooden ones, rusty and risky ones. An endless repetition of precious peeling balconies and waste lots making the occasional gap here and there."

Row after row of winding staircases, of cold-water flats, nurtured a generation of Jews who went on to make significant contributions to the arts and sciences in Canada, from poet A. M. Klein to David Lewis, one of Canada's most eloquent politicians, who learned English poring over Dickens. Others have made a quiet difference, like political activist Leah Roback, white-haired and tireless, a button declaring "Bread Not Bombs" pinned to her coat.

As their lot improved, Montreal's Jews moved out of the streets around the Main and

Time stands still a few blocks away at the Hassidic prayer houses on Jeanne Mance, just round the corner from Nat Levine's grocery shop. But for the small signs outside, they look like any other house on the block. The similarities end at the door. Inside, the rituals of an 18th-century religious philosophy continue.

The everyday world: Daily life for the city's Hassidic community, Canada's largest, is wrapped in Yiddish. Cohesion is one of the distinguishing marks of Hassidism, as is charismatic leadership of the various sects. The *zaddik* (leader) is seen as a healer, confessor, moral instructor and also a practical

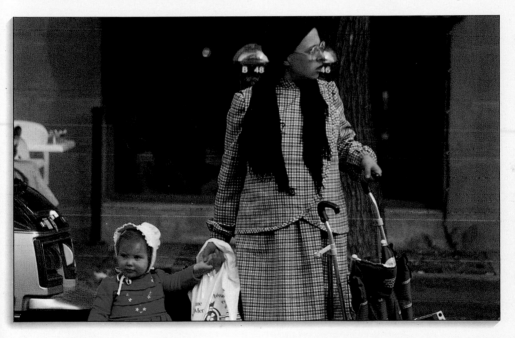

into better homes and neighborhoods. A revitalized wartime and postwar economy created what one social critic called "the social and economic conversion of the Jews."

Jews left the old neighborhood and built synagogues in the new ones. Few of the original synagogues around the Main are still there. Where there was once a synagogue there is now a church or a parking lot. On Fairmount Avenue, Hebrew letters arch across the sky and disappear into the facade of what has now become a French school.

Left, doing business. **Above**, going shopping.

adviser. Central to Hassidism is a determination to persist in their devotion to God and not be distracted by the secular world.

Insular by choice, the Hassidim are an enigma not only to the French Canadians of Outremont, but also to the many Jews who are unfamiliar with their ways. The men walk along streets in their *kapotes* (black silk coats) and *spodiks* (fur hats), locks of hair curled around their ears. Women dress discreetly in modest clothing, children in tow.

Hassidism and secularism clashed in 1988 in a zoning dispute. A sect that wanted to build a new synagogue was pitted against a town council that balked at making the necessary re-zoning changes. Tensions flared when a newspaper article spoke of the "Jewish Problem" in Outremont. For many of the city's Jews, especially Holocaust survivors, the phrase rekindled memories of Nazi Germany. Others recalled the anti-Semitism of Quebec in the 1930s. Insensitive descriptions about how the Hassidim dressed and fear-baiting references to their growing numbers only made matters worse. Both French and English Montrealers were quick to denounce the paper's careless journalism.

Immersed in their Yiddish world, the Hassidim are a minority within a minority.

in the 1960s – a period in which French Canadians, after enduring centuries of discrimination at the hands of an English minority, began to reclaim their past and their status as a majority.

A shifting political scene: Shifts in the Quebec political scene coincided with changes in the Jewish community. A new wave of Jewish immigrants arrived in Montreal, bypassing the Main. Political instability in North Africa led many French-speaking Sephardic Jews to seek a new home. The majority of Montreal's Sephardic community, which now numbers more than 20,000, come from Morocco.

More than half of the Jews of Montreal claim English as their mother tongue. The immigrants who arrived in Montreal earlier in the century arrived in a society dominated by an English-speaking minority. By virtue of a provincial school system that was separated on religious grounds, Jewish children were forced to attend English Protestant schools. The doors to French-language schools were closed to them.

As members of the anglophone minority of Montreal, many Jews found themselves on the wrong side of history when Quebec nationalism arose with the Quiet Revolution

Through the Sephardim, some of the city's Jews saw the "French fact" of Quebec. The Sephardic community's desire to preserve its culture and identity mirrored the goals of French nationalists. Yet many Jews found it difficult to adapt to the new politics, particularly the elderly, used to a time when French was not the official language that it is today.

Anglophone Jewish concerns were heightened with the election of the Parti Québécois (PQ) in 1976 on a platform committed to a

Watching the parade go by: many Jews still preserve their old traditions.

sovereign Quebec. In the aftermath of the PQ's victory, many of the city's younger Jews left for Toronto. But they still gather at reunions featuring slabs of Montreal's smoked meat, and they cart bags of bagels to Ontario after trips to their native city.

An aging population: By 1986, more than 20 percent of the Jewish community was aged over 65. Many Jews, particularly women, live below the poverty line. That there is a "Jewish poor" in Montreal would probably come as a surprise not only to those who hang onto caricatures of Jewish wealth, but also to many in the community itself who associate poverty with Jewish life at the turn of the century.

Yet, as in the past, the community has responded. Services have been created to meet the needs of the elderly. Kosher meals are brought to homes where the infirm can't cook for themselves. In the heart of Côtedes-Neiges, a low-income neighborhood where many Jewish elderly still live, Project Genesis provides storefront services to clients flustered by a French document or frightened by a rent increase.

The Jewish Immigration Aid Service, created in the wake of World War I, continues to help new arrivals. Auberge Shalom is a shelter for battered women where even the most Orthodox Jewish woman can find refuge, as it is run according to Judaic laws. At the Golden Age Association, stooped seniors practice Tai Chi and sculpt stone.

The Jewish Public Library, now in its 75th year of community service, features exhibitions, films, and concerts that celebrate the city's Jewish heritage and links to Israel. Here, grey-haired men scour Yiddish newspapers next to racks of Hollywood videos.

Preserving language: Across the street, next to the YM-YWHA, Yiddish bounces off the stage at the Saidye Bronfman Center. Dora Wasserman's Yiddish theater group has become an integral piece of the fabric of Jewish Montreal, helping to preserve a dying language. Internationally acclaimed, it performs before thousands of Montrealers annually, including works by Nobel laureate Isaac Bashevis Singer, who once wrote "If the Yiddish language is dying, it should only keep dying for the next thousand years."

In a still room at the Montreal Holocaust Memorial Center, candles cast solemn shadows on a wall inscribed with place names etched in the collective memory of Jews. Founded in 1979, it is Canada's first Jewish historical museum and Holocaust educational center. The museum examines not only the destruction of Jewish life during the Holocaust, but also European Jewry as it existed before Nazism wreaked its havoc. Local Montrealers donated most of the artifacts in the museum.

Between one-fifth and one-fourth of the city's adult Jews are Holocaust survivors. Continuity is an important theme: many Jews preserve and continue their traditions and way of life before and during the Holocaust, and they continue to link European Jewry with the community today. A permanent exhibition, *Splendor and Destruction: Jewish Life That Was, 1919–1945*, is one effort to maintain this link.

Contemporary Jews: The Jewish life that was in Montreal is no more. But though demographics and the political landscape have changed the complexion of the community, it still has plenty of color and warmth. The city is home to the Canadian Jewish Congress, a Jewish "parliament" that is national in scope.

Fluently bilingual Jewish Montrealers sit as city councillors. They are leading academics in universities like McGill University, where they were once restricted. Each year Jews take to the streets in a fund-raising March for Jerusalem.

Bonds with Israel are also strong, with many projects linking the city to the country. True to a history of diverse opinion, others have quietly promoted a dialogue with the Palestinians.

When two Jews get together, an old joke goes, there are three opinions. What fate awaits the Jews of Montreal? Some speak of the writing on the wall and nervously point to the resurgence of Quebec nationalism. Others are committed to staying, adapting to a new Quebec as they maintain a religion thousands of years older than the city itself.

Meanwhile, back at Levine's grocery store, it's business as usual. Nat takes another order over the telephone.

Politics are politics and people are people. Contrary to popular opinion, the Québécois are not obsessed with the machinations of independence. Newspapers refrain from spouting invective against confederation, cafés fail to hatch midnight cabals, and every day is certainly not *jour de la révolution.* Lives may contain a heightened level of consciousness about the structures of government, but lives also remain private and voluntary. Politics can be variously a pastime, passion, or obsession; it need never be a birthmark, a chain around the neck. Though tensions surrounding language and culture exist, Montreal is neither Beirut nor Belfast. This is worth remembering.

The city streets are gouged with potholes, and the highways, designed for carriages, discourage the obedience of laws inadequate to the challenges of surviving the commute home. The St Lawrence River is treated like a sewer, the police department maintains its headquarters in donut shops, and zoning laws permit free-for-alls in neighborhoods whose preservation is in doubt. Montrealers are elected to the municipal government to reform or *not* reform, to overhaul or conserve; and citizens, if they are organized and learn how to frame their demands, can usually affect policy in the desired direction.

These are the issues and players of city politics. The mayor, councilors, citizens' groups, the media, children in primary school who use art class to agitate for pollution control: ordinary people dealing with substantial, concrete issues – homelessness, taxes, recycling facilities – in the hope of improving the quality of life in Montreal. Their voices are modified, in proportion to the scale of both the problems and prosperity endemic to Canadian society.

The same cannot be said for the voices currently debating the "large" questions that

are reverberating throughout the country. For many Canadians, and most outside observers, "politics" in Montreal and Quebec means rampant fratricide and divisions in a nation unable to reconcile its linguistic and cultural duality. Politics means language laws, majority rights, Quebec's meandering toward some form of independence from confederation and shouting matches. Moreover, in the 1990s, in the wake of the Meech Lake Accord and a growing frustration in

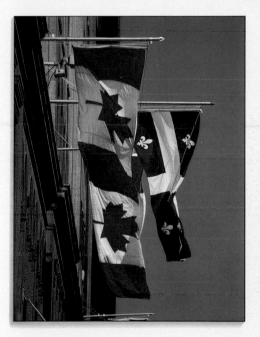

other provinces with both Quebec and the federal government, politics means being impatient, ill-tempered and wishing the mess would resolve itself, for better or worse, and leaving people in peace.

How did the situation deteriorate so rapidly? How did the evolution of Quebec suddenly become a source of implosion for the entire country? Answers to these questions are everywhere; explanations are elusive.

First, a word about Canada. To describe the nation as "massive" is accurate but inadequate. If anything, Canada is *several* massive countries bookended by oceans to the

Preceding pages: Montreal projects a good-time image. **Left,** shamrock, fleur-de-lys and British uniforms mingle in a St Patrick's Day parade. **Above,** putting out the flags.

east and west, a polar cap to the north and the United States to the south. These massive countries – provinces – are home to only 31 million people – who cluster near the extreme southern borders to benefit from milder weather and warming trade breezes.

The term "country" is not being used too loosely here. In 1867, the architects of Canada's political house proposed a "confederation" of the various regions to defend against American territorial ambitions and strengthen their economic potential. No one envisioned a unified nation-state grounded in ideology and chauvinism. How could they have? The pact was agreed when

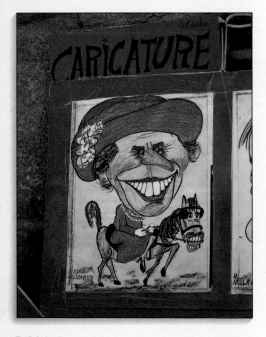

British Columbia wasn't even accessible to Ottawa by overland transportation. (Nor would it be until the cross-Canada railway was completed in 1881.)

If 4,000 miles (6,400 km) separating Montreal from Vancouver seems huge in an age of jetliners and fax machines, imagine how isolated they seemed in 1867. Confederation was political moderation and realism. Canada could *not* be like the United States. But it still could function, and its individual members, granted considerable autonomy over their affairs, could be at once self-sustaining *and* loyal to the large "collective."

How does Quebec fit into the picture? Uneasily. It is at once a founding province and a conquered state. Though the conquering pre-dated the confederation by 100 years, the legacy – English domination of commerce, discrimination against the Québécois and their language – was built into the infrastructures of business and government and lingered until barely a decade ago.

Quebec joined the confederation in 1867 because it hadn't much choice. It has remained a part of the country for far more diverse reasons. More than any other province, Quebec *is* unto itself; it is psychologically, if not literally, a nation, possibly even a nation in the American model. Those who would deny Quebec's exceptional status – an attitude implicitly dismissive of tremendous cultural and economic achievements – only coarsen the debate. Besides, Canada was designed to accommodate diversity. How much diversity, though, and at what cost to existing structures, was never resolved. Quebec's nationalist aspirations have highlighted this ambiguity in the design.

It should be mentioned that Canada's political system, based on representation by population, heavily favors the country's most populous provinces: Ontario and Quebec. Two-thirds of all voters reside in these two provinces. A federal party cannot win an election without the tacit support of Ontario and the full backing of Quebec, whose voters tend to cast their ballots *en masse*. As a result, most of Canada's prime ministers came from the central regions and many of the major leaders have been Québécois. These include Jean Chrétien, the current prime minister, and two other recent prime ministers, Pierre Trudeau and Brian Mulroney.

Ironies abound. First, literally speaking, it is not Quebec that suffers from a lack of power and influence. Such a fate belongs to the smaller provinces, especially those in the west. Second, disagreements aside, the English-Canadian political establishment is obliged to pay great attention to Quebec's demands. By voting in one direction and thereby offering a party the guarantee of a full quarter of the seats in the House of Parliament, the province has become the country's king-maker; governments are elected or rejected and policies – like the Free Trade Agreement – need the good will of the Québécois. In a democracy, this is genuine political power.

Finally, a number of Canada's leading proponents of federalism are themselves French Canadians. Chrétien, Mulroney, Trudeau, and Jean Charest, former leader of the Progressive Conservative Party and now leader of Quebec's Liberal Party, are but a few examples. The ranks are far from closed inside Quebec. There is still plenty of room for alternative voices. Trudeau, Quebec's philosopher-king, tellingly described French Canadians in 1956 as "a people vanquished, business, and by the intellectual and spiritual assertion of Quebec's "self-hood."

Lévesque fired the imagination of French Canadians when he cried: "We are nothing more than an internal colony which lives at the will of another people." The logical next step, argued the Parti Québécois, was independence. *Sovereignty-Association* were the buzz words in those days, focusing on an abstract relationship between the new nation of Quebec and Canada that would make for an economically painless withdrawal from the bower of federal funding.

In 1980 Lévesque's government held a referendum asking the Québécois to decide

occupied, leaderless, kept aside from business life and away from the cities, gradually reduced to a minority role and deprived of influence in a country which, after all, it had discovered and explored, and settled."

Quebec elected its first separatist government in 1976. The Parti Québécois of René Lévesque was the culmination of a 20-year "quiet revolution" (*révolution tranquille*), a period of ferment, marked by outrage at paternalistic English control of Montreal

Left, the French have never appreciated English queens. **Above**, Hôtel de Ville.

the matter. They did; 60 percent voted to remain in Canada. Ironically, the very middle-class that the quiet revolution helped to create regarded independence as too extreme, an unnecessarily radical measure to protect their culture and language. The Parti Québécois, deflated by the defeat, failed to win the 1985 election and was replaced by Robert Bourassa's Liberal Party.

The deciding factor in the independence movement of the 1970s was Pierre Trudeau. As prime minister from 1968 to 1984 (excluding a brief interruption in 1979), Trudeau forged a Canada of his own imagination and intellect. René Lévesque met his equal in this prime minister. For Trudeau, Canada was the sum of its linguistic diversity. He set about recasting confederation through the introduction of a mandatory bilingualism on all levels of the federal government.

Vancouver to Halifax, Windsor to Yellowknife, Trudeau's Canada would be home to both languages, both cultures, a country where tolerance was automatic and, all being equal, no one particular group needed special protection. Trudeau was determined to twist the arms of Canadians until even a Calgarian who'd never met a French Canadian, or an inner-city Montrealer whose

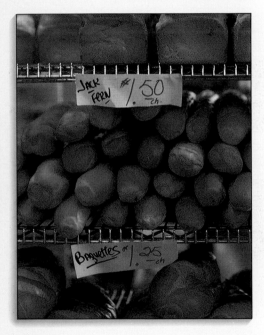

English consisted of pop-song lyrics, would have to acknowledge both the value *and* the necessity of bilingualism. He was also, of course, subtly undermining the Parti Québécois freedom cry.

It worked well, after a fashion. When Trudeau introduced a Charter of Rights and Freedoms to Canada's patriated constitution in 1981, the charter steadfastly ignored any conciliatory gestures toward Quebec's "two nation" ideal, and Quebec steadfastly refused to sign the document. Combatants settled into their respective trenches, and for a few years animosities were left to simmer

while the inevitable evolutions occurred: Trudeau retired from politics, Lévesque died, and the Conservative government of Brian Mulroney came to power in Ottawa. Those commentators who felt that the withdrawal of Trudeau and Lévesque from the scene would deflate tensions were, unfortunately, proved wrong. When the "Quebec Question" flared again in 1988 it was with a ferocity that took most Canadians by surprise, and which left the country reeling.

The spark was the Meech Lake Accord, the Mulroney government's 1987 attempt at a conciliatory constitutional agreement. The accord, which increased the powers of all the provincial governments in relation to Canada's national capital Ottawa, also included a "distinct society" clause that would allow Quebec to opt out of many federal programs and override any supreme court decisions that threatened its security. Meech Lake argued for a different vision of Canada, and though not especially popular west of Ontario, it appeased Quebec and the federal government and seemed a reasonable compromise. All of Canada's provincial leaders signed the preliminary agreement.

The fraternity was short-lived. Within a year Quebec's Bourassa government placed the accord in jeopardy by exercising its privilege and overriding a supreme court decision. Why such a grave matter? The controversy was linked to concerns over previous legislation, Bill 101, the polemical 1977 *Charte de la Langue Française* (Charter of the French Language) that gave the French language primacy in Quebec through several stringent measures, including the barring of English-language schools to new immigrants.

Bill 101 is unquestionably unconstitutional under the terms of the BNA Act – it denies English Quebeckers any right to use English in commercial situations. The law has also been known to produce risible results, with the so-called "tongue troopers" (agents of the *Commission de Surveillance de la Langue Française*) changing long-standing Quebec place names or fining any merchants who put English "Merry Christmas" signs in their windows. English Canadians were enraged.

In 1989, Bill 178 replaced Bourassa's law and banned English from all outdoor signs in

Quebec, even those also in French. It was necessary, claimed the government, to preserve the "rights of the majority." English Canadians were, once again, furious.

The result was a backlash against Quebec. Premiers withdrew support for Meech Lake, jeopardizing ratification. Cities and towns in Ontario began to declare themselves "English Only," and the resentment toward both the Quebec sign laws and Trudeau-sponsored bilingualism intensified. Some people began to question the "two languages" model. Canada, they argued, was multicultural , not bilingual. Canada was also a society grounded in tolerance, a land of "live and let live."

language. Defending the language, therefore, through means like Bills 178 and 101 and enforced French education is a defense of identity. Says writer André Belleau: "We do not need to speak French: we need French in order to speak."

"How can English Canadians understand this?" the Québécois argue. Security and power are birthrights for native English speakers. Privileges are assumed. Not so for French Canadians; they are obliged to create their own political, social, even historical space both within the country and the North American continent as a whole. *Je me souviens* (I remember) is the province's elusive motto.

Quebec, on the other hand, was, according to some, becoming more and more an ideological nation-state, an enclave of tribalism that displayed with pride a "become like us, or leave" mentality.

The issue is all to do with language. Quebec is a society that thinks, reads, and writes in French. Eighty percent of its citizens subscribe to magazines and watch television programs that are foreign to the rest of Canada. Group identity is bound up inherently with

Gallic preferences predominate in Atwater market (left), and in all public signs.

Remember what? Who the Québécois were, who they are and who they will be.

How does all this affect Montreal? The city is the heart of Quebec. It is where the major linguistic skirmishes are being fought. Most of these frictions appear silly. Banning bilingual signs, changing street names, the "language police," Parti Québécois youth leagues that seek out offending merchants. This kind of behavior flatters no one. More encouraging is the debate in the media, where commentators from *Le Devoir*, *La Presse*, *Le Soleil*, and *The Gazette* criticize intransigence and call for clearer thinking from all.

In the 1989 elections, the Liberals returned to power, the Parti Québécois was strengthened in opposition, and a new voice emerged – the Equality Party, an anglophone group that elected four members from predominantly English-speaking Montreal ridings. Although the Equality Party proved evanescent, its presence in the assembly was seen as a healthy development.

However, in the 1994 provincial election, the Parti Québécois won a resounding victory led by Jacques Parizeau, taking 77 seats and leaving the Liberals with only 47. Yet another controversial referendum was held in October 1995, which created massive tur-

But what will be their second language – English or French? According to the Trudeau model for Canada, the choice should be up to the individual: schools, social services, and all government bodies must be available in both official languages. According to the Quebec government, the English language devours other cultures, hence the choice has been predetermined: to live in Montreal is to become a French speaker.

These are very distant views. Common ground is, in one sense, becoming harder and harder to find. A third view wonders if linguistic and cultural exclusivity contradicts the very ethnic wealth of Montreal. In

moil across the country. Although the sovereigntists lost by a remarkably narrow margin, Parizeau stepped down as leader and was replaced by the charismatic Bouchard, who had most recently been leader of the Bloc Québécois in Ottawa.

You need only wander Montreal for a few hours to realize that it is an ethnically diverse city. Besides English Canadians, the "allophone" community includes Italians, Greeks, Jews, people from the Indian subcontinent, the Caribbean and Africa. Each of these communities function first and foremost in their native tongues.

these days of dissolving orthodoxies, as seen in Eastern Europe, and emerging polyglots such as a "United" Europe, when nations are being virtually reinvented by their newest citizens, is the "two solitudes" approach to Canada's problem itself a relic from the past? It seems that, while certain elements of the French and English communities may want their old solitude, it is doubtful that they can have it. Things are changing. And thinking is bound to change too.

Above, bikers cross ethnic and linguistic barriers.
Right, René Lévesque.

POLITICS: INTELLECTUALS VERSUS STREETFIGHTERS

Received wisdom sorts Quebec politicians into two types: the intellectual or the streetfighter. Pierre Elliott Trudeau, former professor of jurisprudence from Université Laval and prime minister from 1968–79 and 1980–84, was the former; his arch-foe René Lévesque, chain-smoking *capo* of the Parti Québécois, was the latter.

The dichotomy is misleading, obscuring the fact that the two flavors are invariably swirled together in Quebec's political figures. Pragmatic, even Machiavellian, arrogant but charismatic – these are the qualities of Quebec's most talented politicians. But, no matter how able, all have been hamstrung by the issue of language, with its anglophone undercurrents.

Trudeau, Quebec's philosopher-king, strongly supported constitutional reform and federal bilingualism, but in 1968 his elaborate courting of Ottawa seemed to many Québécois simple collaboration.

Lévesque, a journalist, foreign correspondent and broadcaster, entered the provincial scene as a Liberal MP in 1960 and fired the imagination of French Canadians when he declaimed: "We are nothing more than an internal colony which lives at the will of another people."
Lévesque emphasized *not* federalism (in which power rests with the national government), but sovereignty-association; *not* bilingualism, but preferential treatment for the Québécois tongue. The hard-talking Lévesque swept into power in 1976 and challenged Trudeau, then Prime Minister, on the destiny of Quebec.

The underlying contradiction of the PQ's controversial language law, Bill 101, is rarely examined. However, if French-Canadian language and culture are as vibrant as some claim, why should extreme measures be needed to ensure a hot-house protection? There's a surprisingly simple answer: much of the long-standing animosity between the Québécois and their English-speaking conquerors still has to be worked out.

Robert Bourassa, the former bureaucratic leader of Quebec's Liberal party, was hoist several times on the petard of language. With his health failing,

Bourassa stepped down as party leader, and was followed by Daniel Johnston, a scion of a family long ensconced in Quebec politics. While the Liberals were clinging to power in Quebec, the traditionally Liberal federal votes of Quebec swung over to Canada's Progressive Conservative party. Brian Mulroney, an Irish Quebecker from Baie Comeau, was elected to a second term in 1988, and managed to deliver Quebec's votes to the Conservatives like a highly relieved gift.

But the Canadian electorate's love affair with Mulroney's Conservatives was not to last, due in part to the collapse of the Meech Lake accord in 1990 and the start of yet another recession.

Towards the end of his term, Mulroney announced his departure from government, and within a few months Kim Campbell, a sassy young woman from British Columbia, found herself party leader and, by default, prime minister of Canada.

The change in leadership was not enough to appease the electorate and in 1993 Quebecker Jean Chrétien was elected Canada's prime minister. The Bloc Québécois, a party committed to the break-up of Canada, became the official opposition.

Jean Chrétien was an old Trudeau man from Shawinigan, Quebec. Not so Daniel Johnston, whose quiet demeanour was no match for PQ leader Jacques Parizeau. In 1994, Quebec elected the PQ, and Parizeau pledged a referendum on independence.

After the 1995 referendum, Parizeau resigned as leader (and premier) and Lucien Bouchard stepped from the federal to the provincial arena to take over the reins of the PQ. He had a tightrope to walk: to PQ hardliners separation as an independent Quebec was imminent. Bouchard's diplomacy would be sorely tested. In 1998, with the resignation of Daniel Johnston, another federal politician switched to provincial politics. Jean Charest, leader of the Progressive Conservatives, took over as leader of Quebec's Liberal party.

Towards year-end, a snap election was called. The liberals lost to the PQ (48 seats vs. 75 seats) but despite dire predictions of the party's annihilation, it won a larger percentage of the popular vote – 43.7% compared to the PQ's 42.7%. Although sovereignty remains a significant issue, a referendum is unlikely to be held anytime soon. ∎

THE LIFE AND TIMES OF PIERRE TRUDEAU

What was it about Pierre Trudeau that fired the enthusiasm of so many Canadians? What did this arrogant, balding law professor from the radical seminar rooms of Quebec tell Canadians about themselves? Whatever it was – perhaps the Canadian ability to be great – Canadians responded in a way no prime minister before or since has dared to dream of. Trudeau was, if only briefly, a genuine national hero in a country largely without them, a rock star of a politician who made crowds swoon and ran the country on the sheer force of his personality.

And what a personality it was. Behind the inscrutable mask of the Jesuit-trained intellectual lay a consummate jokester, given to sliding down banisters, playing with yo-yos and frisbees, and keeping the exhausted press corps constantly guessing about his next move.

His wife Margaret (Maggie), pictured opposite, was almost 30 years his junior, a former flower child who embarrassed Canadians with her own unplanned exploits: running around in a bathrobe at the Rolling Stones' hotel after a Toronto concert, dancing at Manhattan's Studio 54, giving candid interviews in *People* and *Playgirl*. This was the prime minister's wife? But, despite their oddball aura, Pierre and Maggie proved an irresistible pair for normally cautious Canadian voters. Trudeau was the longest-serving prime minister of this century, and he exited the national political scene on his own terms in 1984: rather like a king taking leave of his subjects. He remained on the social scene in Montreal for many years, until the death of his youngest son in a freak avalanche while on a 1999 skiing trip to British Columbia turned him, at least temporarily, into a recluse.

In many ways, Trudeau reflects the uniqueness of Canada. He was born in 1919 to a Québécois father, Charles-Emile ("Charlie") Trudeau, and a Scottish mother, Grace Elliott. The first Trudeau had come to Canada in 1659, and Charlie was a scion of the family, a shrewd businessman who left all three of his children million-dollar legacies at his

death in 1935. Grace was a quiet woman from whom Pierre learned deportment, reticence, and the keen regard for discipline he carried into office. A bachelor until his fifties, he lived with his mother in their old house in Montreal until he was nearly 40. She died in 1973 when her son was in his second term of office.

Trudeau came on the national stage abruptly, rising quickly from his professorship at the Université de Montréal law school to become, in 1967, minister of justice under the Liberal prime minister Lester B. Pearson. When Pearson retired, Trudeau – who was then young, charismatic, and an attractive French intellectual – stepped smartly into the Party's power vacuum, winning a stunning upset at the chaotic leadership conference.

That was perhaps his luck, being in the right place at the right time; his *skill* lay in holding onto power, acquired so effortlessly, for more than a decade. Through some of Canada's most exciting political years, Trudeau was a national fixture: the man the Toronto *Sun*, western Canadians, and Bay Street gray suits loved to hate; the man Canadian children, Québécois, and everybody else loved to love.

The media called it "Trudeaumania" and, while Trudeau never claimed (like John Lennon) to be more popular than Jesus, he could convincingly have done so.

The social exploits of Trudeau are legendary. Before his 1971 marriage, he was seen with a variety of "beautiful young things" on his arm. After the marriage, he had well-publicized arguments with the gallivanting Maggie, a free spirit who hung out with Andy Warhol and took photos of New York celebs. She even had a brand of designer jeans named after her. Despite the trouble brewing in their marriage, the Trudeaus were devoted parents, with a unique talent for having children on Christmas Day – the first two of their three sons were born on December 25.

That little quirk of fate seemed to bode well for Trudeau. The gods were smiling on him. Even the media circus of the marriage breakup in 1977 did not scar Trudeau publicly, as Canadians – by then disposed to suspect the flashy political magician – gave him new credibility as a single father and a martyr to responsibility. But who knows how much he suffered behind the well-crafted public statements of separation?

Much of Trudeau's celebrated arrogance, his unwillingness to suffer fools, whether in the House of Commons or the press corps, stemmed from his own severe mental self-discipline. It was learned early, at the Collège de Brébeuf in Montreal, where Trudeau was known as a scrapper who never backed down in a fight, verbal or physical. He shone at the Université de Montréal, and success took him to Harvard, the Sorbonne, and the London School of Economics. He came to Ottawa in 1965 as one of Lester Pearson's "Three Wise Men" – a trio of Quebec intellectuals of which Trudeau proved himself the ablest. He was arguably Canada's most brilliant leader.

jackets, the fresh rose in his lapel, the disco-age leisure suits. For *Sun* readers, no clothes horse could be considered a serious leader.

But these dismissive second thoughts are not necessarily born of mature reflection. And they cannot be allowed to nullify Trudeau's early success, and the value of the national vision on which it was based. The Jesuit-educated overachiever, a child of strict but loving parents, had risen to international fame. He hobnobbed with royalty, rock stars, and international political meteors.

Yet, unexpectedly, behind the facade of fashionable living and easy brilliance there lived a hardworking scholarship boy, a clever Québécois bookworm who deeply loved his country and his province (in that order) and simply wanted to keep them alive

However, Trudeau's refreshing frankness in debate sometimes appeared merely willful, as when he told a House of Commons colleague to "Fuck off," explaining later that he had actually said "Fuddle duddle."

Late in his series of terms as prime minister, Trudeau's celebrated arrogance took a decidedly peevish turn, and the mania that had fired his early campaign victories was far from fashionable any longer. Indeed, the fashionable thing through the late 1970s was to mock the naivete that had found Trudeau such a compelling figure in 1968. The *Sun*, the reactionary Toronto tabloid long given to hate-filled attacks on anything smacking of reform, consistently called Trudeau "PET" and delighted in reporting on his sartorial fussiness: the flashy

and thriving. Richard Gwyn, author of the biography *The Northern Magus*, said succinctly of Trudeau's character: "Ambiguity is the only consistency."

And Canadians loved Trudeau for being a national visionary long before they indulged in typical Canadian put-downs – the second guessing of anyone who does well; the "Who does he think he is?" put down they learned from the Scots. He showed them who they could be: influential and envied players on the international stage. He showed them what a true national leader, rather than a mediator of regional interests, looked like.

Briefly they followed the lead, relishing his notoriety and the international status the notoriety bestowed on them. But, in their ultimate reaction to Trudeau's vision, Canadians showed him (and showed themselves) that they were not yet ready to embrace greatness. ∎

Left and **above**, Pierre and Margaret Trudeau.

To understand ice hockey is in some sense to understand Canada itself. Across a frozen expanse, enterprising individuals dodge or fight off vicious obstacles, searching for the narrow openings that will bring them glory, And yet the individual cannot succeed – only the team, working together, can consistently send the puck home.

Hockey is raucous but also rule-bound: when individuals flout the laws of the game, they are physically removed from their fellows, placed in the penalty box – the "sin bin" – and the team must struggle on. Fighting is part of the game, but only when it is fair and obvious; dirty play (provided the referee can see it) will draw the penalty every time. Hockey is wide-open and honest, at once rough and graceful, team and individual, a swirling mixture of bone-rattling hits and the poetry of fast skating. It is like nothing else on earth and it is Canada's game. It *belongs* to Canadians, in a way that little else does.

Hockey Night in Canada: Legend has it that Canadians are notoriously self-effacing, finding little to boast about in their own achievements. But when the talk comes round to hockey, Canadians can rightly claim the laurels. Let the propositions be clear: Canadians are the best hockey players in the world, and Canadian fans are the most loyal and discerning. Come Saturday night – "Hockey Night in Canada," as the CBC broadcasters so accurately call it – Canadians of all ages are glued to their television sets, even their radios, dissecting plays and performances in joyous technical detail.

While many Americans view hockey as a cross between all-star wrestling and a roller derby on ice, for Canadians the game is an expression of national aspiration. Our game, our league, our players. What Canadian child has not "skated" around the living room, dumping an imaginary puck into the corner? What youth has not spent an eight-hour day

chipping tennis balls into a foldable net in the back lane, playing until it was too dark to see, too cold to feel toes, and ignoring the call to dinner? For all of them, the hockey announcer's traditional cry, "He shoots... he *scores!*" is a dreamy mantra, a call to glory.

Of course there have been times – desperate times – when the Russians, Swedes, Czechs, and even the Americans put Canada's hockey supremacy to the test. Take 1972, the first Canada-Russia series. It was supposed

to be a cake-walk, a mere workout, for Team Canada. But the Russians came to the Forum in Montreal, the Sistine Chapel of Hockey, and beat "our boys" seven goals to three. Over the next few weeks, Canadians watched in stunned silence as this eight-game foregone conclusion suddenly became a live issue. Teachers wheeled clunky school TVs into classrooms so kids wouldn't miss the day games. Canadians gaped as it took Paul Henderson's goal with 34 seconds left in Game 8 to save their national pride.

But a watershed had been passed. The novelist Mordecai Richler accurately ex-

Preceding pages: hockey in its more genteel days. The game is now a brutal contact sport (**left**) but attracts fans young (**above**).

pressed the feeling that swept from coast to coast after that first series. "We already knew that our politicians lied, that our bodies would be betrayed by age," he wrote. "But we had not suspected that our hockey players were anything but the very best... After the series, nothing was ever the same again in Canada. Beer didn't taste as good. The Rockies seemed smaller, the northern lights dimmer."

There have been other series since then, and Canada has acquitted itself well enough. Canadians also know (don't they?) that the best Canadian players never play on Olympic or series teams because they're too busy earning a living in the National Hockey

the invention of hockey, with at least three cities – Kingston, Halifax, and Montreal – claiming to have witnessed the first game. In fact hockey closely resembles *kalv*, a stick-and-ball game played in the Netherlands as early as the 16th century.

Kingston claims to have been the site of the first North American hockey game on November 25, 1855, but the evidence is a little sketchy. Montreal's claim, though coming 20 years later, lies on firmer ground: on March 3, 1875, two teams gathered to play on the city's Old Victoria Rink. The assembled hearties were mostly winter-idle rugby players, who muscled their way up

League (NHL). They know that the best players in the world still come from funny places like Brantford, Parry Sound, Chicoutimi and Fredericton. They know there is still a large majority of Canadian players in the NHL, the American Hockey League (AHL), even the American college leagues. They go south of the border, they take their money and their education, and that's just fine with most people. Hockey still belongs to Canada, always has and always will.

Montreal's place in the history of hockey is, like its place in the history of Canada, unparalleled. There is a lively dispute about

and down the long rink using (according to one report) "a flat piece of board" as a puck. No record survives of the final score.

Hockey was not popular in Montreal at first, competing with the well-established rugby football, lacrosse and even cricket. Lacrosse, borrowed from the Indians, was by the far the most popular sporting pastime in 19th-century Montreal. *Les toques bleus* – the blue-hatted members of the Montreal Amateur Athletic Association – were often to be seen playing the Indian game in the fields around Montreal. During the 1850s and '60s regular clubs such as the Alma

Mater and the Hochelagas took on the Shamrocks, the Montrealers or the Crescents.

The Canadians who played the first games of hockey probably borrowed many of the game's features from field lacrosse, as well as from the English game of field hockey. And like lacrosse as first played by Native Americans, early hockey had no official boundaries or rules: an indeterminate number of players could range far and wide to set up their goals. They had better be fit, however, since goals were often placed as far as a mile apart. In this respect the early game also resembled primitive forms of English football, games of which often involved en-

ates from McGill University, R.F. Smith and W.F. Robertson, codified the rules of hockey. They specified the approximate size of the playing surface, limited the skating players to eight a side (later six, and now five), and generally gave shape to the game as we know it today. Smith invented the puck by cutting down an India rubber ball that bounced too much for good play on the ice. Permanent winter skating rinks – usually uncovered – were built to make the business of finding suitable ice less hit-and-miss.

Writing the rulebook: Only in 1907 was the International Ice Hockey Federation formed to govern a game that was becoming more

tire towns and ranged for several days over half a county.

The most common setting for a game was some shoveled patch of the frozen St Lawrence River. One reason for the game's early failure to fire the interest of Montrealers was the sheer effort involved in getting a game going. Imagine clearing a field every time you wanted to play lacrosse or soccer.

These difficulties were overcome during the 1880s when two enterprising undergradu-

Left and right, the Canadiens fight it out with their arch-rivals, the Toronto Maple Leafs.

popular by the year. The National Hockey League did not form until 1917 – six years after the Canadiens, the joy of Montreal, had been organized. There were seven teams in the early NHL: the Canadiens and Maroons of Montreal, the Toronto St Patricks (later the Maple Leafs), Chicago Blackhawks, New York Rangers, Boston Bruins, and Detroit Red Wings. From the beginning *les bons Canadiens* were a powerful force.

Le Club de Hockey de Canadiens (as it is officially known) has won more NHL titles than any other team, taking possession of Lord Stanley's Cup 23 times since the old

Governor-General donated the trophy – at a cost to himself of $48.67 – in 1926. The Cup has grown, sprouting bottom layers like a tree grows rings, and *les Glorieux* has been there every step of the way. Its former Montreal temple, the Forum, was so thickly festooned with NHL title banners that opposing players felt distinctly woozy at the sight of its crowded rafters.

Early in 1996, Le Centre Molson replaced the Forum as home for the Montreal Canadiens. A vast amphitheatre built on the platforms of the old Windsor Station, it can accommodate up to 21,247 people. When it opened on St Patrick's Day, more than

150,000 hockey fans waited in line to see their heroes' new base.

As the Cup has grown, so has the league, and the current expanded league has ballooned to over 20 teams that represent cities unthinkable as hockey centers a few decades ago: Los Angeles, Washington, even East Rutherford, NJ. The bloated league has also had more malign effects, extending the season to a ridiculous length and making the playoff procedure an annual league joke. These days the Stanley Cup finals are not likely to begin until sultry mid-May, and it is not uncommon for playoff games to be de-

layed by fog caused by condensing warm air near the ice.

For purists, modern play has deteriorated as well. Forwards are today as likely to dump the puck heedlessly into the corner, letting their linemen scramble, as they are to carry it into the enemy zone on the stick. There may be fewer fights than in the days of "beat 'em in the alley if you can't beat 'em on the ice," but dirty play – vicious hooking, cross checks – has become more common.

Laments like this are the daily currency of sports pages, but they do point to something real: the NHL is probably reaching the limits of its growth. Already some of the players turning pro don't belong anywhere other than in the warlike junior leagues. In their drive to push revenues higher and higher, the leaders of the NHL may be selling the league's glorious legacy down the road.

The Canadiens players have not exactly been above all this: they've produced their share of bad play, goon rookies, and the rest. But they are still the example many fans turn to for peace of mind when all else in hockey seems tarnished. They represent what pro hockey was, and can be again. Such widespread support cannot obscure the fact that the Canadiens are also very much a local product of Montreal, an 85-year family affair between city and club. Indeed, the "H" on their old-fashioned sweaters is popularly taken to initial "*Habitants*," the team's affectionate nickname, when it probably just means "hockey" (as in Club de Hockey).

Les Habs is the team that young Montrealers, indeed youngsters from across Quebec, dream of playing for. There is no other team, and the hometown fans know it. A few of those wide-eyed French Canadian kids grow up to claim that birthright: donning the red and blue sweater, skating out onto the holy ice of Le Centre Molson and putting one away for *les Canadiens*. The rest just keep dreaming.

Many of the best players ever to lace up skates wore the Canadiens' sweater. First and best, perhaps, was Howie Morenz, the legendary "Stratford Streak." An Ontario boy, Morenz anchored the high-scoring 1920s line with two Québécois shooters, Billy Boucher and Aurel Joliat. In the inaugural game at the Forum, on November 29, 1924, the Morenz line pushed in six goals in a 7-1 defeat of the Toronto St Patricks. The stonewall in the Montreal goal was another legend, Georges Vezina (the Chicoutimi Cucumber), who rose to glory at the Forum from a small-town family of 22 children and gave his name to the trophy for goal-tending excellence in the NHL.

In the 1940s, Maurice "The Rocket" Richard, who skated like the wind with the puck seemingly glued to his blade, captained the Flying Frenchmen of the Forum. In those days, Richard's power-play team was so effective – it included Big Jean Beliveau,

The Rocket was a fading blast when the Canadiens entered their greatest-ever period of glory, the epic five-year dominance of the Stanley Cup from 1956 to 1960. The team has won the Cup many times since then, including a hard-fought four-year streak in 1976–79, but the team of the late 1950s was probably the best ever assembled by the venerable old club. The roll call includes many of hockey's most illustrious names: Beliveau, Henri "Little Rocket" Richard, Geoffrion, Jacques Plante (one of the best goalies ever and the first to standardize a face mask), and the coach, a former player called Toe Blake.

Dicky Moore, and Bernie "Boom Boom" Geoffrion – that the NHL was forced to change its rules. With Beliveau and Richard circling the net like angry hornets and Geoffrion unloading thundering slapshots from the point, the Canadiens were regularly scoring two or three goals in the course of a two-minute penalty. Finally, the League altered the rules so that any power-play goal would automatically end the penalty, putting opposing goalies out of their misery.

The game's best seen live (<u>above</u>) but the next best way is on television (<u>left</u>).

There will be arguments about the merits of the two streak teams – the late-1970s club included Ken Dryden, Jacques Lemaire, Serge Savard, Bob Gainey, and Yvon Cournoyer – but there is something elemental about that 1950s dynasty. It reigned before the World Hockey Association (WHA) expansion, before league-parity rules, before the Canadiens became just another business in the NHL, before *English* became the language of the dressing room. For five years this team, composed almost entirely of Quebec boys, could not be knocked off by the best hockey players in North America.

Something else was different in 1976, of course. The Parti Québécois had gained power in the province, deflating the powerful metaphor *les Canadiens* had always provided for downtrodden Québécois. Here was real, not symbolic, power. For many Montrealers, hockey became just a game, no longer a national placeholder capable of provoking the riots on Rue Ste-Catherine that greeted the suspension of Maurice Richard in March 1955.

The villain of the suspension was NHL president Clarence Campbell, just the latest example of a Scot shafting a Québécois. Sportswriter Tim Burke of the Montreal

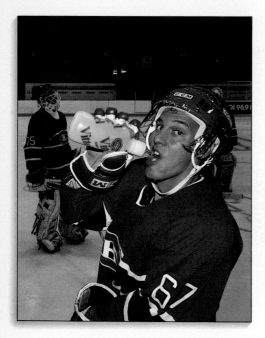

Gazette called the riot "the opening shot of the Quiet Revolution." However, by November 15, 1976, the revolution was over and won, and *les Canadiens* (many of them federalist, not separatist) skated through a game in which the election results dominated the scoreboard, proclaiming the Parti Québécois's stunning victory.

These events, dramatized in Rick Salutin's play *Les Canadiens*, show why the 1956–60 dynasty is a more potent symbol of what *le Club de Hockey* means to Montrealers – a source of fierce cultural pride when all else seems beyond reach. Salutin's play, set in a

miniature rink, reads Quebec's history through the lens of hockey. The musket that kills General Wolfe becomes the first hockey stick. Events are described by a commentator: "the shutout of the French Canadians at the Plains of Abraham… the sparkling teamwork of the Patriotes in 1867… the power play of 1867." But in the play's second act, the mythologising of the Canadiens ends when metaphors for power and Québécois aspiration are no longer necessary. Hockey is hockey; power is in the National Assembly, not the Forum.

However, hockey is still a powerful element in Québécois culture, and the melding of hockey with drama continues. A similar mini-arena setting, complete with commentator, organist and referee, is now used by the *Ligue Nationale d'Improvisation*, which pits teams of uniformed actors against one another in the competitive acting-out of improvised themes. (Penalties may be called for hamming it up.) Many of Quebec's best actors start their careers here, moving up from junior leagues to the televised national games, and then on to even bigger things.

Unfortunately, the other great team of hockey's early years, the Toronto Maple Leafs, has fallen on rocky times. It has not weathered expansion and the modern game as well as Montreal. Sure, the Washington Capitals have been known to beat the Canadiens once in a while, and the Stanley Cup has lately eluded them. But they have never haunted the basement of their division like the hapless Leafs, winners of 11 Stanley Cups in the distant past.

It is perhaps a little hard to imagine now, but there was a time when the Montreal-Toronto hockey rivalry was one of the most exciting in sport. If one were a Canadian, allegiance had to be pledged – Leaf or Hab, and no fence-sitters allowed. And hockey was clearly not the only thing at stake: there was civic pride, the least often examined undercurrent of racial and linguistic enmity.

The writer Roch Carrier distilled these issues in his short story *The Hockey Sweater*. A Quebec kid, a desperate Maurice Richard fan, needs a new hockey sweater and his mother writes away to Eaton's, the famous Canadian store. The resulting parcel holds a

Maple Leafs sweater. *Quel désastre!* His mother will not send it back because it fits him. He is shunned by the other little Rocket Richards, a traitor to Mother Quebec, *les Habitants*, and the Rocket himself. A young priest sends him to confession.

Torontonians have never been quite as hockey-mad as their counterparts to the east, nor have they ever invested so many of their personal and collective ambitions in one team. Toronto hockey has produced its share of heroes – Francis "King" Clancy, Frank Mahovlich, Red Kelly, Darryl Sittler, Dave Keon, Lanny Macdonald, coach Punch Imlach. More recently, however, it became

his coaches with abandon and paying sub-par salaries to his players. After a long legal battle over control of the immensely profitable club, Toronto businessman Steve Stavro became majority shareholder and chairman of the Maple Leafs' board in 1991.

No, the Canadiens, not the Leafs, are Canada's national team. Or they ought to be anyway. Boorish western Canadians have been known to boo the French sections of the national anthem when *les bons Canadiens* are in town. "Some of the players were so angry they didn't want to go out on the ice," Serge Savard said on one such occasion in Vancouver in 1980. The fans in Winnipeg

known for a less glorious personage, the crotchety owner of the Leafs, ex-convict Harold Ballard. Ballard, who went to jail in the 1970s for defrauding his own hockey club of $200,000, was so offensive to everyone that local sportswriters even started a Ballard-Watch pool when he was hospitalized for heart trouble, an ailment of which he eventually died. Legend has it that Ballard's tight-fist kept the Maple Leafs from returning to their rightful place atop the NHL, firing

Left and **above**, hockey now incorporates helmets and body pads to prevent serious injury.

have had a better appreciation of what *Le Club de Hockey de Canadiens* represents: the first time the Canadiens visited Winnipeg after the Jets joined the NHL, all the fans wore tuxedoes and gowns. Despite Winnipeg fans' loyalty, it was not enough to prevent the 1995 transfer of the former Winnipeg Jets' franchise to Phoenix, Arizona.

All in all the Canadiens deserve, at the very least, our respect. The old-fashioned red and blue uniforms, as they glide across the ice, represent not just the best in hockey, but also a window on the tough and tireless teamwork inherent in Canadian history.

PLACES

"I remember." This was the refrain of French troops as they, along with grand hopes of New France, perished on the Plains of Abraham in 1759. *"Je me souviens"* remains Quebec's shibboleth, and it is ubiquitous throughout the province, gracing cultural icons from flags to license plates.

Montreal remembers in a special way the language and culture of its "New France" heritage. As the world's second-largest French-speaking city, Montreal has long been considered the commercial and cultural pivot of Canada and, perhaps more importantly, the garden of Quebec's social and political identity.

From its origins as the first French foothold on a vast and punishing land, to its present status as Canada's most urbane and exciting city, Montreal is a colorful swirl of people, politics, language, and culture. It is here where faith and fur joined hands to transform irrevocably Canada's First Peoples. It is here where Quebec's intellectual and artistic vigor has its most potent expression, and where pride, politics and the past merge in a brilliant and ever-changing tapestry.

Montreal has been called a "phonic" city, with francophones (French-speakers) in the majority, anglophones (English-speakers) and allophones – those whose first language is other than French or English. While wires sometimes get crossed, and communication among these sundry cultures occasionally falters, the city has remained a cohesive, vital, and peaceful social network.

To the surprise of many, London's influential *Sunday Times* reported at the beginning of the 1980s that "Montreal now surpasses San Francisco as the most interesting North American city... There is a swagger about the city that one used to find in San Francisco before it went limp in the early '70s."

But has Montreal fulfilled that promise of excitement to come? To prove that it has, the Places section of this book guides you through the European charm of Old Montreal, the dynamic modernity of Downtown, the astonishing Underground City, and then through the parks and out into the countryside surrounding Canada's most exciting city.

Preceding pages: today's high rises; view over McGill University; winter wonderland. Left, invitation to fitness near the waterfront.

Montreal

800 m / 0.5 miles

OLD MONTREAL

Old Montreal is back. Once the entire city of Montreal, and its business center until late in the 19th century, it is hard to imagine that in 1960 the streets were deserted, the buildings derelict and slated for demolition. Old Montreal came close to extinction.

Then, in 1962 the Viger Commission declared the area historically invaluable. Houses were restored, buildings gutted and renovated, and restaurants, shops and clubs began to spring up to serve tourists *and* Montrealers. Every city inherits styles and traditions, heirlooms bequeathed to the next generation. Old Montreal is modern Montreal's inheritance, and thanks to foresight and initiative it is a *living* inheritance.

The area is a provocative blend of commercialism and history. An 18th-century building houses a thoroughly modern business: banks of computers line a four-foot rubble wall, printers and fax machines operate inside stone vaults. Architects focus their creativity on pre-existing shapes and dimensions and still do excellent work. Electricians wire rooms that smell faintly of paraffin. Painters strip and varnish narrow staircases with cross beams that force tall people to stoop. Old Montreal wants modern entrepreneurs to make history contemporary while making profits for themselves. Atmosphere is abundant, and the location can't be equaled. Why *not* set up shop in Old Montreal?

But there is another side to the restorations. Most Montrealers and tourists descend to the old city to sightsee during the day and dine in the evening. Afterwards they return to their homes or hotels, leaving the cobbled streets quiet and melancholy. But efforts to make the area a functioning neighborhood are beginning to see results, with condominiums and apartments springing up. Old Montreal now boasts over 2,500 permanent residents and a burgeoning

nightlife has started to flourish in the eastern section of the neighborhood.

Old Montreal was once a neighborhood of houses, shops, and churches. It still is an area of public squares – four major squares in a nine-block radius that, until recently, served as community centers, where people gathered to gossip and discuss the business of the day. Their presence reminds the traveler of a vibrancy behind the impressive buildings. What better way to explore Old Montreal than by using the squares as landmarks?

Stand in Place Jacques Cartier and imagine yourself a citizen. The year could be 1790 or 1990. The principal structures still stand, the churches and seminaries still function. The St Lawrence still borders to the south and the mountain to the northwest, and while the walls that protected Montrealers until the early 19th century are gone, the area remains distinct and indivisible. During the summer you can sit in a square for hours watching the merriment. In winter, though, a café seat has advantages.

eft, the eat man ever faces Eglise otre-Dame. ght, ateau amezay.

Heart of tourism: The obvious place to start your visit is **Place Jacques Cartier**. Rectangular in shape, lined with Victorian-style street lamps and cobblestones, the square has a grace and charm that conjures images of women strolling with parasols and men playing absently with pocket watches. The heart of tourist Montreal is here. Restaurants and terrace cafés abound. During the summer, sidewalks, already crowded, dissolve into hives of onlookers gathered around the jugglers, mimes, and acrobats. Artists and *chansoniers* are also plentiful on narrow Rue St-Amable, Rue St-Vincent or any other sonorous alley.

The square slopes up from the St Lawrence River to **Rue Notre-Dame**. There are excellent views of the port, the behemoth freighters being bunkered and provisioned, on any but the foggiest of days. In winter, though, Place Jacques Cartier is subject to the quirky imagination of a city hall decorator who one year festooned **the square** with giant helium-inflated Christmas trees. Recent years have seen a return to more traditional Christmas displays. The features of the lovely old buildings around the square are pleasingly accented by abundant but tasteful lighting.

The square is also the launching point for Montreal's annual **Fête des Neiges** in late January, a brisk but lively winter festival that features ice sculptures in the **Vieux-Port** and ski and snowboard demonstrations in Place Jacques Cartier.

At the top of the square, towering above the buildings, is **Nelson's Monument**, an imposing if odd tribute to England's naval hero. Imposing because it stands 105-ft (35-meters) tall and dates from 1809. Odd both because the Admiral faces *away* from the St Lawrence and, more to the point, that he is there at all. Little in public Montreal escapes political judgement: a memorial to the English conqueror of a French navy is lucky to have escaped intact.

Nelson squares off with a less grand statue of **Vauquelin**, an early French administrator, in tiny **Place Vauquelin**

1 Notre-Dame-de-Bonsecours Chapel
2 Old Seminary Saint-Sulpice
3 Old Court House
4 Youville Stables
5 Bonsecours Market

7 Grey Nuns General Hospital
8 Pierre du Calvet House
9 Hôtel de Ville
10 Court House
11 Bank of Montréal
12 Royal Bank
13 Montréal Stock Exchange
14 Château Ramezay Museum
15 Notre-Dame Basilica
16 Centaur Theater
17 Convention Center
18 Expotec

at the crest of the incline. From this square, once the site of the town jail and the public flogging ground, "new" Montreal sprawls in all directions. Vauquelin, it should be noted, *is* facing the river, though his position may have more to do with keeping the bitter north wind to his back than anything else.

Place Vauquelin is bookended by important buildings. To the west is Montreal's former **Palais de Justice**. The old court house, dating from 1856, was designed by John Ostell, the man responsible for the magnificent twin towers of **Notre-Dame Basilica** on **Place d'Armes**. The style, known as classical revival, was extremely popular in Montreal at the time, particularly the thick columns and, when it was added in 1890, the cupola dome. The court house is now occupied by government offices.

Across the street, at 100 Rue Notre-Dame, is a later bastion of canon and code. This massive, suitably dour building was used until quite recently for criminal cases, and it features massive columns fronting a lovely bronze door. Above the door are bas-reliefs detailing the history of criminal law. The Latin inscription over the cornice reads: "He who transgresses the law shall seek the help of the law in vain." Hardly comforting words for a defendant! The **Nouveau Palais de Justice** currently showcases the talents of Québec's finest young artists. It is home to both the art and drama conservatories, where aesthetic laws are transgressed daily.

East of Place Vauquelin stands Montreal's stately **Hôtel de Ville**, a second-empire structure with slender columns and the mansard roof so common in Québécois architecture. The building, which dates from 1860, survived a major fire in 1922, and today it boasts an extra storey. During the holiday season, tiny lights outline the building's striking architectural features in a dramatic but seasonal silhouette. It was from a second-storey balcony that Charles de Gaulle addressed a crowd

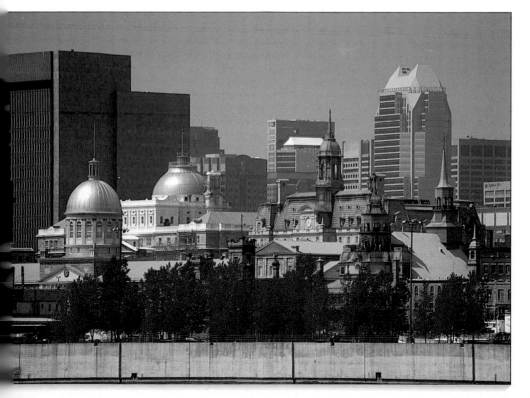

that crowded Place Jacques Cartier in 1967. De Gaulle roused the Québécois with his cry *"Vive le Québec libre!"* The crowd heeded his words.

Château Ramezay, across from the city hall, is the most famous of the many restored houses around the square. Built in 1705, this low-lying fieldhouse has over the years served as offices and warehouses for the *Companies des Indes*, the official residence of British governors, a court house, school, seat of government, even a headquarters for the American army under Montgomery and Benedict Arnold when they briefly occupied Montreal in 1775.

Benjamin Franklin stayed in the house while on his mission to persuade Lower Canada to join the American revolution. The Château survived these incarnations nicely, and it still boasts the three-foot walls and deep stone vaults ordered by its namesake, Claude de Ramezay, the 11th governor of Montreal. Today, it is a museum of life in 18th-century Montreal.

The rooms of Château Ramezay are worth exploring. Among the more curious artifacts are stern portraits of pioneer officials, religious icons, maps, a 1750 manuscript of liturgical chants translated into an Amerindian language, rugs, business ledgers, a reproduction of the head offices of the *Companie des Indes Occidentale* in Nantes, France. The building was the North American headquarters of the French West India Company from 1745 to 1760.

A series of rooms recreates the interiors of diverse living quarters in New France. These include the offices of the governor, a dining room, kitchen, and servants' quarters. All the rooms contain period furniture, and some pieces are very fine, especially the cabinets. There are regular special exhibitions.

In the whitewashed vaults and narrow passages of Château Ramezay's basement is an attempt to do justice to the Amerindians who were displaced by Europeans. The predominant feature of the exhibit is a 19th-century photo col-

Fête des Neiges at Place Jacques Cartier.

the exhibit is a 19th-century photo collection showing "civilized" Indians smoking pipes in suits and ties.

Two other prominent examples of restoration include the **Maison du Calvet** (1770), with its distinctive high chimneys and steep roof to prevent snow from accumulating, and **Maison Papineau** (1785), known for its wood facade painted to look like limestone.

Both houses are well known for their historic namesakes, but Calvet is the infamous of the pair. Pierre du Calvet was an administrator who betrayed the French, first to the British in 1759 and then to the Americans in 1775, for which he was duly imprisoned. Upon his release several years later Calvet sought financial compensation from the Americans for his trouble, but was refused. Next he sailed to England to protest his term in prison. Tragically, his ship sank en route, and Calvet kept his traitorous status for perpetuity.

The Papineau family, in stark contrast, is among Quebec's most honored.

Louis-Joseph Papineau, the leader of the 1837 rebellion in Lower Canada, was born in this house, and six generations of the family, including many distinguished politicians and businessmen, have occupied it.

Maison Papineau was also the residence chosen by Eric McLean of the Vigor Commission to begin the renewal of Old Montreal. In the early 1960s **Rue Bonsecours**, which holds both houses, was dreary and vaguely disreputable. When workers began to restore Maison Papineau, they eliminated two brick storeys and replaced all the windows. They also stripped the walls of 19 layers of wallpaper. The refurbished Maison du Calvet has become a trendy bed and breakfast – the Pierre du Calvet, complete with excellent restaurant and quaint coffee shop.

Arguably the most charming street in Old Montreal is **Rue St-Paul**. Cobblestoned, the air smacking of the St Lawrence River 100 yards to the south, and lined with 18th-century buildings

vic pride
ssoms
th.

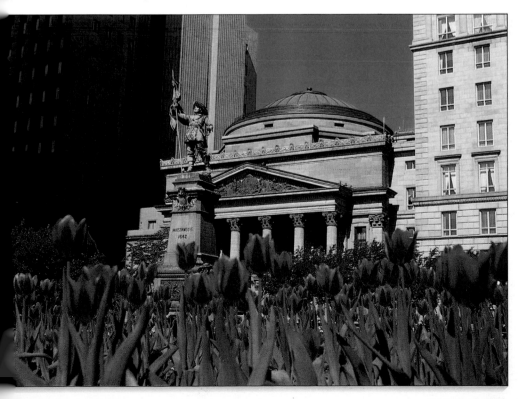

authentic without being precious, at once current and deeply historic. The three most prominent structures are **Rasco's Hotel**, the **Marché Bonsecours**, and **Notre-Dame-de-Bon-Secours**.

In its day, **Rasco's Hotel** at 295 Rue St-Paul was considered among the finest hotels in North America. Named after an Italian, Francisco Rasco, who emigrated to North America in the early 1800s, it was constructed in 1836 and featured a lavish restaurant that was "the place to be" in 1840s Montreal. A ballroom and concert hall were available for the cultured and/or wealthy.

In 1842 Charles Dickens, on the visit that would eventually produce *American Notes*, stayed at the hotel with his wife. Dickens' observations about Montreal, though simple, still ring true: "Montreal is pleasantly situated on the margin of the St Lawrence, and is backed by some bold heights, about which there are charming rides and drives. The streets are generally narrow and irregular." Rasco's Hotel, abandoned for decades,

was restored in 1982 and currently houses government offices. Look for the name between floors of a simple, almost spartan, greystone building.

The **Marché Bonsecours** was once the most photographed edifice in Montreal. It boasts attractive facades, especially on the river side, and a Renaissance-style dome (1864) that was the first to be erected in the city. Remember that Montreal was, and still is, a port. Ships moving down the St Lawrence from Quebec would have spotted the dome and Notre Dame church before anything else. For a sailor, riding an autumn storm and fatigued from months at sea, these markers became emblems of security and shelter, visible even in his dreams.

The Marché was primarily a market and exhibition center. The vagaries of history, however, forced it to function briefly as both house of parliament (1849) and, between 1852–78, the city hall. For the last 30 years it has served as offices for civil servants, but in May, **Trotting out Rue St-Paul**

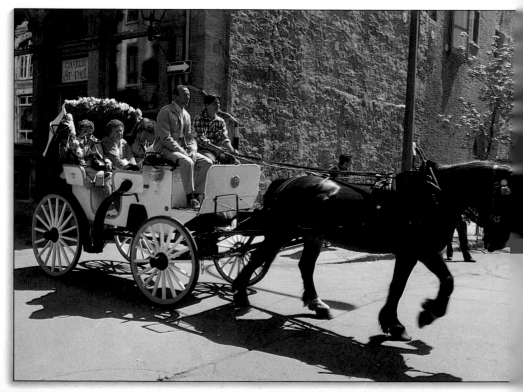

130

1996, it reopened as a public market, complete with farmers' stands. It runs from mid-May to mid-October.

No symbol of Montreal's maritime heritage is more poignant than **Notre-Dame-de-Bon-Secours**. One must stand at the water's edge in the **Vieux-Port** to appreciate the church's impact. Rising above the clock tower is a statue of the Virgin Mary, her outstretched arms welcoming ships into port. For hundreds of years seamen from Montreal made a pilgrimage to Notre-Dame-de-Bon-Secours to pray for safe passage.

Little wonder, too, that the lively and busy interior of the "sailor's church" has a decidedly nautical look: there are votive lamps shaped like vessels, and carvings of ships – many donated by seamen – hang from the ceiling. *Secours* translates to "assistance" or "help," but the church's name in English – Our Lady of Divine Assistance – lacks all the resonance of the original.

The first church on the site was founded in 1671 by Margeurite Bour-

geoys. Various incarnations followed, and the current building dates from 1772. Typically Québécois features of Notre-Dame-de-Bon-Secours include the arched door, wooden belfry, and *oeil-de-boeuf* (a small round window in the gable). Interestingly, Saint Marguerite – she was canonized by Pope John Paul II in 1982 – returned from a visit to France in 1672 with a tiny wooden statue of the Virgin Mary. Against all odds the statue survived numerous fires and is now kept in a house on Rue Sherbrooke.

Marguerite Bourgeoys is a legend in Quebec. The museum dedicated to her life in the basement of Notre-Dame-de-Bon-Secours is a site of veneration for many Catholics, especially older people who can recall an era when the Québécois Catholics were among the most devout and pious in Christendom. Her life is, naturally, shrouded in myth and folklore. The museum is modest, consisting largely of showcases that use miniature dolls to re-enact the key scenes of Saint Marguerite's long and active life. The

rché nsecours.

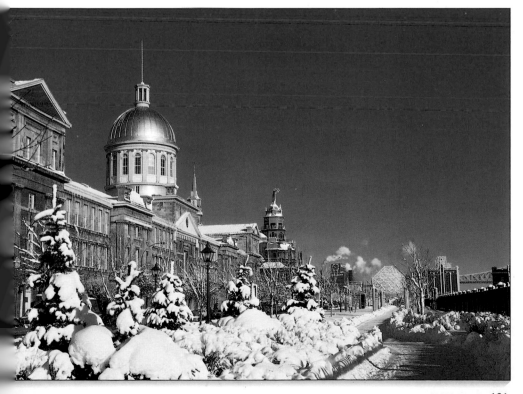

A LIVING LANGUAGE

The leading French dictionary, *Le Petit Robert*, defines linguistic purism this way: "The excessive concern for the purity of language, in accordance with an intangible and idealistic model." It is characterized by a desire to freeze a tongue at a certain stage of its evolution. Purism is autocratic. Worse, it is uninteresting.

Québécois, the French spoken in Montreal and throughout the province of Quebec, is anything but pure. Major French dictionaries published in Paris once took it upon themselves to denounce Québécois as a bastardization of the original tongue. They couldn't have been more misguided. Montreal French is a language crackling with vitality. Anglo-Canadians, Greeks, Africans, Asians, even the occasional transplanted US citizen, seize the French tongue and contort, distort, and otherwise twist it into new, unimagined shapes. Compound this with the ribald, earthy, but always original *joual* of the Québécois themselves, a street-wise dialect bursting with word-puns and wit, and the linguistic climate is far from dull.

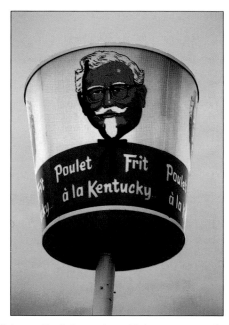

A major concern of linguistically sensitive francophones, however, is that the verbal climate is a bit too interesting, Québécois French, they sense, is fast becoming overrun by anglicisms: English words incorporated into day-to-day vocabulary. Where else, for example, do people go for drives on *le weekend* as long as *le traffic* isn't too heavy and they can *faire du parking* with success. Surely in Quebec such an excursion should occur at *la fin de semaine* – as long as *la circulation* isn't too heavy, of course, and they can *faire du stationnement* with success?

Yes, Montreal French is rife with English expressions. Many people are, after all, fluently bilingual; such a gift leads inevitably to a casual mingling of languages, especially with so much of the popular culture emanating from just across the border in the United States. A musician is *super-cool* if *le mood* that night is good. In the mornings people eat *les corn-flakes*, slip on their *sportwear*, and go *faire du shopping*. A *rough and tough* guy usually wears *son tee-shirt* or *son pull* (pull-over sweater), and will spend evenings at a friend's *living* (living room) drinking *les Ex* (Molson's Export beer). At work, especially in an age of technology, one attends *un briefing* or *un meeting* to do some planning or perhaps engage in *un autre brainstorming* session. Later on the executive will relax with *un coctail* at *un night-club*. *C'est OK* to stay late to *voir le show*.

Even people are stirred into the linguistic stew. An Englishman in Quebec? Easy: *un rosbif!* And in certain parts of English Canada, a Québécois is known as a *peasouper*, in honor of the province's love of pea soup. We are, apparently, what we eat.

Quebec French is also characterized by certain expressions. Besides the accent, a Parisian will usually be able to identify a Québécois by phrases like *nous autres* (the rest of us), *J'ai-pas* (I don't know), the musical *binbin* (*bien, bien*: very, very good) plus the bookend greeting *Salut!* (Hi/Bye) instead of the more formal *bonjour* and *au revoir*. There are also literally thousands of words that are unique to Quebec. Experts estimate that, of the 200,000 active French words, 8,000 to 10,000 originated in North America. Of those, however, the average Montrealer may incorporate 300 to 500 into his or her vocabulary. A few samples will whet the appetite: a *bête puante* (smelly animal) for a skunk, a *p'tit blanc* for a whiskey, *une sacoche* for a handbag, a *char* for an automobile. How about a *chanteur de pomme* (singer of apples) – a playboy who seduces women using glib, sickly-sweet language!

The Montreal accent is particularly noteworthy. Many visitors to the city, both French and those who've learned the language in school, are shocked at first by what they hear. More precisely, the shock is with what they don't *understand*. A thick Montreal accent is a marvel. It is skitterish, lightning-quick, and sounds initially as if the speaker is using his or her nose rather than mouth. The tone is harsh but decidedly musical. Listen closely, extract the odd words of dialect, and what will emerge is a gregarious and engaging tongue almost totally lacking in the pretense of Parisian French. Québécois French doesn't sound like a textbook. It sounds like people! ∎

dolls wear traditional costumes and smile sweetly. A more interesting activity, included in the price, is a climb up the creaky wooden staircase to the aerial chapel and observation tower.

The view of the harbor from here is impressive. Visible to the south, astride the St Lawrence, are Expo 67's two most famous, or infamous, landmarks: Buckminster Fuller's 20-storey geodesic dome (previously the American pavilion and now the Biosphere – an intriguing interpretive center on the ecosystems of the St Lawrence and the Great Lakes) and architect Moshe Safdie's cubic apartment complex Habitat. The latter, a startlingly ugly and awkward living space, consists of 158 units hoisted into place like building blocks. The panorama north of the mountain is also fine, weather – and wind – permitting. The tower and museum keep regular hours. Notre-Dame-de-Bon-Secours is open to visitors year round.

A tour of Place Jacques Cartier would be incomplete without a walk along the sweeping arc of **Rue de la Commune**, once Montreal's waterfront, and a glance inside the Vieux-Port. Little of interest remains in the old port, except a curious art-deco clock tower and, at the far end of Old Montreal, the **Harbor Commission Building**. Notre-Dame-de-Bon-Secours and the harbor commission building frame the entire area.

Rue de la Commune was once a bustling thoroughfare lined with carriages and transport wagons. It had a promenade where strollers could watch the ships unload onto railway cars as thickets of masts swayed in the swell like compass needles. It is quiet now, largely inactive. But history is painted on the facades of the warehouses: J. Alfred Ouimet – Importater; Borque – Wholesale Grocer; Standard Paper Box. Condominiums are beginning to take root in some of these derelict buildings.

Place d'Armes: The expansion westward from the houses of Place Jacques Cartier to the skyscrapers of **Place d'Armes** represents, in broad terms, the

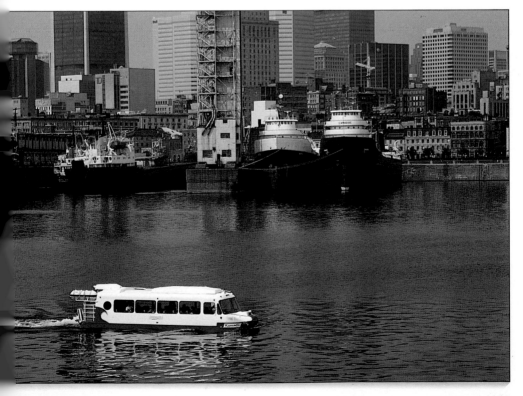

transformation of Old Montreal from an 18th-century French colonial outpost to a 19th-century English business center. Keep in mind that pre-1759 Montreal was a walled city, even though the hilly topography of the region left many of the taller buildings, including both churches, fully exposed to cannon fire from the St Lawrence River.

The ramparts had four main gates, including one off Rue Notre-Dame. The walls that were 18-ft high and 4-ft thick (5.5 by 1.2 meters). Historians emphasize their flimsiness, and it is generally accepted that they wouldn't have slowed the enemy for very long.

When the ramparts came down in the early 1800s, the symbolism was inescapable. No longer defensive, no longer insular, Montreal was now open for business with the rest of Canada and, thanks to the St Lawrence, the outside world. Place d'Armes was where the major transactions occurred.

But first a word about the streets between the two squares. For many tourists, and most locals, Old Montreal in summer means eating, drinking, and music. The narrow lanes, barely wide enough for a car, are lined with restaurants and cafés, along with Quebec's beloved *boîtes à chanson*. **Rue St-Paul**, **Rue St-Vincent** and, further west, **Rue St-Pierre** are good to wander.

Watch the crowds, see where they are heading. Then, knowing which spots are popular and which are not, decide either to follow fashion or *set* it. Among the more popular restaurants are *Auberge Le Saint Gabriel* on Rue St-Gabriele; *Le Muscadin, Le Grill* with its lovely courtyard in summer, *Chez Queux*, and *Brocherterie du Vieux-Port*, all on Rue St-Paul. For totally different experience, *Stash's Café Restauracja Polska* offers good inexpensive fare with the motto: "Anything tastes better with vodka."

Also on St-Paul, combining pub atmosphere with lighter fare, are *Le Keg* and *Chez Brandy*. Restaurant *Sawatdee* further along St Pierre is worth mention as it offers tasty, reasonably-priced Thai food. For less expensive dining, *Giorgio* offers Italian food in a fortress-like building at the foot of Rue St-Laurent. *L'Usine de Spaghetti*, near Rosco's Hotel, also has fair prices.

Finally, worthy of mention if only as an aside, is the *McDonald's* at the intersection of Rue Notre-Dame and St-Laurent. A plaque outside the restaurant informs the history buff that here lived Antoine Laumet de Lamoníe (1658–1730), founder of Detroit *and* governor of the state of Louisiana. Lamoníe was certainly a busy man.

Visiting a *boîte à chanson* is virtually mandatory on any trip to Montreal. Literally a "music box," these beerhalls are boisterous, frothy, *joie-de-vivre* establishments where musicians, often solo guitarists, run through the current repertoire of Québécois folk songs, anthems and the latest chart hits. The packed houses sing along, applaud, proffer requests that are adopted, deferred, or rejected out of hand – all depending on the tone and direction of the night.

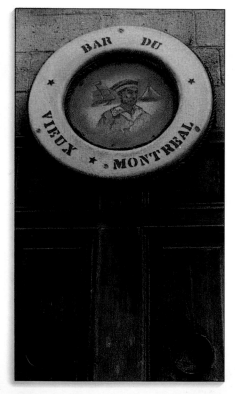

Invitation i the Old Po

Boîtes are authentically Québécois and impervious, by and large, to the encroachment of technology on music. A guitar, a microphone, pitchers of beer, a convivial audience: what more is needed? The quintessential *boîte* in Old Montreal is *Les Deux Pierrots* on Rue St-Paul. A lively mix of chansonniers and rock sing-alongs is hugely popular. Come early – there are long lineups an hour before the music begins.

Finally, don't forget about the **Vieux-Port**. Though largely unused as a port, the park by the St Lawrence offers long summer evenings of music and dance. With the Montreal skyline as a backdrop and the river, active with ships and sailboats, flowing gently past, the setting alone makes the park worth a visit.

Montreal's historic growth: Back to Place d'Armes. To stand in the square is to witness in visual terms the historic growth of Montreal as a city. The casual mingling of commerce with religion is, at first, rather disconcerting. Notre-Dame Basilica and the adjoining semi-

nary appear lost among the banks and, by modern standards, miniature office towers. But, after a while, the congruities between the buildings make the juxtaposition jar less. Perhaps there is also in Quebec a resigned acceptance of the "business of faith," and vice versa.

Maisonneuve, whose statue adorns the square, would certainly not have blessed this marriage of God and Mammon. As the founder of Montreal, Paul de Chomeday de Maisonneuve definitely deserved a memorial in a prominent location. But why Place d'Armes, while Admiral Nelson gazes so incongruously upon the city hall in Place Jacques Cartier? The statue depicts Maisonneuve holding the banner of France. He is surrounded by other pioneers, including Jeanne Mance, Louis Hébert and Lambert Closse.

All the figures are, in turn, surrounded by the likes of the Bank of Montreal, the New York Insurance Company, and the Bank Canadienne Nationale. Are Montreal's founding fathers (and moth-

e former
tel Viger,
w a civic
ilding.

ers) at all uncomfortable with the company? Though Maisonneuve's expression is dour, the limestone otherwise reveals little.

Parked along the southern rim of the square, rain or shine, snow or sand storm, is Montreal's venerable fleet *des calèches* – horse-drawn carriages. They are hard to miss. If the sound of wooden wheels rattling over cobblestones doesn't prick up the ears, the bellow of the drivers certainly will. "*Un calèche, Monsieur?*" they will shout across Place d'Armes. Or, sizing up the mark as a tourist: "Ride through old Montreal for you, Sir?" In high season the competition is fierce, and drivers fan out across the square like angry bees. In winter the men sit stoic inside their vehicles, watching their breath dissipate into the frigid air. Under these circumstances the invitation to visitors is more matter-of-fact, without conviction.

Touring Old Montreal in a carriage can be charming. Try it during the winter, with a bear skin protecting the lower body and, ideally, a flask of something warm tucked inside the pocket. During the busy months it is often best to wait until evening to hire a carriage. The streets are full of moving shadows; shafts of light seep between drawn curtains, water trapped between cobblestones glistens under the yellow street lamps.

A few words of advice for the would-be rider. First, bargain. The price quoted for a tour is not necessarily the bottom line, especially in off-season. The carriages are restricted as to where they can travel, so be realistic. Finally, use a ride to experience the atmosphere of Old Montreal at different times of the day and year. *Don't* hire one to sightsee. Always do that on foot.

Place d'Armes is also home to the ubiquitous tour buses dropping visitors off for cursory tours of Notre-Dame and its environs. The traveler aboard one of these buses who aspires to jump ship couldn't choose a better place to do it than the square, a launching point for just about all the most interesting areas

A forest of flags on Rue St-Paul.

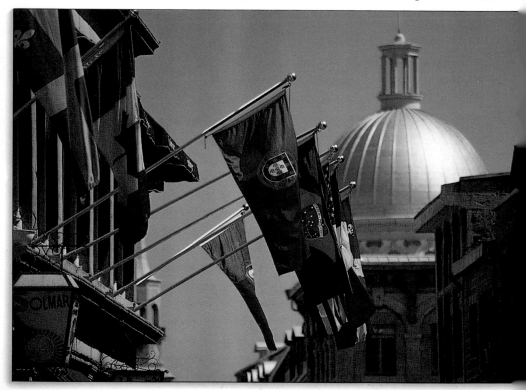

of Old Montreal. Mutinies of this kind are to be encouraged.

Notre-Dame Basilica on Rue Notre-Dame is Montreal's most famous church. The first chapel, built within the fort in 1642, was covered with bark. The current structure (1829) is a little more grand. A contemporary Montreal poet describes the church in winter:

In laden February, on Rue St-Jacques
we are dreaming the breeding of
  lilacs
and shuffling on ice toward Notre-
  Dame.
Suddenly the cold bright square
the two arms of her towers and the
  walk
into the blue sunrise of her altar.

The twin arms of her towers are magnificent, the mark of greatness in architect James O'Donnell's design. Each measures 227 ft (69 meters), and they were completed only in the 1840s by John Ostell, who succeeded as architect after O'Donnell's death. The plainness of the exterior was both aesthetic and practical. Quebec lacked the stoneworkers to do the work. The decision to leave the facade unadorned was, in the context, a wise one.

The west tower of Notre-Dame houses a 12-ton bell that it took a dozen men to ring. Even today, powered by electricity, the bell is used sparingly. The basilica, still considered among the finest examples of the Gothic revival style in North America, was visited by architects from other cities to learn from O'Donnell's mastery.

The interior of the basilica is majestic. Designed by Victor Bourgeau, who also worked on the Mary Queen of the World Cathedral in Dominion Square, it is at once massive and welcoming, a feat achieved by the original use of woodworking and carpentry. Bourgeau encouraged local artists to use traditional methods and tastes. The result is a glittering, and at times overwhelming, use of paints – the aqua-blue nave, for example, is delicate and refined – and ornately carved wood statuary.

Notre-Dame
Basilica.

Note especially the main altar, which is perpetually bathed in flowers, and the figures of Jeremiah and Ezekial at the bottom of the pulpit. The wraparound balconies are also splendid. They serve to narrow the distance between the worshipper and the sacristy. Also worth noting is the haunting presence of giant pipes in the organ loft. The effect, achieved by back-lighting the organ (also done with the "sunrise" behind the altar), is stunning: fingers of bluish light arc upward into the nave.

Notre-Dame keeps long hours to satisfy the tourists, admirers, and worshippers who wander the aisles. Services are held several times daily, and those who are lucky might hear the organ. The sound is sonorous and celestial.

Adjacent to the west wall of the basilica stands – miraculously, some say – Montreal's oldest building. The **Vieux Séminaire de Saint-Sulpice** dates from 1680. The Sulpicians, the order that founded the seminary, at one time wielded enormous power in New France.

In 1663 the Société de St-Sulpice took over missionary duties from the Société de Notre-Dame, becoming, in effect, the landlords of *all* the island of Montreal. Even Maurice Duplessis would have envied such power. Today, more than 300 years after arriving, the Sulpicians – no longer *seigneurs*, no longer even the moral arbiters of life in Montreal – still own and operate the fieldstone seminary.

The seminary clock, by the way, was installed in 1701. It is considered the first public clock in Canada. Though the works were replaced by electronic movements in 1966, it still functions only periodically. Setting one's watch by it would be unwise.

If Notre-Dame asserted francophone values, the **Bank of Montreal** building across Place d'Armes was an anglophonic retort. The neoclassical design of this 1847 structure offers an ornate facade that boasts six Corinthian columns with pediment sculptures – discernible only through lenses of some

Notre-Dame Basilica.

sort – of a sailor, a colonialist, and two Amerindians, one a "noble savage" and the other a recalcitrant hell-bent on rejecting civilization. The facade was designed by local architect, John Wells.

The interior of the bank is stunning. The lobby is spacious, the colors gentle and the light soft at all times of day. The atrium in particular, linking the older part of the building with a 1905 addition, is lovely, lined by eight Ionic columns of Vermont granite with marble bases. The walls of the atrium are made of pink marble from Tennessee. In the majestic front hall one discovers another 32 columns, also of granite, and counters of marble. Gold leaf covers everything, and elaborate chandeliers hang from the ceiling.

The interior gets its grace from both the simplicity of the design and the continuous presence of natural light streaming down from massive windows. The bank's architects worked directly from models of Italian churches: it is hard not to remark upon the "basilica"

he Vieux
eminaire.

style of the structure. A provocative gesture? Artistic inspiration? Also worth a look is a fine statue of Patria in the atrium. The marble statue is a memorial to Canadians who died in World War I.

The Bank of Montreal offers visitors a small museum off the main lobby devoted to numismatics – money, to the layman. Displays of banknotes, coins, a collection of elaborate 19th-century piggy banks and other interesting memorabilia are to be found. Tours are available in both official languages.

In tone and proportion the Bank of Montreal headquarters sent a message: on **Rue St-Jacques**, the street crossing the north end of the square, business would be calm, orderly and efficient. The result was the "Wall Street of Canada," an appellation applied to "St James Street" as it was called by anglophone Montrealers.

Until only 20 years ago, Rue St-Jacques was Canada's financial center, a street of busy Victorian buildings swathed to varying degrees in stucco, wrought-iron, columns, and elaborate porticos. A trolley down the middle of the road serviced office workers.

Among the many stately edifices are the **Molson's Bank** 288 St-Jacques and the **Bank of Commerce** across the street. An intriguing facade back at 230 offers pillars and statues and, for the moment at least, little else – the building *behind* the facade has been demolished. The Molson's Bank, built in 1866 using brewery profits that today fuel, among other things, the Montreal Canadiens hockey team, is impressive, as are all the offices at the corner of St-Jacques and Rue St-Pierre. None, however, quite stack up to the **Royal Bank**.

Like it or not – and many Montrealers consider the building an exercise in ostentation – the former head office of the Royal Bank at 360 St-Jacques is a must-see on any tour of the business district. Constructed in 1928, the Royal Bank was for a brief period the tallest structure not only in Canada but the entire British Empire.

The exterior is grand but austere, even sober. Not so the interior. The architects who designed the building were said to have had in mind the Medici Palace in Florence, Italy. They certainly had grandiose ambitions. The main doors are framed in bronze replicas of coins and lead into a lobby noted for its coffered ceiling and the marble steps which ascend to the main hall. Arches are covered with reddish limestone and walls are decorated with the coats of arms of Canada's provinces. Again the ceiling is ornately coffered. There are marble walls, bronze screens and the mosaic tiles on the floor are inlaid with Canada's royal coat of arms.

The effect is either dazzling or disheartening, depending on aesthetic tastes. Both in size and decoration, the Royal Bank begs comparison with the Bank of Montreal building. To the untrained eye, they are both formidable.

In the 1880s many commercial businesses followed the fashion and moved their offices further west to **Place Victoria** at Rue St-Jacques and Rue McGill. The square was for a brief period a prestigious residential address and one of Montreal's prime shopping districts. Barely 20 years later, however, department stores, lured by the rapidly growing English community along Rue Sherbrooke, moved again to the current "mecca" of Rue Ste-Catherine. Place Victoria faded rapidly, only to be revived again by the building of the World Trade Center. Opened in 1992, its 19th-century facade fronts a stunning office complex with a soaring sunlit atrium, the Hotel Inter-Continental and the Nordheimer Building, and a restored music hall in which Sarah Bernhardt performed in 1880.

The historical demographics of commercial life in Montreal are a study in skitterishness and insecurity. Only the stalwarts, the banks and loan companies, had the presence of mind to stay along St-Jacques; until, that is, recent political developments precipitated a wholesale rethinking of location.

The Stock Exchange tower in Place Victoria.

Place d'Armes features other prominent buildings. Dozens of offices and banks, many of them still functioning, line the streets on and around the square. But the area is also the focal point for Montreal's considerable newspaper industry. Within a few blocks can be found the offices of nearly all the major newspapers, and one significant ghost.

The *Montreal Star,* once the city's largest English paper, resided at 245 St-Jacques in the heart of the business district. Though the *Star* ceased publication in 1979, the *Montreal Gazette,* the current flagbearer, has offices on Rue St-Antoine and in the old *Star* building on St-Jacques. The *Gazette,* launched in 1778, is the city's oldest newspaper. *La Presse,* North America's best-selling French daily, has both its original and modern home at the corner of St-Jacques and St-Laurent. The old *La Presse* building is quite stately.

Also in Old Montreal, appropriately isolated from the larger community, are the old offices of the erudite and influential *Le Devoir.* If the other buildings *look* like the offices of large, busy, mass-appeal publications, then *Le Devoir,* groomed for a different class of reader, was appropriately solemn and demure. Its former digs are at 211 Rue St-Sacrement.

Banks, business, newspapers: the markers of the new 19th-century industrial city as delineated by Dickens in England, Zola in France, James and Dreiser in the US. Place d'Armes is the product of these modern realities – Second Empire Paris, Victorian London, the architectural landscape of reconstruction New York and Chicago. But, among the soaring edifices on the square, none are more impressive, more substantial, than the towers of Notre-Dame. The panorama is appropriately skewed. Peaceful co-existence is unspoken motto of Montreal. Even the old warrior Maisonneuve, though compromised by location, appears resigned to the fact.

Origins, health, religion: Montreal began in **Place Royale** and **Place**

ld house, ow a estaurant, in ôte du eaver Hill.

d'Youville. These two squares intersect each other at the site of Pointe-à-Callière, where Samuel de Champlain landed in 1611 and declared the spot a "place royale." Thirty years later, Maisonneuve chose that same site to erect the fort that became Ville-Marie. An obelisk at the eastern end of Place d'Youville – Place Royale runs north to south, d'Youville east to west – commemorates the event. The inscription emphasizes that Maisonneuve ordered the simultaneous construction of a fort, a chapel *and* a graveyard. Health, religion, and death: the basics.

It is difficult to imagine how Ville-Marie looked nearly 400 years ago. The St Lawrence has been pushed back for landfill, a small river that ran alongside the fort is now underground, and the dense forest that made reaching Mount Royal an arduous journey is today a forest of skyscrapers, the walk made tricky by rush-hour traffic. When Maisonneuve shifted the village to Place d'Armes – 300 ft (100 meters) north – it was a move inland, away from the dangers of the St Lawrence. Things have changed dramatically.

But **Pointe-à-Callière** remains the literal birthplace of Montreal, and the surrounding streets are its oldest neighborhood. A plaque in Place Royale calls the site the "first public square of Montreal," affixing the date 1657 to its creation. In a sense the "community" of Montreal also dates from that year. Before 1657 Ville-Marie was a wildly remote fort inhabited by a singular group of people: adventurers, traders, missionaries, soldiers and their officers.

Though it was where they lived, Ville-Marie was not their home. Instead the fort was variously a potential market, potential mission, potential conquest. The stake these pioneers had in the colony, while considerable, was not likely to produce citizens and samaritans. That required settlers, ordinary people devoted to establishing a life for themselves and their children. Communities are the sum of citizens, not con-

Café society

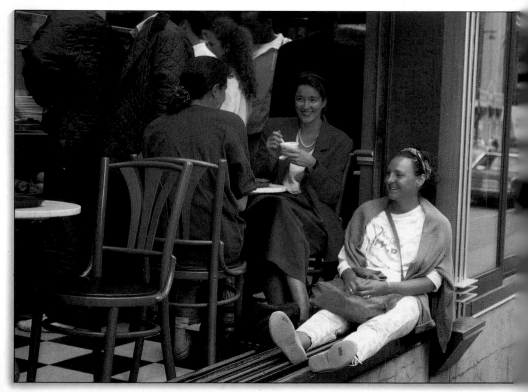

quistadors. In European society the traditional symbol of a town was a public square. So, too, in Montreal.

As part of the city's 350th anniversary celebrations in 1992, the **Musée d'Archéologie et d'Histoire de la Pointe-à-Callière** was opened on the site where Montreal was founded in 1642. State-of-the-art multimedia techniques in the modern Eperon building present the city's earliest history. The site is above a crypt, believed to date back to the first cemetery, where 17th- to 20th-century artifacts are on display. Visitors pass through this subterranean gallery on their way to the old customs house, now part of the museum.

Despite its importance, this was for many years the least known and least explored part of Old Montreal. Since the mid-18th century, attention had been drawn east to Place d'Armes and Place Jacques Cartier. However, a transformation has been taking place here since the early 1990s, and both visitors and Montrealers are finding many reasons to acquaint themselves with the area once again.

At the southern end of **Place Royale** is a grandiose statue of **John Young** (1811–1879), the harbor commissioner credited with making the city a world-class port. Young's gaze still encompasses Rue de la Commune and the eastern docking facilities.

Keep in mind that the river, which today appears distant from Old Montreal, once flowed precariously near the shops and warehouses along the Commune. Photos from the period tell the story: floods, especially in late winter, submerged the lower streets in 3 ft of water. Though landfill curbed the St Lawrence's reckless power, stinging winds and sleet remind the visitor of the seaway's proximity.

Place d'Youville, Old Montreal's largest square, commences at the statue and runs west four blocks to Rue McGill. Besides Pointe-à-Callière, the square's other main attraction is the **Centre d'Histoire de Montréal**. Formerly a

oyal Bank
Canada.

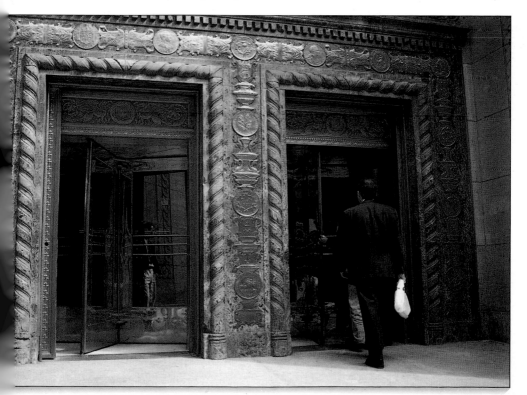

stylish 1915 firehouse, it combines Dutch and English architectural styles. Now a museum of Montreal history, it is worth a visit for anyone interested in studying the city's growth.

Place d'Youville was once the site of the parliament for both Upper and Lower Canada. The building, erected after the 1837 rebellion, lasted only a dozen years before rioters, protesting an unpopular British bill, burned it down.

Canada's pre-1867 legislature was housed briefly in the Marché Bonsecours, then resumed its quixotic search for a home: Kingston, Quebec City, and finally the current capital Ottawa. There are a number of restored buildings on the square, the most famous of which, the **Hôpital des Soeurs Grises**, runs off Rue Normand. The old hospital traces its origins to 1693, the year François Charon de la Bare resolved to begin a "house of charity" for Montreal's sick, poor and handicapped.

In 1753 Maria d'Youville, who founded the Sisters of Charity, extended the project into a hospital under the care of the sisters, known locally – no one is quite sure why – as the gray nuns (*soeurs grises*). Though the hospital moved to Rue Dorchester in 1871, many of the original structures escaped demolition and were restored in the late 1970s. The restoration was superbly done, and the hospital's west wing, including the remains of the original chapel, are visible on Rue St-Pierre.

The courtyard facing the square is also charming. As well, a delicate stained-glass window along Rue St-Normand brightens an otherwise austere, functional exterior. Both Hôpital des Soeurs Grises and the adjoining **Écurie d'Youville** (d'Youville Stables) are currently finding use as multi-purpose facilities. The courtyard of the stables, surrounded by 19th-century buildings, is a pleasant place for a cold drink in the summer.

The bottom of St-Pierre, also off the square, is a heartening example of successful urban renewal. Until recently empty, the block now houses luxury apartments, law offices, architectural firms, even a fancy cheese and chocolate shop. It is also the location of a small museum devoted to Marc-Aurèle Fortin (1888–1970), an important Québécois painter. Fortin's watercolours of the St Lawrence in all its seasonal variety are famous in Canada.

Further west, at the extreme edge of Old Montreal, are blocks of impressive 19th-century warehouses and customs houses. **Rue McGill** in particular has several fine buildings, including the ornate former headquarters of the Grand Trunk Railway at 360 and the Wilson Chambers Building at 474, near Place Victoria. The third customs house at 400 Place de la Commune features a clock tower and a small cross above its turret. The building is designed from the Beaux-Arts classical style.

The streets north of Place d'Youville were in limbo for many years, but gentrification is now taking place, particularly at the west end of Rue St-Paul.

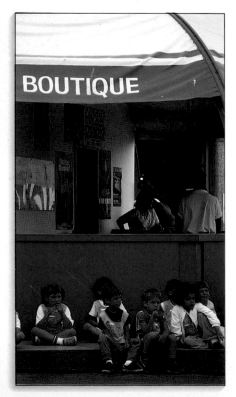

Tomorrow's customers.

However, some buildings remain derelict, awaiting an entrepreneur to restore them to life. Wandering along Rue St-Pierre, Rue St-Nicolas and Rue St-Francois-Xavier, especially at night, can be an eerie but wonderful experience.

Imagine a movie set once the crew has left for the day. Restaurants, antique and craft shops and even the occasional apartment block are sprinkled among the stone skeletons. The more willing the explorer, the more intriguing the explorations.

The area also boasts the **Centaur Theater** at 453 St-François-Xavier. The theater, which is host to Montreal's leading English-language company, occupies a 1903 Beaux-Art structure that was home to the city's stock exchange until 1966. Before the Centaur building, the stock exchange was located in the old *Le Devoir* offices just around the corner. Before *that*, well, Montreal's 19th-century wheelers and dealers carried out their business in a Rue St-Paul coffee shop!

Buildings in Old Montreal change function far more quickly than they change facades. Why shouldn't they? Historic neighborhoods often atrophy because they fail to meet modern needs, but a neighborhood needn't lose its soul to remain vital. Old Montreal has been struggling to retain its shape – or, better, to find a new identity – for over 30 years. Though the struggle is not over, the future is bright. Both the Vieux-Port and Old Montreal have seen massive, and ongoing restoration projects.

Three previously mentioned examples of the overhaul are the opening of the archaeological and history museum in Place Royale, the Montreal History Centre in Place d'Youville, and the restoration of the Marché Bonsecours. The Vieux-Port de Montréal has also been revamped for the city's 350th anniversary. Take time to admire the neoclassical old greystone warehouses along Rue la Commune, overlooking the port. They are a rare example of waterfront planning in North America.

The port stretches over a mile (2 kilometers) along the St Lawrence River and is a hive of activity, virtually year-round. An attractive park runs alongside it, with a pedestrian walkway and a bicycle trail that goes to and even beyond the Lachine Canal, a journey of at least 6 miles (10 kilometers). Anyone with a sudden urge to cycle after arriving at the Old Port can rent bicycles, or even skates, at the Place Jacques Cartier entrance to the port.

Besides a few remaining shipping activities within the port, there is an Imax Cinema where three-dimensional movies are shown on a seven-storey screen, a popular flea market open from early May to early September, SOS Lanyrinthe, a 1.25 mile (2 km) maze of obstacle-filled foggy corridors, a 2-mile (3-km) maze, and the Magic and Illusion Houdini Theater, in which levitation, metamorphosis and extra-sensory perception are highlights of an intriguing one-hour show. And don't forget that during the Just for Laughs Festival, the Jacques-Cartier Pier becomes a non-stop comedy routine.

A range of boat tours leave from the Old Port, including traditional harbor cruises with Croisières AML, glass-topped tours through the locks of the Lachine Canal on Bateau Mouche, exhilarating rafting tours with Les Descentes sur le St-Laurent. The former control tower for barges on the Lachine Canal now operates as a tourist information center for the Old Port from mid-May to mid-September.

Two of the privately funded projects to have helped the revival of Old Montreal since the early 1990s are the World Trade Centre and the Intercontinental Hotel. The revival is ongoing, funded by both the public and private sector. Cobbled streets continue to be restored, as do more and more of the buildings along Rue St-Jacques and Rue McGill. Old Montreal is an integral part of any traveler's visit to the city and growing into a comfortable and dynamic living space for its own citizens.

Pedal powe

Festival City

Montrealers start the summer months with a bang: the International Fireworks Festival features pyrotechnical wizardry with a twist: music! Try to imagine Tchaikovsky's *1812 Overture* to salvos of Roman candles and bombs, this by the inventor of the Roman candle and director of the Festival, Giovanni Panzera. Over the years, Montrealers have been treated to the very best in the field, with competitors from China, Japan, Spain, France, Italy and the US.

Then follows the International Jazz Festival, one of the main events of this type in the world. A small organization only 10 years ago, the Montreal Jazz Festival has become a 10-day extravaganza with over 500 musicians on outdoor stages and indoor concerts playing to throngs and throngs of onlookers. Jazz legends such as Oscar Peterson, a native Montrealer, team up with jazzmen the like of Pat Metheny, Dave Brubeck, Wynton Marsalis and Dizzy Gillespie, plus top players from Africa, South America and the Caribbean.

No sooner has the Jazz Festival come and gone than the Just for Laughs *(Juste pour rire)* comedy festival takes over, bringing together comedians from the US, Britain, France, Belgium and Canada. Comedy is a big ticket in Québécois culture: comedians have so pervaded everyday life that they often star in television commercials. Comedian André-Philippe Gagnon with his one-man rendition of the popular hit *We are the World* even made it into the "inner sanctum" as a guest on American television's *Johnny Carson Show*. Just for Laughs organizer Gilbert Rochon has created a comedy school in Montreal in order to ensure the future success of the genre.

Montreal is also the home of the only circus school in North America, l'Ecole Nationale de Cirque, whose students are featured in the Cirque du Soleil, a one-of-a-kind circus (only one ring and no elephants or tigers) that has won acclaim for its high-flying theatrics in many an international competition. The Cirque du Soleil unfolds like a play, each act building on the other. In one popular act, a clown dons ski boots and, on a trampoline, conducts the *1812 Overture*.

Talent is definitely one of the city's major exports if one considers the MSO, the Montreal Symphony Orchestra, acclaimed as "the best French orchestra in the world today" under the baton of Swiss maestro Charles Dutoit. Montreal has also sent a great many names off the pop chart: Luba, Men Without Hats, The Box, singers Daniel Lavoie, Roch Voisine, Céline Dion and Ginette Reno. Montrealers Maureen Forrester, Louis and Gino Quilico and Joseph Rouleau have also made a name for themselves in the great opera halls of the world.

In dance, Montreal has produced many successes, among them La La La Human Steps, Ballets Eddy Toussaint, Marie Chouinard, Ginette Laurin and Margie Gillis. In theater, a new breed of directors, such as René-Daniel Dubois, René-Richard Cyr and Robert Lepage, have staged collective works in an assortment of unlikely venues, including old firehouses, abandoned warehouses, train stations and disused chapels.

Theatergoers are constantly enthralled by challenging productions, such as a six-hour play, *La Trilogie des Dragons*, that was staged in an abandoned warehouse in the Old Port. A brand-new festival has been added to Montreal's already impressive roster. Théâtre du Monde is a month-long festival from late April through to late May which presents provocative contemporary theatre from around the world.

Montreal has also taken improvisation to new heights: actors from France, Belgium and Switzerland now participate in improvisation "play-offs," a form of theater popularized by the *Ligue nationale d'improvisation*, a takeoff from the National Hockey League, complete with teams, striped shirt referees, and organ background. Teams of actors are given a theme on which to improvise. The audience is responsible for the scoring and the critique. They show their disapproval in no uncertain terms by throwing galoshes on the "ice."

Summer finally winds down in Montreal with the International Film Festival, where bleary-eyed film buffs rush from one showing to the next in an effort to keep pace with 200-plus films. ∎

DOWNTOWN

The St Lawrence River is a confluence of seas and lakes, a brackish bridge between the Atlantic Ocean – Europe's border – and the Great Lakes that are the watery heart of North America. Montreal's downtown is also a meeting place, a concourse of commercial enterprises, businesses, and residential neighborhoods. North America and Europe mingle freely in every district to produce a lively jumble of restaurants, shops, churches, architectural styles and ethnic communities. Together, they create a vibrant picture that reflects the historical diversity of Montreal.

The first settlers built their homes snugly against the St Lawrence River in the area now called "Old Montreal." Though the river was an important source of livelihood, it was also what drove citizens to higher ground. Persistent flooding in the 19th century prompted city-dwellers to move north, where the views from the mountain and the beauty of the surroundings enticed them into permanent settlements.

The downtown has undergone three eras of expansion. The first came during the late 19th century when English and Scottish fur traders accumulated fortunes and the city center shifted west from Place d'Armes to Dominion Square. In this period, waves of immigrants caused an expansion eastward, lengthening the parameters of the inner city. As a result, the area north of Rue Sherbrooke was transformed from farmland into affluent urban neighborhoods. The majority of Montreal's famous churches and illustrious buildings were built in this initial expansion.

Predictably, the subsequent period of growth began after World War II, extending through the building boom of the 1950s, whose architectural aesthetics have not worn well. This rapid development radically altered and in some cases destroyed certain downtown neighborhoods. Under the prolonged leadership of Montreal's mayor Jean Drapeau, the city underwent a third period of expansion during the 1960s and '70s, a period marked by bold and often dazzling architectural experimentation. Many "world-class" projects such as the Métro, Expo '67, and the 1976 Olympic facilities were built during Mayor Drapeau's mayoral reign.

The Underground: Montreal's urban development, however, has produced not only a vibrant surface life, but also an intriguing subterranean world. Begun in the 1960s and apparently based on an idea by Leonardo Da Vinci, Montreal's "Underground City" currently includes one railway station, two bus terminals, 10 métro stations, seven major hotels, 1,200 businesses, 1,600 boutiques, 200 restaurants, 40 bank branches, two department stores, some 30 cinemas and theaters, and numerous other outlets.

In a city with dramatic temperature fluctuations, the underground downtown

:ceding ges: Place ; Arts.

t, ;hitectural itrasts.

ht, image he lerground /, home to intless itiques.

Downtown Montreal

320 m / 0.2 miles

Boulevard Saint-Laurent

R. Ontario

R. Evans

ST.-LAURENT

Boulevard de Maisonneuve

Rue Sherbrooke

Québec National Library

Rue Jeanne-Mance

Avenue du Parc

Rue Milton

Avenue du Président-Kennedy

PLACE-DES-ARTS

McCord Museum of Canadian History

McGill College

Les Terrasses

Avenue McGill College

MCGILL

Rue Mansfield

McGill University

PARC RUTHERFORD

Avenue Docteur Penfield

Rue Peel

Rue Stanley

Rue de la Montagne

Avenue du Musée

Montréal Museum of Fine Arts

Concordia University

Boulevard de Maisonneuve

Rue Simpson

Avenue Docteur Penfield

Côte des Neiges

Rue Sherbrooke

Collège de Montréal

Rue Saint-Marc

Rue du Fort

Canadian Center for Architecture

Marguerite d'Youville Museum

Rue Saint-Mathieu

Rue Guy

GUY-CONCORDIA

Rue Bishop

Rue Sainte-Catherine

Av. Overdale

Boulevard René-Lévesque

Autoroute Ville-Marie

LUCIEN-L'ALLIER

GEORGES-VANIER

Rue St.-Martin

Av. Lionel-Groulx

R. Chatham

Versailles

Place Victor Hugo

Rue Guy

Rue St.-Jacques

Rue Notre-Dame

Rue Peel

Rue de la Montagne

Rue Saint-Antoine

Windsor Station

BONAVENTURE

La Laurentine Building

Canadian Imperial Bank of Commerce Building

Square Dorchester

Place du Canada

Mary Queen of the World Cathedral

Central Station

Sun Life Building

Tourist Info

Place Mount-Royal

Rue Sainte-Catherine

Rue Cathcart

Avenue Union

Post Office House

Christ Church Cathedral

Place Ville-Marie

Rue University

Rue Belmont

Rue Mansfield

Côte du Beaver-Hall

Saint Patrick's Basilica

Rue de la Gauchetière

SQ VICTORIA

Rue Saint-Antoine

Rue St.-Jacques

Rue McGill

Rue St.-Paul

Rue St.-Jacques

Rue St.-Pierre

Rue St.-François-Xavier

Rue Saint-Urbain

Rue de la Gauchetière

Convention Center

PL. D'ARMES

CHINATOWN

OLD MONTREAL

Boulevard Saint-Laurent

Rue Notre-Dame

Rue St.-Paul

Rue Saint-Urbain

Spectrum de Montréal

Complexe Desjardins

Complexe Guy-Favreau

Boulevard René-Lévesque

Rue Jeanne-Mance

Place des Arts

Rue Saint-Alexandre

Rue de Bleury

Rue Côte

Rue Université

offers a warm (or cool) and waterproof environment. Glittering with chrome and smooth marble, it resembles a labyrinthine but opulent ant colony. Shops, businesses and services are linked by Montreal's impressive and efficient transit system, the Métro – a network of 65 stations individually designed by prominent artists and architects. Entrances to Montreal's remarkable substratum are found throughout the downtown area, and in all subway stations.

The downtown core is large, bordered roughly by Avenue Atwater, Rue St-Denis, Rue St-Antoine, and Rue Sherbrooke (*see map*). Dividing it into five main areas makes for a relatively easy tour. These areas are: Rue Sherbrooke and Golden Square Mile; Dominion Square (now known as square Dorchester); Rue Ste-Catherine; Chinatown; and St-Laurent and the Main. Even in fine weather, you'll probably want to make use of Montreal's excellent *Métro* to access these areas. We'll begin our tour at the northern edge of downtown – that is, at the foot of Mont Royal along Rue Sherbrooke.

Expansive era: The **Golden Square Mile** was the name bestowed upon the neighborhood enclosed by Boulevard René Lévesque, Rue Guy, Rue Université and Avenue des Pins. In 1900, the 25,000 residents of this square mile controlled a staggering 70 percent of the wealth of Canada.

The buildings that remain from that period recall a grand and expansive era in Montreal's history. The most obvious symbol of this golden age is the **Ritz-Carlton Hotel**, on Sherbrooke and Rues Drummond (*see page 156*).

Imagine Rue Sherbrooke nearly 100 years ago when the Ritz-Carlton towered over the three-storey mansions and stately elm trees that lined the boulevard. Today Rue Sherbrooke is lined with many modern hotels, including the Westin Mont-Royal (formerly known as the Four Seasons), office towers, art galleries in converted turn-of-the-century houses, and exclusive shops such as the famous **Cartier** and Canada's own **Holt-Renfrew**.

Perching gargoyles: There are also a few elegant apartment houses, including the imposing granite edifice just across the street from the hotel. The **Château Apartments** were built in 1925 for Senator Pamphile du Tremblay, a former owner of the influential *La Presse* newspaper. The building is intended to resemble a castle on the Loire River in France, and it has some amusing details. The gargoyles perching on window ledges hold onto coats of arms, and side turrets and crosses carved from stone adorn the corners of the building. It also has a lovely interior courtyard.

This château-style design, with its decorative turrets, facades and porticos, can also be seen in many public and private buildings throughout Quebec. It represents the dominant architectural trend in the province during the first half of the 20th century.

Next door to the Château Apartments is the **Erskine and American United**

Church. Built in 1863, the church and its neighbor share a moody, almost medieval ambience. The severity of the rusticated stone exterior contrasts the warm tones and circular floor plan of the church's interior. The exquisite stained-glass windows are from the Tiffany Studio in New York.

Next to the church on the north side of Rue Sherbrooke is the **Museum of Fine Arts**. Founded in 1860, this is Canada's oldest museum. This edifice, known as the Benaiah Gibb Pavilion, has a classical design and is faced in Vermont marble – a theme carried through to the lobby, which is dominated by an elegant marble staircase. The building was originally quite small and, although an extension was completed in 1977, it was unfortunately not well matched to the original and suffered from a lack of natural light.

Happily the matter was rectified in 1991 when the museum was expanded to the Jean-Noël-Desmarais Pavilion, just opposite on the south side of Rue Sherbrooke. This new building is a stunning vision of white Vermont marble, designed by Moshe Safdie, and it is connected to the original building by an underground tunnel.

The museum's permanent collection consists of a wide range of paintings, sculptures and drawings from North America and Europe. There is a good sampling of European art from the 17th century onwards, including works by El Greco, Rodin, Dalí and Picasso.

Canadian Art is represented by Inuit woodcarvings, soapstone sculpture and paintings by the Group of Seven – a seminal group of Ontario landscape painters – and contemporary artists like Paul-Emile Boranas, Jean-Paul Riopelle and Betty Goodwin. The museum also houses a fine collection of decorative arts from around the world.

On the north side of the road, to the west of the museum, is the **Church of Saint Andrew and Saint Paul**. This is one of the many examples of Gothic revival architecture in Montreal, and it

Tiffany window in the Erskine and American Church.

154

is best known for its stunning stained-glass windows. Two windows, located in the rear (left) and donated by the Allan family, are believed to have been done by Sir Edward Burne-Jones, the famous Pre-Raphaelite painter.

The Golden Square Mile: Adjacent to the Museum of Fine Arts is **Avenue du Musée**, probably one of the best preserved streets in the area. It has little traffic, and modern construction has made only a modest impact. The pleasures of residential architecture are subtle enough, and a stroll through this neighborhood can transport you back to a different, slower-paced age.

The status and wealth of these homes sets the imagination to wondering what life must have been like during the area's zenith in the first decades of the 20th century. One exhibit of paintings at the Museum of Fine Arts, borne out of a similar curiosity, discovered works by Cézanne, Toulouse-Lautrec, Degas and Gaugin among the private collections of Montreal's former elite. Men who had expanded their wealth as rapidly and haphazardly as had Canada itself – through railways, shipbuilding and natural resources – built extravagant homes for their families and furnished them expensively. At that time, it is said, 70 percent of Canada's wealth was controlled by about 100 people living in this square mile.

Remember that in those days the neighborhood would have been appropriately removed from the hustle and bustle of the downtown. With the slope of Mont Royal affording stunning vistas and trees providing the requisite privacy, and with the Ritz-Carlton only minutes away on Rue Sherbrooke and Ogilvy's Department Store three blocks further south on Rue Ste-Catherine, life would have been both tranquil and convenient for the residents.

The southern face of the mountain or the forests tucked into its plateau would have been ideal for a summer promenade. Hospitals and social clubs were close by, and excellent schools – such as

Dali's Lobster at the Museum of Fine Arts.

The Grande Dame of Sherbrooke Street

Every major city deserves a Ritz-Carlton Hotel, but few are lucky enough to have one. Montreal, however, is one of those "lucky" cities. Since its construction in 1911, Montreal's Ritz-Carlton has been a measuring stick for elegance and civility. The hotel is a symbol of old-world gentility in pleasant contrast to the sterile, hermetically-sealed towers that pass for gracious accommodations today. The fact that the Ritz-Carlton Hotel hasn't changed much in its 80-year history is precisely why it is such a special place.

In the early 1900s, Charles Ritz was thought to be the owner of the best hotel in all of Europe. The Ritz in Paris, in fact, rivaled the equally splendid Carlton of London. It was Charles Hosmer, president of the Canadian Pacific Telegram, who thought Montreal could be well served by bringing together the rich traditions of these two great hotels.

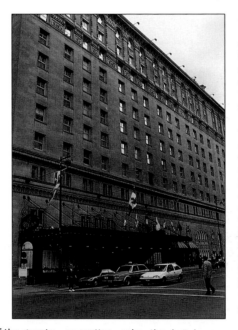

Charles Ritz was finally convinced, but not without making stipulations unheard of at the time. He demanded that every room in the hotel have a private adjoining bathroom and a telephone. He also insisted that every floor be equipped with its own kitchen and that the concierge be available at all hours to fulfill the needs of the guests – no matter how ludicrous. As if that wasn't enough, he also mandated certain changes in the hotel's interior design and decorations.

His instincts were proved to be sound; the Ritz-Carlton became synonymous with top-quality service and the hotel assumed the status of a North American landmark.

An illustrious and historic moment in the hotel's early history came in 1916 when C.F. Sise, Bell Telephone's Chairman of the Board, made the country's first transcontinental telephone call from the Ritz-Carlton to Vancouver. It was also during those early years that the hotel played host to world-class luminaries such as the Prince of Wales, Queen Mary of Romania, and Hollywood stars Douglas Fairbanks and Mary Pickford.

Though the hotel's bright lights were dimmed during two world wars, its luminary status among the city's English speaking elite picked up again in the 1950s and early 1960s, and today rooms command more than $200 a night.

While out-of-town guests were enjoying the fine service of the Ritz-Carlton, the hotel also established itself as an "unadvertised" private club for Montreal's anglophone business moguls. In the Ritz Bar, the Café de Paris, or the courtyard garden, Le Jardin du Ritz, business and political decisions – big and small – were sealed.

The Ritz-Carlton was so closely associated with Montreal's business community that Canadian novelist Mordecai Richler immortalized the hotel in his novel *Joshua Then and Now*. His characters, attracted to the cozy charm of the Ritz, mourn its passing as a covert club in a humorous send-up: "The incomparable Ritz where once impeccably schooled brokers could conspire over malt whiskies and dishes of smoked almonds to send dubious mining stock soaring…"

A lot has changed since then. A shifting political atmosphere in the 1970s changed the business face of Montreal, and the Café Paris today offers visitors a smoky atmosphere and crowded but animated conversation against a piano backdrop. Nowadays, just about anyone can get into the Café Paris, which, although no longer "private," is nevertheless rather "elite." Any yet, the Ritz still stands strong.

In a way, one can admire the hotel as much for its stubborn self-confidence as for its elegance. The lobby is small, the bar is crowded, and both the number of rooms and functional facilities are modest. The Ritz-Carlton has no gym, no pool, not even the now mandatory disco. If, however, you are of international fame, count on devoted service. You will get two staff members to each guest!

What was good enough for guests 60 years ago, the hotel believes, is, with few modifications, good enough today. Status is not size; excellence is not gurgling fountains in a lobby. These qualities of status and excellence, elegance and charm, are, the Ritz-Carlton suggests, more subtle and elusive than we may care to believe. The hotel seems to be right. The lineup of Rolls-Royces and custom-built Lincolns indicates the message continues to be communicated where it counts. ∎

Trafalgar Girls' School on Docteur Penfield and McGill University on Rue Sherbrooke – absorbed the progeny of the Montreal's affluent.

The business community that centered around Dominion Square and Rue St-Jacques in Old Montreal always had a job for favored sons. And neighbors on the Golden Square Mile were, naturally, the right kind of people – other business tycoons, bankers, various anglo-politicians, possibly foreign dignitaries from the consulates; even the rare wealthy French Montrealer who had been lured into the area by a beautiful home. Elegant living, propriety, and social networks: along these steep narrow lanes life was, for a while, perfect. This was where all the newly gentrified Canadians wanted to live.

Dorchester Square: A gradual shift of commercial enterprises from Old Montreal to areas further north allowed Dorchester (formerly Dominion) Square to assume a predominant position in the downtown plan by the late-19th century: the presence of corporate headquarters, a large hotel and a center of transportation helped secure its place. Though today many large office towers line Boulevard René-Lévesque, and the southern portion of the square was renamed Place du Canada, Dorchester Square retains a symbolic importance.

It is one of the few green spaces left in a forest of brick and concrete and is always quite busy, especially during the summer. Office workers take their lunches under the tall elms while commuters stream across the square to Windsor Station. The stateliness of an older Dorchester Square remains, redefined by the number of glass and concrete skyscrapers that vie for attention.

The square, once a Catholic cemetery, was officially made a public park in 1869. For years it was the site of Montreal's immense "ice palaces" and the center of the city's elaborate winter carnivals. Today there are a number of statues on the green, including those of the Scottish poet Robert Burns, Sir

One minute to catch the train at Windsor Station.

Wilfred Laurier, Prime Minister of Canada between 1896–1911, and a particularly well-executed monument commemorating the soldiers who fell in the Boer War. There is also a fountain that was dedicated at the time of Queen Victoria's diamond jubilee.

The highlight of the square is the justly famous **Sun Life Building**. Begun in 1914, its present form did not fully emerge until the completion of the two wings in the late 1920s. Variously described as an immense temple or wedding cake, the building was once Canada's largest, and it helped firmly establish the former Dominion Square as Montreal's new downtown center.

The **Windsor Hotel** deserves some attention, albeit brief. Once among Montreal's finest hostelries, the Windsor spanned an entire city block and had a sumptuously decorated interior. A series of fires resulted in the hotel's demolition, and today only a late addition to the original remains. Designed in a 19th-century Parisian style, the Windsor

Building now houses offices. On the site of the old hotel is the **Bank of Commerce**, a tall 1962 glass tower with an extraordinary narrow base.

On the southeast side of the square stands **Mary Queen of the World Cathedral**. Its dome, once considered imposing, is now adrift in a sea of skyscrapers. If the cathedral's exterior looks familiar, that's because it was modeled after St Peter's in Rome – note the similar line of statues on the portico and the Greek columns. Mary Queen of the World Cathedral is only a quarter of the size of its Roman model and lacks, perhaps, a significant measure of grandeur. There was strong opposition to the plan to replicate St Peter's, particularly by the church's primary architect, Victor Bourgeau, the man also responsible for the interior of Notre-Dame Basilica. Bourgeau lost the argument and the aesthetic judgement of the church is still just a matter of opinion.

The cathedral, which took 20 years to build, was completed in 1884 and quickly became the center of worship for downtown Catholic residents. Its interior is bright and airy. The altar canopy, a reproduction of Bernini's *Baldacchino* in Rome, is probably the most notable aspect in an otherwise uninspired design.

At the far end of the square, at the corner of Rues Peel and de la Gauchetière, is the architecturally uninspiring **Marriott Château Champlain Hotel**. A rather lifeless concrete tower, it was described by one travel writer as an "immense cheese grater."

Saved from the wrecking ball by a group of concerned Montreal citizens, **Windsor Station** dominates the southwest corner of Dorchester Square. The site for the station was chosen for its elevation, away from the St Lawrence's menacing spring floods. From a distance, the station looks like a fortress fitted out with arched windows and rusticated stone.

Designed by New York architect Bruce Price, the building is a celebra-

Bath-time f[...] Brother André, founder of S[...] Joseph's Oratory.

tion of strength and solidity. Its quasi-Gothic style and castle-like design are reminiscent of other structures built for the Canadian Pacific Railway by Price. A number of wings were added as the railway company grew, with the final wing completed in the 1950s.

Windsor Station's imposing exterior is not, however, matched by its interior. Recent renovations have left the waiting area cold and uninteresting.

Next is **St George's Anglican Church**, which was built to accommodate Montreal's west-end Protestant population. The church was completed in 1870 and is the square's oldest remaining building. It is certainly worth venturing inside simply to admire the carved woodwork that covers the interior. The entire ceiling is also exquisitely carved and has managed to survive the years gracefully.

St George's illustrates the immense wealth of the Anglican community in Montreal, and it merits comparison with the lovely cathedral on Ste-Catherine.

From its steps the view of Dorchester Square is magnificent: the dome of the cathedral is best appreciated from this angle – what, perhaps, the Catholic bishop had in mind!

One can also gain a fuller appreciation of the **Dominion Square Building** located to the north between Rues Metcalfe and Peel. Its distinctive design is actually Florentine. Though the facade has been renovated to match the commercial storefronts on Rue Ste-Catherine, from the steps of St George's, one can still appreciate the gracefully arched upper windows that look out over the green.

If Dominion Square serves as a symbol of 19th-century Montreal, **Place Ville-Marie** represents the city's modern face. The complex, located just east of the square on Boulevard René-Lévesque, looms up behind the Sun Life Building. Place Ville-Marie's cruciform shape – unabashedly symbolic in an overwhelmingly Catholic city – figures in many travel brochure photos. The

Mary Queen of the World Cathedral, with permanent sentinel.

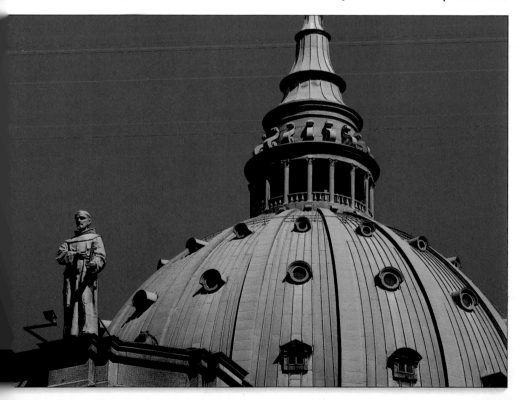

project was one of the first by the now world famous I.M. Pei, who later caused a stir with his glass pyramid addition to the Louvre Museum in Paris.

The feature making Place Ville-Marie particularly distinctive is the vast underground city beneath which, as conceived by city planners in the 1960s, links the complex with other plazas and the subway system. Place Ville-Marie is, in a sense, the prototype for this radical urban development. Ironically, the underground city concept has also come under fire by critics who complain of the dehumanizing effects of too many sunless days!

Place Ville-Marie is a complex of four buildings, dominated by the 45-floor **Banque Royale Tower**. These structures are connected by walkways and open-air plazas that host numerous outdoor cafés during the summer.

Rue Ste-Catherine: At any time of the day or night, it seems the heartbeat of Montreal originates from somewhere along Rue Ste-Catherine. Especially for

Montreal anglophones, Ste-Catherine has been the main shopping district of the city since the latter years of the 19th century. The electric tram that formerly ran along the street enabled the many customers to shop in comfort – from Ogilvy's all the way to the Bay.

Today, commercial businesses have spilled onto the stately graystones and row houses – once private residences – on Rues Crescent, Bishop and de la Montagne. Even a brief walk will reveal noteworthy architecture, elegant shops, massive department stores, and, like it or not, some of the seedier aspects of downtown Montreal.

Until recently, most Montrealers would have argued that Rue Ste-Catherine begins further east with Le Forum, the former home of the beloved Montreal Canadiens. However, the street is relatively quiet until it intersects with Rue de la Montagne.

Located at the corner is **Ogilvy and Sons**, one of the city's best known department stores. The original granite structure still stands on the northeast corner, but the store has moved to the 1910 building on the west side of de la Montagne. A plaque on the newer building states that Ogilvy and Sons was established in 1866, making it one year older than Canadian Confederation.

At the corner of Drummond and Ste-Catherine is the classically styled **Bank of Montreal**, built in 1921. Architecture buffs can walk north on Drummond where they will encounter a number of buildings that, though erected at the beginning of this century, are still in excellent condition.

Another famous department store that once thrived on Ste-Catherine was **Simpsons**, located at Rue Metcalfe. Simpsons was a mainstay of Canadian commerce. It was a classic "family" department store selling everything from shoes to furs to Inuit sculptures, with cafés and restaurants for the weary but unsatiated shopper.

In the early 1990s The Bay bought out Simpsons, a longtime rival, and the

Where woul a modern c be without shopping malls like Montreal Trust?

magnificent Art Deco building is now occupied by a chic fashion store and a movie theatre complex consisting of 14 cinemas and an Imax theater.

Next door is **Place Montreal Trust**, an example of the most recent thinking on urban architecture in the downtown. This shopping complex, an alternative to the labyrinthine underground city model of the 1960s, attempts to maintain a street presence – an active blend of shoppers, pedestrians, onlookers, commuters, even the proverbial "hanging out" crowd – and still allow for the ease of indoor shopping. Place Montreal Trust and other complexes like it represent the city's continuing struggle to temper its harsh climate through experimentation in "living spaces".

The intersection of Avenue McGill College is next. Take a moment to admire the view of **McGill University** as it ascends the steepening slope of Mont Royal. At the foot of Avenue McGill College is the underground entrance to **Place Ville-Marie**. This wide boulevard has recently been revitalized by a number of large building projects. New skyscrapers have helped shift the city's business district in a more easterly direction. Decorated with rows of lights in the winter, Avenue McGill College has an expansive, nearly grand feel. Watch for some amusing outdoor sculpture on the sidewalks and in the plazas.

Philips Square is the closest thing Ste-Catherine's has to a center. From the small green, Canada's two largest department stores are in plain view. The **Eatons** building is a two-block-long structure. Like its once-thriving rival Simpsons, Eatons is an all-purpose department store best known for its grand 9th-floor café, a lovely spot for afternoon tea. **The Bay** is housed in a smaller red sandstone building with a large modern addition attached.

Though a sense of proportion on Philips Square – befitting a classic downtown green – has been diminished by ungainly buildings and tacky billboards, the nearby older edifices and, in particu-

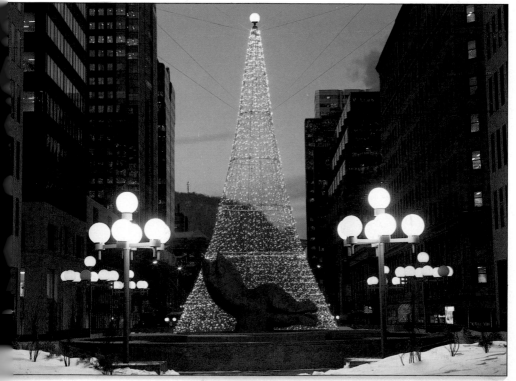

re de ël, Place le-Marie.

lar, **Christ Church Cathedral**, still offer a measure of grace and dignity. The church stands out prominently against the modern structures around it.

Designed by Frank Wills of Salisbury, England, in 1857, Christ Church is considered one of the finest examples of Gothic architecture in Canada. The building is cross-shaped, like many 14th-century English churches, and its exterior design reflects a careful and graceful balance in design. The lovely narrow spire is made of treated aluminium, the original stone having been removed because of its weight. Grace and balance are also evident in the church's interior, primarily of stone except for the ceiling. There are carved heads of saints above the doors and the arcades of the nave are capped by leaves representing indigenous trees.

Maison des Coopérants, the elegant modern glass tower behind Christ Cathedral, ingenuously incorporates the lines of the church's apses and windows in its design. During the day the spire is reflected in its tinted glass; at night Christ Church is a shock of black outlined in the gray tones of the city.

Tucked between the church and Maison des Coopérants is the exclusive French restaurant **Le Parchemin**, a Parisian-style home done in the same speckled granite as Christ Church. One needs a thick wallet, or a slim credit card, to enjoy Le Parchemin's cuisine.

On Philips Square stands a rather large, even grandiloquent statue of **King Edward VII**. The proverbial Edwardian gentlemen is an appropriate spiritual mentor for the area. Sharing the square with The Bay is **Birks**, one of Canada's oldest jewelers, and the Canada Cement Company. Housed in well-preserved structures, they are, like the Anglican Cathedral, reminders of the old English money that built so much of the city.

Continuing east on Ste-Catherine, the shops become less interesting and certainly less grand. You might even notice a few unpleasant *parvenus* – pornographic movie houses and sex shops –

McGill University: beauty behi bars.

that settled in the area during the boom of underground shopping in Montreal and haven't yet been driven away. These blocks are best walked through to reach **Place des Arts**.

A worthwhile stop, though, would be **St James United Church** at the corner of Rue St-Alexandre. Unfortunately the facade of St James was inauspiciously covered over in an attempt to "integrate" it with the commercial face of the rest of the street. The best view of the church, from St-Alexandre, reveals a modest sized Gothic edifice set in a quiet tree-lined green.

The architect, Alexandre Dunlop, decided on a rather unique design for the interior. He chose a horseshoe arrangement, a design known as "Akron" in honor of a city in Ohio where it was first used. The style is also very much like the 18th-century convocation halls at Oxford and Cambridge Universities in England. The curved wood balcony and central chandelier are striking and the general effect is very pleasing.

The final stop point on Ste-Catherine is **Place des Arts**. The complex, famous for the sweeping curves of its design, is actually composed of two buildings that contain a total of three concert halls. The larger of the two, **Salle Wilfrid-Pelletier**, is home to the Montreal Symphony Orchestra. Completed in 1963, Place des Arts is an example of the innovative architectural atmosphere that ruled in Montreal under mayor Jean Drapeau. The hall has a permanent collection of works by modern Canadian artists, including two large tapestries designed by Robert La Palme and Micheline Beauchemin.

There are two more theaters in the smaller pyramid-shaped building, officially opened in 1966. Through an unusual design technique, the floors and ceilings of both theaters are suspended from thousands of springs, enabling the halls to be used simultaneously without fear of sound interference.

Adjacent to Place des Arts is the Museum of Contemporary Art. It has

The Montreal Symphony Orchestra.

had a peripatetic history, with three homes since its founding in 1964 before finally moving to this 44,000-sq-ft (4,088-sq-meter) space above the Place des Arts parking garage. Post-1940 works of art from both Quebec and elsewhere are attractively displayed throughout the museum's eight rooms.

Directly across the street stands **Place Desjardins**. Grouped around a central atrium, the complex contains three office towers, a hotel, along with the ubiquitous floors of shops and restaurants. A three-dimensional wood sculpture by the Québécois artist, Pierre Granche, serves as a centerpiece in a brown concrete interior. The atmosphere is either serene or sterile, depending, perhaps, on your perspective.

Chinatown: Historical Chinatown differs dramatically from the present-day neighborhood. Rue de la Gauchetière, St-Laurent, and the small streets radiating from them were once home to the thousands of Chinese who began emigrating to Canada in the late 1800s. By

law, the first immigrants were men only. Social and economic discrimination forced the community to band tightly together, creating a self-reliant ghetto that tended to attract some less than wholesome enterprises, including brothels and gambling dens.

The proximity of Chinatown to the downtown, combined with the ramshackle condition of many of the residential buildings, made it a prime target for development. In the past 15 years a number of the more interesting older edifices have been demolished. In their place today are large government office buildings, multi-use indoor complexes, and, quite frequently, barren parking lots. Old meets new in Chinatown, but not quite as harmoniously as in other parts of the city.

For the sake of our tour through the downtown, it is easiest to call this neighborhood Chinatown. Historically, however, the area belonged to another immigrant group, the Irish, and even once went by the name of "Little Dublin."

Chinatown.

Interestingly enough, the two churches in "Little Dublin" have very different histories. **Église du Gésu** (Church of Jesus) on Rue Bluery between Ste-Catherine and René-Lévesque was an important site for Montreal's francophone community. For many years a Jesuit university, College Saint-Marie, was located just south of the church.

Its reputation as a center of rigorous intellectual activity, in the Jesuit tradition, was widely known throughout Canada. Many members of the French Canadian elite were educated there during the early part of the century, including poet Emilé Nelligan. The school, eventually taken over by University of Quebec at Montreal, was finally demolished in 1977.

Église du Gésu, modeled after its namesake in Rome, was built in the Italian baroque style. It was designed by an Irish architect, Patrick Keeley, and completed in 1865. The interior was renovated in 1983–84, and the murals and frescoes decorating the walls were repainted and restored. The original parquet floor at the front of the church is striking, as are the imposing oil paintings of saints on either side of the altar, done by the Gagliardi brothers of Rome. The other church, **St Patrick's Basilica**, stands as a monument to the faith and building skills of the Irish community.

Across the street from St Patrick's at 454 de la Gauchetière, is the **Unity Building**, an excellent example of the Chicago School of architecture (typified by the designs of Louis Sullivan) and the only one of its kind in Montreal. Though the building is in a state of disrepair, its uniquely projecting cornice is quite distinguishable, despite layers of dirt.

To begin a tour of Chinatown proper let's begin at the corner of de la Gauchetière and Rue Bluery. Standing on the northwest corner is the lovely **Southam Building**. Constructed in 1912 by the Southam Company – owners of many of Canada's largest newspapers – it was sold in 1960 to a number of small busi-

s in all
hinatowns,
od looms
rge.

nesses. Luckily, this delightful edifice remains intact.

There is a wealth of stone sculpture decorating the brick facade. Above the front entrance stand four women carrying coats of arms, each figure with different features, and a different coat of arms. Two of the women are supported by full-bodied cupids reclining in amusing positions. Myriad naturalistic carvings elsewhere – such as animals and leaf motifs – are certain to delight.

After another block, de la Gauchetiere turns into a bricked pedestrian walkway opening onto a large outdoor plaza between Guy-Favreau and Palais des Congrès. The massive buildings on either side of the plaza act as barriers: in the absence of any large trees or shrubs, the square looks rather barren, even in the summer. At one end stands the **Chinese Catholic Church**, saved from demolition because of its status as a historical monument. Though the original church dates from 1835, it has undergone many reincarnations.

At the other end of the plaza stands the **House of Wing**, believed to be the oldest building in Chinatown. It truly speaks of another era: erected in 1825, its exterior looks its age. House of Wing, once the British and Canadian School, is now a noodle and cookie factory.

De la Gauchetiere from Rue Côté to St-Laurent is adorned with two brightly colored ceremonial gates. Anyone who is familiar with traditional Chinese architecture will recognize the gates (vestiges of pre-Socialist China) as markers announcing the entrance to an important avenue, one that the emperor might travel. In China, the gates were meant to ward off evil spirits; in Montreal's Chinatown, however, they signal the beginning of the pedestrian mall lined with many restaurants and other commercial enterprises.

Try to come to Chinatown on the weekend. On Saturday and Sunday afternoons the streets teem with families. Chinese and non-Chinese alike eat sweets, gaze in display windows and

For ethnic groups like the Chinese, bilingual living comes naturally.

search for those hard-to-find Chinese delicacies in shops and bakeries. The best way to explore this area is with chopsticks. Restaurants are in abundance and they permit the curious epicurean to sample everything from Cantonese *dim sum* to spicy Szechuan beef. You can also snack on fried dough and mooncakes while you go shopping for Chinese herbs or inexpensive cotton clothes. Most restaurants hang their menus in the window and advertise various daily specials.

From the eastern gate of Chinatown on St-Laurent, you are just one block away from the **Monument National**, a building worth examining for its handsome facade. Since it was built in 1894, the Monument National has always functioned as a theater and was once the site of important cultural and political activity. This solid, gray granite edifice now houses the National Theater School. Its students' performances, often of high quality, are presented in the Nouveau Palais de Justice in Old Montreal.

A few blocks up St-Laurent brings the traveler to "The Main," the final leg of the downtown tour. If by this time you are also on *your* last leg, pay attention to the many signs advertising cafés, bars and smoked meat houses.

Microcosm of Montreal: The essence of what makes Montreal unique in North America is to be found on **Boulevard St-Laurent**. The street is a microcosm of the city itself, a neighborhood bursting with ethnicity, old-world charm, and the daily comings and goings of immigrants and their children. More and more, St-Laurent is also becoming the chic place to shop and eat; still, the street remains indomitably without pretense and has an energy all its own.

St-Laurent has always symbolized both division and unity in the downtown. It is still the east/west dividing line of the city's addresses while also being the central street of the St-Louis district. For many years, francophones lived primarily east of St-Laurent, anglophones to the west.

ontreal's
etro is an
ficient way
getting
ound.

Succeeding waves of immigrants changed the nature of that division and expanded the street into a thriving commercial district. The street became known as "The Main" when Russian Jews settled in droves during the 1920s. When much of the Jewish community moved out, Greeks, Hungarians, Portuguese, and, most recently, Latin Americans moved in.

In the winter, the boulevard is decorated with giant, red-striped candy canes. In the summer, however, crowds are its decor, especially during the annual food fairs and ethnic festivals. One reason the street has managed to retain its charm is because many of the older facades have been utilized rather than torn down.

There is a mix of high and low, chic and oh-so-normal that keeps the area both unpretentious and unpredictable. Discount shoe stores stand next door to hip cafés, while Greek bakeries and art galleries share old warehouse space. Come to St-Laurent to walk, browse, and, most importantly, to eat.

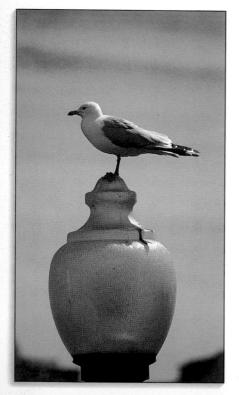

"The Main" is known for its smoked meat delis, and delis are known for lots of honest food at honest prices. Try **Schwartz's Delicatessen** (officially the *Charcuterie Hébraïque de Montréal*) at 3895. Schwartz's was first opened in 1927, and it is said to be the only restaurant that still makes its own smoked meat. Rubin Schwartz brought his curing recipe with him when he emigrated from Romania. **Moishe's Steakhouse** at 3961 opened in 1938 on the site of the restaurant where Moishe himself had been a busboy.

A good place to admire the old buildings of St-Laurent is between 3640 and 3712, once called the **Baxter Block**. The attached buildings have impressively large arched windows and still retain the original central heating system. Also worth checking out is **Cinéma Parallèle** at 3684, which houses a café and arts cinema. At 3950 are the **Shubert Baths**. Built in 1931, the baths were a necessity for the many people without bathrooms in their homes. The swimming pool is still open today.

Finally, one block over from St-Laurent on St-Urbain, is one of the city's most beloved cafés, **Santropol**. Its quirky interior, oversized sandwiches, and lovely summertime outdoor garden has secured it a place in the hearts of many Montrealers.

It is worth remembering that, unlike other neighborhoods in a city, a downtown is likely going to be a haphazard mixture of the residential, the commercial, the old and the new, the interesting and the mundane. Montreal is no exception. While Dorchester Square, the Golden Square Mile and The Main are by far the most vibrant areas, especially historically, along virtually every street, every alley, an inquisitive traveler will find something that surprises, astonishes, pleases.

These sorts of discoveries can be as exciting as learning about famous monuments or exploring churches. Even in a sea of office towers, you never know what treasure may lie in their shadows.

Left, waterfront visitor. Rig[ht] spring com[es] to Christ Church.

BOHEMIAN MONTREAL

A few blocks east of the business district and north of Old Montreal lies a street of Victorian townhouses with a mixture of businesses: cafés, croissanteries, boutiques, bookstores, a couple of theaters and cinemas. There are many streets in Montreal with a similar mix, but none have the easy charm of **Rue St-Denis**. It is the place where Montrealers seem to feel most at home, and casual observation gives the impression that the café crowd has indeed made a second home here.

One is tempted to say that nowhere else in Montreal has so Parisian or European a flavor, but the truth is that nowhere is more essentially Montreal. This is the focal point of many of the festivals that now fill the summer months and the area where, traditionally, Québécois separatists gather whenever nationalist feeling runs high. Recently the provincial government has begun to promote it as a place for visitors as well, but fortunately it has been saved from the dreadful fate of turning touristy. With UQAM (the university) such a dominant presence in the area, and laws in place that restrict changes to the 19th century facades, it seems doubtful that it will be spoiled in the near future.

UQAM (pronounced *Ooh-kwam*) stands for *l'Université de Québec à Montréal*, which occupies the striking building at the corner of Rue Ste-Catherine. The architect, Dimitri Dimakopoulos, incorporated the steeple and south transept of the old Eglise St-Jacques (1859) into his modernist design, to preserve something of the district's Victorian past in a building that otherwise embodies the modern hip atmosphere of the street.

UQAM enrolls about 22,000 students a year, and, as one of the five campuses of Quebec's youngest university (founded 1968), it has never been a conservative influence. English-speaking scholars spill into the area from the McGill annex, which lies a few blocks west. With the constant patronage of academics, the local cafés, theaters, restaurants and bookstores flourish.

From UQAM come the intellectuals and the students, but the artistic crowd also makes Rue St-Denis its turf. One of Canada's three major ballet companies, **Les Grands Ballets Canadiens**, and the Québécois dramatic company **Théâtre du Rideau Vert** (Green Curtain Theater) have their home here. The **Théâtre St-Denis**, just north of Rue Ste-Catherine, belies its ordinary exterior with a seating capacity of 2,500, making it the largest playhouse in the city after Salle Wilfrid-Pelletier at nearby Place des Arts.

For filmmakers there is a permanent facility just off St-Denis at the **Cinémathèque Québécoise** at 335 de Maisonneuve Est. Besides a repertory cinema and a large reference library, the building houses a museum following the history of filmmaking equipment.

Preceding pages: Rue St-Denis market. Left, and Right, shopping on St-Denis.

Heaven knows where all the other people come from, but they all seem equally to belong here, whiling away hours in endless conversation over wine at a sidewalk café; sitting on the front steps of a duplex flat, watching the world go by on a warm summer evening; sifting through *La Presse* over coffee and croissants on a Saturday morning. The natives are obviously extremely comfortable here.

Guidebooks still refer to the Rue St-Denis district – roughly the section that runs from Rue Ste-Catherine to Rue Sherbrooke – as the Latin Quarter, a name borrowed from the *Quartier Latin* in Paris between the Sorbonne and the Seine, a district renowned for its bohemian atmosphere. Both francophone and anglophone Montrealers have adopted this nickname as it evokes the right connotations: Rue St-Denis has a gallic flair, and a youthful, gently bohemian personality that attracts personalities – and anyone who loves café society and *la dolce vita*.

The cafés are, of course, not cafés at all, in a strict sense, as they pour out far greater quantities of beer and wine than coffee. Tables are usually placed close together, decors are attractive but secondary, prices are reasonable. A few offer a complete menu. At the corner of Rue Emery, **Le Faubourg St-Denis**, perhaps the largest bistro on the street, serves full meals in a dining area behind the sidewalk café. Although there are many cafés which provide music, for the most part conversation and people-watching constitute the entertainment along St-Denis.

As pleasant as it is to simply stroll the sidewalks, it's often rewarding to explore further. If the weather is fine, the garden terrace at the rear of the **Café St-Sulpice** can be magical, when furry white flakes of pollen from some hidden source swirl about in drifts so thick that it seems to be snowing. Water splashes into a rock pool from a fountain at the far end of the terrace. Empty in the late afternoon, after the lunch crowd leaves, the vacant chairs await a crowd that will arrive late in the evening and stay until 2 or 3am.

There are those who prefer a down-home ambience rather than the more contemporary sounds and surroundings of many of the Latin Quarter's eateries. **La Binerie Mont Royal**, on Avenue Mont-Royal between rues St-Denis and Drolet, has been a longtime favorite with Montrealers. Run by the same family since 1938, its Québécois fare runs from *fèves au lard* (baked beans and bacon) to *ragout de pattes et de boulottes* (meatball and pig's feet stew). The place is always packed, and it presents plenty of opportunities for rubbing shoulders with people from all parts of the city, and quite literally, all walks of life.

The making of St-Denis: The particular spirit of the St-Denis district is the product of a fate that drove the street from riches to rags and then back towards riches. The street was originally carved out of the estates of two leaders of the 1837 rebellion against British rule, **Wall art.**

Denis-Benjamin Viger and Louis-Joseph Papineau. St-Denis became the main street of a posh residential district named the "Faubourg St-Laurent," one of Montreal's first suburbs when the city overflowed its old defensive walls. Once home to the premier of the province and the elite of the business class, most of the original buildings were destroyed by the Great Fire that devastated Montreal in 1852.

Some of the wealthy moved north and west, but the district remained fashionable until this century. The Victorian elegance of some of the townhouses can be discerned in neoclassical and art nouveau embellishments on some upper storeys (particularly the Mendelson Apartments at Boulevard Maisonneuve.)

In 1897, the **Université Laval** opened a center next to the Eglise St-Jacques, which was then Montreal's cathedral, and so first drew academic life to the area. The **Bibliothèque Nationale du Québec**, which maintains the official archives of the province, was erected in 1915, and it still resides behind its stately Beaux-Arts facade on the west side of St-Denis, now sandwiched between busy cafés. The Laval center gained independence as the **Université de Montréal**, but it abandoned the area in the 1940s for its opulent new campus in Outremont.

Meanwhile, many large residences had been converted into rooming houses, and the clergy had opened homes for the growing numbers of the sick and destitute. Lacking the academy, St-Denis fell victim to the same urban decay that most of east Montreal began suffering as the folks with money settled down in the suburbs.

In the 1960s, city planners made brave attempts to revitalize the area by making it a transportation crossroads. But the construction of the Voyageur bus terminus on Rue Berri only congested the roads. In 1966, the Berri-de-Montigny Métro station opened (now Berri-UQAM) at the corner of Rue Ste-Catherine. It was the main transfer point on the slick new subway system, but for

A beer in
ohemia.

the most part easy access to underground shops left commuters without any special reason to venture up to the streets to patronize local business.

Money, if not respectability, returned to the district during the late 1960s and '70s as St-Denis cafés gained notoriety as the hotbed of separatism and radicalism. Enterprising restaurateurs began to move in and renovate. Among the first was **Le Faubourg St-Denis**.

There was no lack of vitality, as the street would explode with celebrations and demonstrations every year on the Québécois feast day: **Fête Jean-Baptiste** (June 24, now the *Fête Nationale*). The scene looked much the same whenever the Montreal Canadiens hockey club won the Stanley Cup, a pretty regular event in the 1970s. Among the intellectual and artistic community that gathered here, the youth of Montreal defined themselves no longer as "French Canadians" but as "Québécois."

The opening of UQAM in 1979, and a slow but steady effort to push the heart

of downtown east toward St-Laurent, has had a positive effect. Today the area flourishes, with a steady influx of visitors from far and near to add to the local clientele. All summer long, one international arts festival after another keeps the street busy and interesting.

Still, the traces of a less prosperous past are visible in the less savory flavor of some businesses along "la Catherine": strip clubs and off-color bookstores still pepper the busy central artery. The clubs seem to be able to resist the perennial efforts of politicians to get rid of them. Legislators are eager to clear away at least the more lurid street signs but, ironically, the very laws that so carefully guard freedom of expression under Canada's new charter of rights also make it next to impossible to draft legislation that would eradicate the smutty language on storefronts.

Fortunately, the pleasant atmosphere of Rue St-Denis is in sharp contrast to that of some of the neighbors. In fact, the sector north of Rue Sherbrooke to Avenue du Mont-Royal is increasingly becoming a fashionable, upscale shopping area. Antique stores and boutiques sell fine Québécois tapestries and woodcarvings or handicrafts in pewter and pottery, as well as more pricey European imports, such as Tiffany lamps and art deco furniture.

Other boutiques specialize in contemporary and futuristic designs in furnishings. Trendy clothing stores, and some excellent new and rare bookstores (mostly but not exclusively selling books in French) are sprinkled along the whole length of the street.

Rue St-Denis is most alive during the summer festivals, of which there seem to be no end. Among these events, the most important is the **Montreal International Jazz Festival** (*see page 179*), but St-Denis is also a focus for the **Just for Laughs** comedy festival, the **Festival International de Nouvelle Danse**, held every two years, the **World Film Festival** and the **International Mime Festival**. Each of these is among the

Braces for sale.

largest in its medium and draws performers and fans from around the globe.

Tens of thousands mill along the street during the Jazz Festival, held every year in the first two weeks of July. For much of the festival, the street is closed to traffic and becomes a carnival arcade. It seems the whole city comes out to hear the free concerts at temporary stages set up at the intersections, and to watch unofficial street performers juggle, mime and eat fire. With 1,000 musicians from five continents, and up to 50 concerts daily, the festival has helped to make avid jazz enthusiasts out of Montrealers.

Prince Arthur and Duluth: Festivals brighten up a city wonderfully, of course, but on **Rue Prince-Arthur** there is an ongoing celebration of basic human pleasures: people and food. Citizens of Montreal claim to excel at enjoying life together, and they have tried to resist the tendency of other modern cities to bury the human scale under megaliths and speedways. The restaurant district on Prince-Arthur, though a bit more con-

trived than St-Denis, represents a small triumph for the pursuit of simple pleasures in the heart of the big city.

Just north of the bistros of St-Denis, the restaurant mall runs west from **Square St-Louis** to **Boulevard St-Laurent**. In 1981, the city closed these five short blocks to vehicles, paved them with brick, and spruced them up with trees, poster-pillars and a small fountain. It also encouraged new restaurants to forgo a liquor license and allow customers to bring their own bottle of wine with them. The opportunity to dine well for less money held obvious appeal for this city full of epicures, and the street has flourished.

Restaurants offering a wide range of ethnic menus, especially Greek, Vietnamese and Italian, line the mall, interspersed by a few small boutiques. Québécois cuisine is harder to find. Most of the big Greek restaurants that dominate have a similar atmosphere, price and menu, serving kebabs, stuffed grape leaves, grilled chicken, swordfish, and shellfish from the Maritime provinces or the tiny Îles-de-la-Madeleine.

On weekend nights the mall fills up with a meandering crowd of diners, often distracted by jugglers, musicians and sketchers who find here an ideal forum to show off their skills. Diners at second-storey windows get a view of the whole parade of life below. Tables arranged out on the mall itself let customers eat under the sun or the stars, or in the shade of a parasol.

Many restaurants here and elsewhere in Montreal no longer bother to display a sign that says "*Apportez votre vin*" (Bring your own wine). It is nevertheless worthwhile to check with the staff, since most Greek restaurants – and many others – encourage patrons to run into a liquor store or the local *dépanneur* (a corner grocery) and pick up a bottle of something to bring inside.

There the waiter will gladly uncork and serve it as though the wine had been ordered from the menu. (There is a *dépanneur* on the north side of Prince-Arthur, and around the corner on the main street, St-Laurent, there is a well-stocked provincial liquor store.)

Access to the mall from St-Denis is through **Square St-Louis**, a block north of Rue Sherbrooke. This small, pretty park with lots of benches around a broad Victorian fountain provides a treasured spot for locals to while away the summer hours, or in winter to skate on the paths that the city floods over. Well-preserved and sometimes ornate 19th-century townhouses border three sides of the square.

The easy charm of Rues St-Denis and Prince-Arthur give the impression that Montrealers are "at home" in these wandering streets, bohemian retreats and quiet, beguiling cafés.

Originally homes for the more well-to-do of French society, a number of these houses have been bought by Portuguese families in recent years. The small front gardens are undoubtedly more lush and colorful than they were under their original ownership.

Rue St-Denis market.

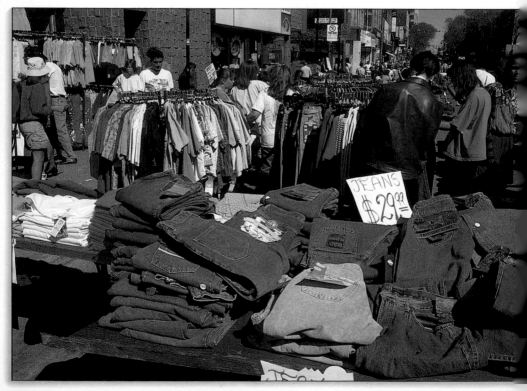

THE JAZZ SCENE

For 10 days in early July, the Montreal International Jazz Festival books 1,000 performers from around the globe into venues all over the city. What makes this festival extraordinary is that these venues include not only pricey clubs and concert halls but also whole streets, blocked off to let thousands hear free concerts at stages erected at major intersections on Rue St-Denis and Rue Ste-Catherine. These nightly block parties lend the city a euphoric jazz atmosphere that makes the festival the highlight of Montreal's summer – and one of the best jazz events anywhere. With an attendance exceeding 1,500,000, the festival now rivals Montreux and Monterey. One concert alone attracts 400,000 fans each year.

In Montreal, the term "jazz" is defined fairly loosely, so that performers like Joan Baez and Van Morrison have made the bill. But most acts belong much more obviously within the jazz orbit.

Ever since the days when Montreal was the only major city on the continent not subject to Prohibition, nightlife has flourished here. But jazz has held an insecure foothold in a town that has generally preferred dance music like swing or rock'n'roll. Still, great jazz was heard in a handful of clubs throughout the 1930s and '40s.

The heart of the jazz scene throbbed away at "the Corner" where St-Antoine crosses de la Montagne, the home of the Café St-Michel and Rockhead's Paradise.

The most renowned performer to emerge from this era is the pianist Oscar Peterson, who began his career at 17 playing swing in the Johnny Holmes Orchestra at Victoria Hall in Westmount. He created his own sound in a trio that performed in the Alberta Lounge opposite Windsor Station, and he later found fame in the US. Trumpet player Maynard Ferguson also started with Johnny Holmes, and he likewise found success in the States after forming his own band.

Sixty years ago, in the days of gang wars and rampant vice, there were hundreds of nightclubs open 24 hours a day. Jazz prospered with a small audience and the passionate devotion of its performers. They sustained the energy of Montreal's jazz until about 1954, when Mayor Jean Drapeau started to clean up the city. The heavy pressure on nightlife and competition from television and rock'n'roll finally smothered the jazz scene. The story has been recounted by critic John Gilmore in a history of jazz in Montreal called *Swinging in Paradise.*

Within the context of the cultural revival that accompanied the "Quiet Revolution" of the 1960s, the Jazz Libre quartet pushed free jazz to its limits. Its style was related to John Coltrane's but even further radicalized by a heavily separatist-socialist ideology. On the other hand, Vic Vogel's Big Band began to play much more mainstream jazz in 1968, and the group remains a popular staple of today's scene. A fusion band named UZEB has been gaining a following in Quebec for the last decade, and in France its record sales rival Miles Davis.

The jazz audience in Montreal has been expanding ever since Alain Simard, then aged 29, presented the first jazz festival in 1979. The vibrancy of the festival does not represent the state of things during the other 11 months of the year, but unmistakably there is new life in today's jazz picture. Charlie Biddle, who came from Philadelphia in 1949, plays bass with some of the best talent around at his own two establishments Biddle's Bar and Ribs (2060 Aylmer) and 318 Ontario Est in the Latin Quarter. Visitors to Old Montreal can enjoy jazz acts at L'Air du Temps. More recent additions to the jazz scene include Café Thélème and Café Sarejevo, in the lower Plateau, and Upstairs, a student hangout near Concordia.

There are other signs of new enthusiasm, including a local jazz label called Justin Time Records and a degree program in jazz studies at McGill University. Even the son of the Provincial premier, François Bourassa, heads a prize-winning trio.

Finally, Les Ballets Jazz de Montréal adds another dimension altogether to the portrait of jazz in the city. To music ranging from Gershwin to Pat Metheny, sometimes exploring social themes such as gender relations and nuclear holocaust, it has presented exuberant and accessible ballets to audiences worldwide, and it ranks among the three major ballet companies in Canada. ∎

Westmount and Outremont

A Montrealer would probably scoff at the idea that Outremont and Westmount share any physical or, worse, historical affinities. They might point out that Westmount is where well-to-do anglophones (English Canadians) have always lived as the majority voice in the community. Outremont, on the other hand, has been home to French Canadians (francophones). These neighborhoods, in many ways, are considered to be the "two solitudes" of Canada.

On the surface, it appears that Westmount and Outremont are worlds apart. And yet, a look into the origins of these cities within the city reveals common ground. Both communities were born out of the impulse to escape from the more crowded and sometimes dirty conditions of 19th-century city living. Both began as farming communities that developed at a slow pace around the sloping inclines of the mountain. Leaders of each community defended their power to control construction, landscaping, architectural styles, and zoning. Most of all, they sought to preserve the privileged relationship each had with the mountain and the unique landscape they lived in.

Westmount is built on both the western slope of Mont Royal, known as the *petit montagne*. Though the area is surrounded on all sides by the city of Montreal, it is a significant parcel of land, covering nearly 1,000 acres (405 hectares). **Outremont**, on the other side of Mont Royal, is the incorporated city to the north. Though smaller in area, to the eye it shares much in common with Westmount: gracious residences, leafy parks and lively commercial districts.

In the 1670s, the Sulpician Order established an outpost on what is now Rue Sherbrooke Est, today considered the dividing line between the city of Montreal and Westmount. Two circular defense towers stand on the north side of the street in front of the Grand Seminaire as reminders of this early settlement. Eventually, the order began to cede lands on the *petit montagne* to farmers. Old Indian trails and horse tracks connected these farmers to the city but, by any standard, they were isolated, and it wasn't until the mid-1800s that the community on the *petit montagne* grew in size.

As transportation gradually became more efficient, Scottish and English fur traders, much taken with the splendid views, clean air, and lower rates of taxation, began to settle in the area. In 1869 the first English school was established in what was then called the village of Côte St-Antoine.

As more people settled in and around the village, a movement developed to preserve the residential, non-industrial character of the community. In 1890, the Côte St-Antoine Improvement Committee was formed and, composed of mainly anglophone residents, created a city plan for municipal buildings and

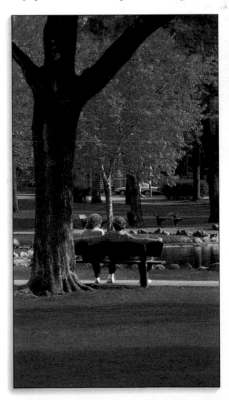

parks. The committee was successful at regulating commercial development, and for many years it banned the "gathering of families under one roof" in apartment houses.

Its enthusiasm was fueled by a desire for a peaceful residential community and a deep distrust of the Montreal city government. In a vote that was very nearly defeated, the city council changed the name of the village to Westmount in 1895, and the city of Westmount received its charter in 1908. As the population became more homogeneous, a distinct enclave of middle-class anglophone Montrealers was established.

Westmount residents appear to have been strict teetotalers at the turn of the century and avid sportsmen. In fact, they seem to have been absolutely wild about sport. Westmount established a golf course, a Toboggan and Snow Shoe Club, a Cricket Club in North America was established in Westmount in 1913 and the town hosted the 1894 Canadian Speed Skating Championships.

Significantly, it was the site of what is thought to be the first lacrosse match ever played under lights and, as every Canadian nationalist knows, lacrosse, not hockey, is Canada's national sport. Today, the city is renowned for its parks; a reflection, no doubt, of this long tradition of outdoor pursuits.

It was also the Sulpician Order that was the original owner of much of the land which is today the city of Outremont. The Order began to yield large portions of its land in the early 1700s, but population growth was very slow owing to its distance from Montreal, the crowded fortress by the St Lawrence River. For many years the farms of the Outremont produced "Montreal melons" and prospered by selling them to hotels in New York.

In the mid-1800s the two largest landowners, besides the St Viateur religious order, were two farming families by the name of Bouthillier and Beaubien. The Beaubien family's power, quickly translated into political influence when a son went on to become an important mayor of Outremont.

Outremont's population quadrupled between 1900 and 1911. While the first settlers were primarily Scottish and English, newcomers included French Canadians attracted to the less expensive homes as well as the proximity of Catholic churches. Jews also moved in and set up shops along Rue Van Horne.

Like Westmount citizens, Outremont residents, fueled by the fears of overdevelopment, formed a "beautification committee." They were successful in obtaining more park land and regulating the size of apartment buildings. In its greatest coup, the committee persuaded the utility companies in 1914 to bury their telephone and electrical wires underground, thus eliminating unsightly poles and wires on the streets.

Today, Westmount and Outremont are still fairly homogeneous compared with the rest of the city. About 19 percent of Outremont's population is anglophone, while the percentage of

Traditional Westmount staircase.

francophones in Westmount is roughly the same. For inner city neighborhoods, they both are exceptionally lovely, full of green spaces, elegant architecture and plenty of personality. Their cultural identities have not been compromised and, for the residents of each, a wonderful balance has been struck between urban living and an appreciation of nature's beauty.

The Municipal Center: Cutting a large swathe from north to south, **Westmount** comprises two districts. The central portion shares more in common with the atmosphere of Montreal's downtown, while upper Westmount hangs precipitously, hugging the sides of the *petit montagne*. In a recent survey by the city designed to track historical buildings, it was revealed that a remarkable number of 19th-century structures have survived in Westmount. Little demolition has taken place except at the southerly edge of the city around the Boulevard de Maisonneuve.

The municipal center of Westmount is loosely arranged on the English "green" model. The City Hall sits on a triangular site at the apex of two streets: Chemin de la Côté St-Antoine and Rue Sherbrooke. Across the street is the beautifully landscaped **Westmount Park**, the municipal Library, Conservatory and Meeting Hall.

Westmount City Hall, located at 4333 Côté St-Antoine, is an imposing Tudor-style structure surrounded by colorful beds of flowers. One of its architects, Robert Findley, was also responsible for the design of Westmount's other municipal buildings.

Nearby is the **Library**, which opened in 1899 and was Canada's first free library. It is distinguished by an unusual Romanesque style, leaded-glass windows and delightful bas-reliefs which glorify "knowledge." The attached **Conservatory**, built in the 19th century, still functions, and it beautifies Westmount's parks and streets with its winter-grown plants. **Victoria Jubilee Hall**, although echoing the design of the

city hall, is intended to resemble English medieval buildings and is used for a variety of public functions.

Going up the mountain: West of the municipal area is the oldest building in Westmount, located at 563 Côte St-Antoine. Because this street cuts across the lower half of the mountain, it made early construction on the steeper inclines extremely difficult.

Maison Hurtubise was built in 1688 by Pierre Hurtubise on land granted to his father by Maisonneuve. The house, the last remaining farmhouse from the 17th century in Westmount, reflects the style typical of residential architecture of the time, recognizable by its steeply gabled roof, fieldstone walls, small panes of glass and dormer windows. Because the house was built so far from Montreal (Ville-Marie), early inhabitants named it *la haute folie*.

The Boulevard is a particularly lovely street, lined with imposing homes of every shape and size. These homes mirror not only the eclectic tastes of their

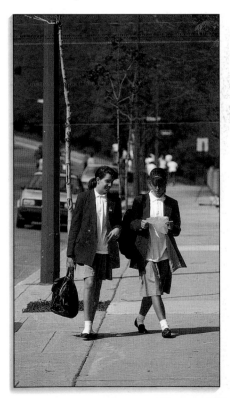

ming home
m Penfield
enue
hool.

PARC DU MONT-ROYAL

Yes ou can see it from just about anywhere in Montreal: buying a newspaper at the local stand, gazing idly out from a kitchen window, taking the dog for its nightly walk. Mont Réal – or, as Montrealers call it, *la montagne* (the mountain) – looms up in the middle of the city like a natural obelisk emphatically proclaiming Montreal's presence. The mountain lends a poise and dignity to Montreal by drawing the city, like a billowing skirt, close to its stalwart legs.

For Montrealers, the mountain embodies a kind of grandeur, a place where nature's sublime and wild moods play freely across a landscape untouched by the heavy hand of urban development. Mont Royal is more than a park. It is like an unmistakable family trait – the mountain is a cherished feature of a rich and vibrant history.

It was here in 1535 that explorer Jacques Cartier was led by Indians through wooded hills and up rocky crests to the summit. It was to here that the 17th-century *habitant*, one mile away, turned his gaze each morning as he walked through the dawn toward his fields. And it is here, today, that all of Montreal's ethnic groups can be found sunning, sledding, strolling, folk-dancing and picnicking.

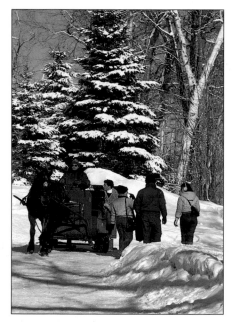

That Mont Royal is not covered by a network of roads, walks, cafés, electric cable cars and vast amphitheaters is largely owing to the aesthetic sensibilities of Frederick Law Olmstead, the man hired by the City of Montreal in 1874 to design the park. Olmstead, who also designed Manhattan's charming Riverside Drive and the elegant Morningside and Central parks, firmly believed that nature was a source of spiritual sustenance and that parks, if properly designed, could provide urban dwellers with relief from the oppressive routines of metropolitan life.

Olmstead urged Montreal to preserve its gracious mountain and warned voracious developers that in dealing with Mont Royal "as if it had the impregnable majesty of an alpine monarch, you only make it ridiculous." So far, he has been heeded, although the developers still harbor hopes.

Most of Mont Royal's pleasures can be taken advantage of in any season: a stroll through its 500 acres (200 hectares) along winding trails, a walk to the summit for a look at the 100-ft (30-meter) cross. The cross is now electrified, but the original was raised in 1643 by Paul Chomedy de Maisonneuve when the fledging colony of Ville-Marie was saved from a flood. You can also take a jaunt to one of the park's two lookouts (at the chalet or along Camillien Houde Parkway) for a spectacular view of central Montreal, the St Lawrence River and the Montérégian mountains.

Near the chalet are monuments to the explorer Jacques Cartier and to King George VI, as well as carvings entitled *La Sentinelle* and *Les Sans-Abris* (to the homeless). Visit the *Musée de la Chasse et de la Nature* for exhibits on local fauna and flora. In warmer months horse-drawn carriages *(calèches)* are a relaxing way to traverse the park, and free nature walks *(randonnées)* are conducted in French and English. In winter, skaters take to Beaver Lake (an artificially made pond) and cross-country skiers travel along tranquil tracks. Tobogganing attracts shoals of enthusiastic children.

Like Highgate and Brompton, the grand cemeteries of London, the Mont Royal cemeteries contain ornate mausoleums, sinuous trails and almost suffocatingly lush vegetation. Covering half the mountain, these resting places are eloquent, in a rambling sort of way, on the subject of French-Canadian genealogy.

Beneath the soils of Mont Royal Cemetery, which is Protestant, are the remains of some remarkable Montrealers: Sir John C. Abbot, prime minister of Canada; Sir Allan Hugh, a shipping magnate and political wheeler-dealer; Anna Leonowens, governess to the king of Siam; and Sir George Simpson, fur-trade financier.

Next door in the Catholic cemetery of Notre-Dame-des-Neiges are more illustrious and interesting Canadians: Calixta Lavallée, the composer of the national anthem *O Canada*; Wolfred Nelson, a leader in the 1837 rebellion; Sir Georges-Etienne Cartier and D'Arcy McGee, the fathers of the Canadian Confederation; and Pierre Laporte, the minister who was tragically murdered by terrorists in the 1970 FLQ crisis. ∎

original owners, but also more recent technical advancements in construction. Wreathing the top of the mountain are **Sunnyside Avenue** and **Summit Circle**. No. 14 Sunnyside Avenue, built in 1911 for Charles A. Smart, a member of the Quebec Parliament, is thought to be one of the most impressive residences in all of Westmount.

On Summit Circle is the **Westmount Lookout**, a small park and viewing area. It affords a breathtaking panorama to the west and the flat plain and volcanic hiccups of the area's mountains. The houses around the lookout seem precariously sturdy at best; the dramatic views from their living rooms would never appeal to anyone afraid of heights.

Above is the wooded peak of the *petit montagne*. In 1928 McGill University sold the land, once site of a botany lab, to Westmount, stipulating that it could never be developed. It is now a sanctuary for hundreds of species of birds.

Avenue Greene and Lower Westmount: Commercial enterprises in Westmount are clustered along **Avenue Greene** as well as **Rue Sherbrooke**. Here there is a mixture of convenience stores, banks and restaurants, all catering to the needs of the community. There are a few upscale antique and clothing shops, but Westmount residents seem to prefer to spend "big money" downtown. Avenue Greene was refurbished with brick sidewalks and flower pots in the early 1970s and retains an unpretentious charm. **The Double Hook** bookshop, located at 1235a Greene Avenue, was the first shop in Canada to sell exclusively "Canadian" books.

Sometimes referred to as Lower Westmount, the streets below Sherbrooke are full of interesting rowhouses. While obviously less grand than the residences on the mountain, these display everything from the fortress style to mansard roofs, with numerous examples of stone and wood designs.

Of particular note are the **Towers** at 4130–40 Dorchester (Westmount's first terrace), and those at 47–41 Holton (which show the classic Montreal pattern of alternating units).

Toward Montreal downtown via Rue Sherbrooke is **The Mother House of the Sisters of Notre-Dame**. Now the campus of **Dawson College**, Quebec's largest *anglophone cejep* (junior college), it is impossible to miss. An awe-inspiring edifice designed by J. Omer Marchand in 1904, its distinctiveness is derived, in part, from the well-judged use of pale-colored stone and a flamboyant Beaux-Arts style. At one time the building was used simultaneously as a hospital, retirement home, school and headquarters for the religious order.

Outremont: Outremont's boundaries are roughly defined by the commercial Avenues Van Horne and Laurier and the residential Chemin de la Côte Ste-Catherine and Rue Hutchinson. These boundaries are not strict, however, and the neighborhoods which stretch beyond them are deemed, at least in the classifieds, to be "adjacent" or "outer" Outremont. Today, being on the edges

of this chic section of Montreal is good enough to secure a higher rent from prospective tenants or better sale of a home. An address in Outremont tells people a lot about you: it means that you are most likely a francophone, most likely a dyed-in-the-wool urbanite, and wealthy enough to be able to afford this great in-town location.

It wasn't always this way. Before the gentrification that took place in the 1960s and '70s, Outremont's streets, such as Avenues Laurier and Bernard, and especially **Avenue Van Horne**, were common, ordinary car lanes. They were even considered to be on the shabby side. The area around Van Horne was once semi-industrial and is still referred to as "lower" Outremont.

Older residents remark that Avenue Van Horne, the district's northern boundary, still has the original character of the neighborhood. There you will find a modest array of shops and restaurants, row houses built more closely together, fewer parks and smaller yards.

Waiting for the mailma

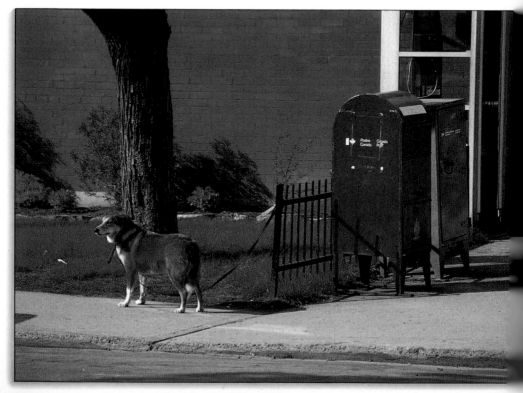

Outremont's attractions: With a good pair of walking shoes, you can journey into the francophone version of "the elite." The following sights represent merely a taste of Outremont and will lead you into some of its more interesting neighborhoods.

Outremont's municipal center is rather understated. The **City Hall** and **Public Library** are located off Côté Ste-Catherine. Ironically, the city hall is housed in a stately private residence thought to have once been a trading post of the British-owned Hudson's Bay Company. It is one of the oldest buildings in Outremont, constructed around 1800. The library is also located in an old private home behind city hall, but it is a rather inadequate facility for such an established community.

The finest architecture in Outremont is found in its public buildings: schools, cinemas and churches. One of the most striking buildings is **Académie Querbes** at 215 Rue Bloomfield. Designed by J.A. Godin in the Beaux-Arts style and completed in 1915, the building lends a distinctly European atmosphere to the otherwise typical North American residential architecture which surrounds it. Today, it houses a primary school.

Residents had to fight hard to save the **Outremont Cinema** on Rue Bernard. Plans to convert it into a multi-use complex were blocked by a public awareness campaign and petition drive. The bas-reliefs on the outside of the building are remarkable, despite the considerable damage they've suffered because of harsh weather. The interior is abundantly grand, reminiscent of Montreal's old theaters including the Strand, Loews and the Capitol.

At the corner of Avenues Laurier and Bloomfield is the imposing **Eglise Saint-Viateur**, which was completed in 1913. Its Gothic-Revival style is strongly represented in the church's facade which towers above the modest apartment buildings surrounding it. Interestingly, the sides of the church aren't as well constructed as the front – a frequent

afy
tremont.

feature of buildings where the architect concentrated on the facade.

At Côte-Ste-Catherine and Avenue D'Indy are two other interesting public buildings. **Eglise Saint-Germain**, which stands at the intersection of these two roads, was built in 1931 and has a magnificently large bell tower as its centerpiece. The other building, facing out on Côté Ste-Catherine, was once the Pensionnat du Saint-Nom-de-Marie. Designed in 1903, its most striking feature is the classically designed portico, which incorporates a remarkable number of other architectural styles.

The residential areas of Outremont are generally organized around a number of parks. The houses around **Parc Outremont** are beautiful simply because of the fine construction techniques and the regularity of their design. The unique detailing makes them interesting to look at: one can see a variety of stained-glass designs, wood and iron trims, and stone bas-reliefs inserted into the brick facades.

The houses around **Parc Outremont** have the best vantage point with which to view the changing seasons on the mountain. **Parc Joyce** and **Parc Pratt**, which take their names from the farmers who once owned the land, also afford views of the mountain and the campus of the **University of Montreal** and **St Joseph's Oratory** which rest on its northern face.

Also on the mountain, on the edge of Outremont, is the Protestant Mount Royal Cemetery. Its sylvan landscape attracts species of birds found nowhere else in Quebec.

In these idyllic settings, many famous French Canadians have lived, and still live. The leader of the Parti Québécois, Lucien Bouchard, lives in Outremont, and former Prime Minister Pierre Trudeau grew up on Rue McCullough. The popular Québécois writer Maurice Tremblay also lived in Outremont.

Finally, there is a lively contrast between the quiet, tree-lined residential streets of Outremont and its commercial areas which hum with activity day and night. Along **Avenues Laurier** and **Bernard** is a wealth of clothes shops, cafés and mouth-watering bakeries.

Many buildings on these two streets have been recycled from parking facilities into multi-use centers or from garages into galleries. Here you can take your cat to a "post-modern" veterinary clinic or buy the latest in light fixtures or kitchen utensils. On Avenue Laurier in particular, one will also find some very fine French-language bookshops.

Westmount and Outremont as two solitudes? Perhaps. But polar opposites? Hardly. Both communities possess an abundant sense of pride and independence, considering themselves unique and indivisible. They *are* desirable places in which to live. They are not, however, the unchanging bastions of the civilized. The age of insular living spaces has passed. Modern Montreal is a diverse, multi-racial city, and Westmount and Outremont increasingly reflect this bounty.

Outremont Cafés

When the word "café" is mentioned, images of smoky brasseries, sun-dappled terraces, or brooding artists bent over manuscripts come to mind. This tableau is enmeshed in the cafés along Avenues Bernard and Laurier in Outremont. For a taste of Europe, step into one of these cultural enclaves, most of which hum day and night. Experience the "café culture" of Outremont and savor a café-au-lait with a delectable pastry.

The cafés on the busy thoroughfares of Avenues Bernard and Laurier range from the refined to the humble. From the exquisitely decorated to the unadorned, each has a distinctive ambience and a devoted clientele. What they all share, besides delicious coffee, is their neighborhood role as meeting places.

Café Romolo, located at Jeanne-Mance and Bernard, is just outside the official limits of Outremont. Its unique character and fine coffee draw a steady crowd, many of whom live in Outremont or, perhaps, simply frequent the Rialto Cinema which is just around the corner.

The Romolo is recognized by its long picture windows and the pool tables that dominate one of the two rooms. At small tables with plain wooden chairs people read newspapers or converse in small groups, their heads ringed in a haze of smoke, the smell of which mingles with the potent fragrance of fresh coffee. Smooth, frothy café-au-lait is served in tall glasses as in Italy and Spain; sugar and cinnamon sit on the tables. The café also serves espresso, alcoholic beverages, and pastries which the owner "imports" from the Greek bakery next door. Café Romolo is open all day, every day. Students, artists, and a host of "nine to fivers" come in for a quick coffee, a game of pool, or just a quiet break in which to read the newspapers or write a letter.

Le Bilboquet, at 1311 Bernard, is renowned for its ice cream, sorbet and frozen yogurt. The café is closed for a portion of the winter, but is kept busy all summer long. Its breezy interior is accentuated by an art-deco green-pink-and-black tiled floor.

Another memorable café – forgive the pun – is the Café Souvenir at 1261 Bernard. Huge maps of

European cities adorn the walls of this cozy little restaurant, with its strong French ambience. It's an especially popular neighborhood café for those who like to drop by for coffee and a simple, but always satisfying, meal. A little further down the street, locals head for Le Café de la République at 1051 Bernard when they feel like sampling something from the delectable array of desserts that are always on offer.

La Croissanterie is located on Rue Hutchinson, one block east of Avenue Laurier. Nestled within a residential area, the café's daytime customers are generally neighborhood regulars. They stop in for a sandwich, homemade pastry or a cappuccino made strong with a frothy mound of hot milk and a generous dash of cinnamon on top. The café's interior is an eclectic environment: a full-sized African statue stands alongside plants, fondu pots, and the well-hidden remnants of a previous restaurant's interior. Large ceiling lamps and fans, together with large picture windows, give *a pleasant, airy feel.

While there are a few cafés on Avenue Laurier, La Petite Ardoise appears to be many people's favorite. Its wood-paneled interior emits a cozy glow that warms the spirit just as the café's imposing bowls of café-au-lait warm the body. The rich coffee-milk medley served here is a little more expensive than at other places, but it is worth the extra cost. Homemade pastries are also featured, and a variety of sandwiches and full meals are served. Along the stretch of exposed brick, local artists display paintings and collages for sale, while a bulletin board at the back announces gallery openings and other cultural events. In the summer, a small back garden is transformed into an outdoor terrace, and patrons are encouraged to eat and drink at a leisurely pace. The café's refined atmosphere is softened by the relaxed pace and neighborhood familiarity.

Cafés in Montreal play an important role in promoting social cohesion because, while they are an essential part of a francophone's cultural identity, many of the city's newer immigrants – Greeks, Italians and Africans – are increasingly drawn to them. For anglophones, cafés are a special treat, serving as reminders of how "un-American" this North American city truly is. ∎

ST JOSEPH'S ORATORY

The word "oratory" means house of prayer – and St Joseph's Oratory is just that, albeit a very big one. St Joe's cupola, rising 790 feet (263 meters) above sea level, is a vast, imposing, but familiar sight towering high above Montreal's rooftops. Celebrated as one of Christendom's outstanding monuments of faith, this is the Grand Central Station of devotional Catholicism in Montreal. Built in honor of Canada's patron saint, the shrine hails over 3 million visitors a year and rivals devotions to the Lourdes and Fatima shrines.

From the foot of the 278 stairs which lead up to the entrance, St Joseph's Oratory is an overpowering presence. The gigantic oratory exudes an unselfconscious resignation to its own monumentality – much like a whale placidly accepting its behemoth dimensions. An architectural arrogance characterizes this oratory, whose cumbersome haunches make the other edifices in Montreal seem like sidedishes.

The oratory of Mount Royal is (as the famous Canadian cleric, Cardinal Tisserant, noted) "the world's capital of devotion to Saint Joseph." While this proclamation alone draws several million pilgrims to St Joseph's stately doors, simple curiosity also propels several thousand pairs of feet toward the shrine. For the devotional Catholic, St Joseph's is a religious event, a holy place, a sacred duty. For the mere visitor the shrine offers an intriguing glimpse into a Catholic culture that, at one time, permeated almost every aspect of French-Canadian life.

Whether religious inspiration or anthropological curiosity propels you to this site, a visit to this oratory inevitably means an encounter with stairs – plenty of them: 99 from street level to the entrance of the crypt-church and 179 more up to the basilica proper. Pilgrimage groups usually gather around the bronze and granite monument to St Joseph located inside the main gate and, drawing a few deep breaths, prepare a steep ascent toward the celestial structure. Some pilgrims, as act of penance and reverence, will make an edifying and excruciating climb on their knees

up to the church-crypt. The stairs at St Joseph's are not properly *scalae santae* or holy stairs which, when ascended on the knees, are a way in which Catholics can obtain indulgences (divine pardon) for past, present or future sins. This rather painful practice, however, currently remains a devotional act intended to purify the soul for an encounter with the saintly patriarch.

The crypt-church, the first stop on the way up, was completed in 1917. It derives its name from its vault-like appearance and, one is tempted to add, its vault-like feel since the ponderous stone walls create the sensation of being sealed underground. The stained-glass windows depict gospel episodes in which St Joseph features prominently: the Flight into Egypt, the Birth of Christ, the Circumcision, Life at Nazareth, and so on.

Adjoining the crypt-church is what is called a votive chapel designed for private devotions. St Joseph's importance for the Catholic church is reflected in the eight plaques which display the saint's titles: Guardian of Virgins, Terror of Demons, Protector of the Church, Hope of the Sick, Patron of the Dying, Comfort of the Afflicted, Mainstay of Families and Model of Workmen. (A busy saint!) In addition to preserving virgins and deflecting devils, St Joseph heals through miracles. The crutches and braces scattered throughout the chapel are "testimonies" left by pilgrims cured by the oil found in a basin beneath the statue of St Joseph. (The oil is also on sale in the gift shop.)

In the center of the votive chapel is the flickering of more than 3,500 vigil lights, candles lit either in memory of the dead or as a request for blessing. The wrought-iron railing contains a "holy relic," a tiny particle of St Joseph's clothing, allegedly authenticated and venerated for its miraculous healing powers. Behind the main lamp rack is the resting place of Brother André, the founder of the oratory who died at the age of 91 and who was finally beatified by Rome – one step below Roman Catholic sainthood or canonization.

Brother André was the innocuous doorkeeper at Notre-Dame College, a boys' school across the street from the Oratory, before he turned celebrated founder of St Joseph's. A museum displaying artifacts related to his origins, childhood and service in the oratory is located two stories below the basilica. The exhibits include a peculiar "exact" replica of the austere cell Brother André occupied while a doorkeeper and a "thoroughly authentic" reproduction of the hospital room in which he died on January 6, 1937.

Heading upwards again, visitors climb toward solid Canadian granite, staunchly defending the oratory against time and the elements. A brief pause here under the Renaissance-style facade affords not only a bird's-eye view of Montreal but also a chance to catch your breath before advancing into the real caverns of the behemoth.

Aesthetic sensibility has always been one of the great human mysteries, and exactly what was running through the minds of the Basilica's designers will indeed mystify many. Although almost grotesquely huge, St Joseph's exterior is nevertheless stately, and its Romanesque-Renaissance style is also curiously appropriate for a religious monument. St Joseph's bowels, however, are strangely barren, and they exude about as much charm as an airplane hangar. Inside, the awful 1960s art combines with an alienating functionalist modern design to create an understatement so overwhelming that the act of passing from the outside to the inside can be quite jarring to the senses.

A closer look at the sanctuary (if you're up to it) can tell you much about

the Catholic liturgical innovations inspired by Vatican II (1962–65), the second international meeting of Catholic bishops and clergy to discuss the church's role in the modern world. (The first meeting was in 1870.) Unlike the altars in some of the older churches in Montreal, where the priest celebrated Mass with his back to the congregation, St Joseph's altar is placed forward on its platform and the rituals of the Mass are performed by a priest who faces the people. This new altar arrangement was intended to establish not only a closer tie but also a greater accountability between clergy and laity. Yet the incredible size of the basilica is hardly conducive to intimacy. This is the world's seventh-largest religious floor space: St Joseph's is able to accommodate up to 12,000 people at one time. Standing room only, of course!

Back outside, there's still plenty to see of the oratory. Secluded gardens ranging beyond the basilica and out into the mountainside encourage meditative meanderings. Many visitors choose to follow Louis Parent's famous Way of the Cross, a series of prayers performed in front of 15 stone tableaux representing the stages of Christ's death and resurrection.

Each station's foliage was carefully chosen to reflect a mood. At the third tableau, where Christ is shown falling on the way to crucifixion, the predominant color is red to connote the flow of blood. Where Veronica wipes the face of Christ, the colors are delicate pastels to suggest tenderness. And at the 13th station, where Christ is taken down from the cross, the colors are bland and austere, conveying grief and desolation.

By far the most endearing and interesting of St Joseph's offerings, however, is the tiny shrine to Brother André, dwarfed beside the looming Oratory. Inside, cracked walls stand behind the faded paint of once garish religious statues, and the floors groan as bended knees approach them. Simple, humble and worn out, the chapel is endearing in a dusty sort of way and is a welcome contrast to the pomposity of its grandiose cousin next door. Here too are weathered plaques thanking St Joseph for his intercessions, some dating from the chapel's earliest days.

Finally, a trip to St Joe's wouldn't be complete without a visit to the "gift shop" back at the bottom of the hill. Here almost every kind of Catholic religious paraphernalia can be found, from four-foot statues of St Joseph, whose heart (assuming the statue is plugged in) will glow an ethereal rose, to miniature versions of the saint that are specially designed for the dashboard or refrigerator.

There are almost 100 varieties of rosary to choose from, those made of expensive red crystal have beads shaped like hearts while an economy model is made of lightweight plastic.

Here, with people pawing through bins of plastic medallions, glow-in-the-dark rosaries, and laminated holy cards, St Joseph's commercial side is brazenly exposed. While celebrating the transcendent human soul, the shrine is also a monument to a culture capable of generating a commodity from even its most "immaterial" aspects. ∎

STADIUMS AND GARDENS

Travel east along Rue Sherbrooke and the **Olympic Stadium** looms up suddenly amid rows of unassuming duplexes, as though a mollusc-shaped starship from another galaxy had settled down in the suburbs. Futuristic, majestic, impractical and incredibly expensive, controversy still surrounds the "Big O" long after the memory of the 1976 Olympic Games has faded.

Roger Taillibert, the French architect who designed the stadium, claimed that sports arenas are the cathedrals of our age. The metaphor appealed to a city with a history of building magnificent churches: St Joseph's Oratory on Mount Royal boasts a dome larger than any except St Peter's in the Vatican in Rome.

But the plan for the new sports dome – designed to assert the city's modern, cosmopolitan flair rather than its Roman Catholic history – was far more ambitious, and ultimately it demanded even more financial sacrifice. And just as the slow construction of St Joseph's depended upon the personal charisma of Brother André, so the sudden realization of the Big O was only possible through the force of one personality: the irrepressible Jean Drapeau, Montreal's mayor from 1954 to 1986.

Drapeau gets credit for sheer visionary ambition. The Olympic Stadium's revolutionary design boasts a leaning tower 55 storeys high from which a flexible Kevlar roof descends along cables over the playing field. Tower and stadium alike are imaginatively modeled in fluent curves that soar at beautiful and seemingly impossible angles.

But Drapeau must also shoulder a large part of the blame for the Big O's other unofficial nickname: "the Big Owe." Montreal's stadium just may be the most spectacular sports arena in the world – but there is no question that it is the most expensive. The price tag of $1.2 *billion* gives it the distinction of

being the world's most costly building. The price tag means that each of its 70,000 seats cost more than $17,000. In 1984, an accounting firm determined that the Big O had cost only slightly less than all the other domed stadiums in North America put together – and that was before it had a roof.

Yet Mayor Drapeau had promised Montreal "modest games" that would pay for themselves through revenues from tickets and souvenirs. He remains notorious for his assurance that the Olympics could no more run a deficit than a man could have a baby. Predictably, local cartoonists enjoyed depicting the former mayor heavy with child.

The reasons for the exorbitant price-tag are easy enough to find in hindsight. The concept of a retractable canopy roof suspended from a tower leaning at 45° had never before been attempted on this scale. Since the top of the tower had to be centered over the stadium's roof, the circular opening in the center of the stadium slants slightly toward the tower,

**eceding
ges:
tanical
rdens; fun
La Ronde.
ft, picnic
lle St-
ène.
ht,
mpic Park
wer.**

so that the end of the ellipse near the tower's base is lower than the far end. The pleasing asymmetry of this design made the task of casting the huge, irregular concrete ribs of the stadium extremely tricky and delicate – and, of course, expensive.

But the real construction headaches were caused by the rigid deadline that Olympic Games always impose upon the host city. The clock ticked away as the builders waited for detailed plans from the architect. In the end, they built most of the complex in just two years, between 1974 and 1976. At the opening ceremonies, Montreal had a magnificent stadium, but there was still no tower and no roof. Nevertheless, in the giddy flush (and relief) of the moment, the city gave Drapeau a standing ovation. The tower would take another decade: it was not completed until 1987.

Does the city's professional baseball team, the Montreal Expos, need so extravagant a home? Defenders of the Olympic Stadium ask: does anybody worry about how much the Pyramids cost? Or the Roman Coliseum (which, as it happens, would fit onto the Big O's playing field)? Drapeau once reminded his critics that the ancient Athenians had rebuked Pericles for building the Parthenon instead of warships.

Only one other professional baseball team plays under a retractable roof: the Toronto Blue Jays. Montrealers acknowledge that Toronto's "Skydome" is tidy and efficient – like the city around it – but Montreal's stadium makes an impression that few monuments can match. For once, however, Torontonians have the last laugh. Due to ongoing problems, the Olympic Stadium's roof is now kept tightly closed.

A visitor need only ride the funicular cable car that runs up the spine of the tower to the observatory deck to appreciate the architect's imagination. One might say that the tower combines the grace of the Eiffel Tower with the eccentricity of the Leaning Tower of Pisa. While the top of this concrete tripod

Waiting for the game to begin.

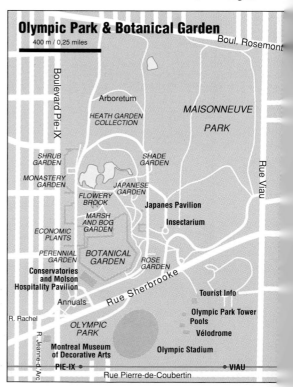

Olympic Park & Botanical Garden

400 m / 0,25 miles

Boul. Rosemont

Boulevard Pie-IX

Arboretum

MAISONNEUVE PARK

HEATH GARDEN COLLECTION

Rue Viau

SHRUB GARDEN

SHADE GARDEN

MONASTERY GARDEN

JAPANESE GARDEN

FLOWERY BROOK

Japanes Pavilion

MARSH AND BOG GARDEN

Insectarium

ECONOMIC PLANTS

PERENNIAL GARDEN

BOTANICAL GARDEN

ROSE GARDEN

Conservatories and Molson Hospitality Pavilion

Rue Sherbrooke

Annuals

Tourist Info

R. Rachel

OLYMPIC PARK

Olympic Park Tower Pools

R. Jeanne-d'Arc

Vélodrome

Montreal Museum of Decorative Arts

Olympic Stadium

PIE-IX

VIAU

Rue Pierre-de-Coubertin

overhangs the roof of the stadium, the hollow base forms the roof of the Olympic Pools, with wing-like lobes that spread out on either side. Come equipped for a dip, as the spacious pools are open to the public year-round.

Thirteen stories of office space fill up about two-thirds of the tower's neck, with a three-floor observatory at the summit where the tower broadens as its three corners begin to sweep apart. The exterior double-decker cable car carries up to 90 passengers and, as it emerges into the open air about a third of the way along its path, it offers an increasingly spectacular view of the eastern horizon.

From the observation deck at the summit, the view extends about 50 miles (80 km) and includes an unobstructed westward view of Mont Royal and the city skyline, with the St Lawrence River winding around from the left. There is also a vertiginous view into the stadium.

The cables that suspend the roof pass down from a niche (where the roof is stored) only a few feet below the deck,

affording a unique perspective on the operations that raise and lower the 65 tonnes of fabric. Forty-six winches must operate in precise synchronicity in order to unfurl the roof over an area that measures more than 200,000 sq. feet (18,500 sq. meters). When lowered, the canopy stretches over the playing field into a tent-like cupola.

For all this nifty engineering, the retractable roof did not entirely eliminate rain delays. If an unexpected shower occurred in high winds, the game had to wait until the winds let up before the roof could be unfurled. In fact, the roof could not be lowered in winds stronger than 15 mph (25 kph), while the roof of Toronto's Skydome can operate in winds up to 40 mph (65 kph). As it took almost 45 minutes to drop the roof into place, the stadium officials normally let weather predictions determine whether the roof should be lowered for an event, rather than waiting for the rain.

Some baseball fans criticize the sightlines at the Big O, which was designed

The Olympic Stadium.

more with track and field in mind. In any case, the stadium plays host for all kinds of events now that the roof allows the stadium to be used year-round. Trade shows, rock concerts and Canadian football attract crowds to the stadium's stands. Special events, such as the visit of Pope John Paul II or the spectacular production of Verdi's *Aida* that came complete with a 40-foot sphinx, live elephants, and over 1,000 singers, can have an unforgettable impact in this setting – one that sometimes converts even die-hard pragmatists to Drapeau's grand ambitions.

Spreading out from the base of the Olympic Pools, the **Vélodrome** was built to accommodate the cycling events at the Olympic Games. However, another celebratory spin-off from the city's 350th anniversary resulted in the conversion of the space into an unusual life-sciences museum called the **Biodôme**. City botanists, biologists and zoologists have created four different ecosystems under one roof: a tropical jungle, a polar

environment, a northern forest and the habitat along the St-Lawrence River. Characteristic plants, animals and birds have been installed within each micro world. Thanks to cleverly sited underwater cameras, visitors can even observe beavers hard at work inside their elaborate lodges.

The Botanical Gardens: The Biodôme will complement the glories of nature already on display across Rue Sherbrooke. As sports fans roar inside their concrete cathedral, 26,000 species of plants repose in tranquility at the **Jardin Botanique**. If Montreal, with its harsh winters, seems an unlikely setting for one of the world's largest botanical gardens, consider the pleasure of sitting in the warmth of the tropical greenhouse, among the pineapple plants and the orchids, during a December blizzard. However, most of the two million people who visit every year are more interested in the houseplants and exotic gardens than they are in a chance to come in from the cold.

Located on a 180-acre (73-hectare) rectangle across the street from the Olympic Park, the gardens have been steadily evolving since Brother Marie-Victorin founded the project in 1931. A modest statue of him stands to the right just beyond the main gate.

Although a total of nine greenhouses protect the tropical flora from the elements, spring and the fall are still the best seasons for a visit, since the vast majority of plants are divided among the various outdoor gardens. Different plant groups bloom each month between April and October.

Even those visitors who can't tell a begonia from a rhododendron can enjoy a stroll among the blooms, but those who prefer a chauffeur can take a guided tour on the mini-train. With about 30 plots in which the plants are grouped according to particular themes, a trip through the gardens is a little like moving through a series of stage or films sets. Some gardens are as much educational as sensory experiences.

Botanical Gardens.

The monastery garden has displays of medicinal herbs in an arrangement that recreates the quiet enclaves of medieval monks in the age of Charlemagne. Information panels offer useful trivia about such topics as the aphrodisiac power of absinthe and the laxative properties of licorice. The poisonous plant section is only a few feet away. These plots are located just beyond the neatly arranged perennials and test gardens, to the left after the entrance.

Winding paths, ponds thick with lilies, rock gardens, and a "flowery brook" make a poetic setting at the center of the gardens. An assortment of birds live among the aquatic plants in the ponds. In the Alpinum, flora from the world's mountain ranges are gathered together beside a quaint waterfall. When the flowers bloom, choruses from *The Sound of Music* pop into mind. Beyond the ponds that lie behind the Alpinum, the Arboretum is more like an open park, with its trim heaths, dwarf spruces, shade trees and chestnuts. In the fall the maples

begin to turn splendid colors, and the dense assembly here provides a convenient way to go "foliage peeking."

The Chinese Garden is the largest outside Asia, with seven pavilions built in the Ming Dynasty style around a central lake. The Botanical Gardens staff worked closely with the City of Shanghai on this project. The Japanese Garden is all serenity, with bubbling streams full of carp and a tea room.

The greenhouses recreate the climates of the warmer parts of the globe: an equatorial rain forest has the musty bouquet of orchids; then a hot, dry desert with human-sized cacti, and a Mexican villa with a popular collection of carnivorous plants including the famous Venus fly-traps.

Several permanent and temporary exhibitions are housed under glass here as well. A computer controls the climate of each of the ecosystems in the exhibition areas. There are also trivia-quiz computer games for the kids to play, and audio-guides in French and English.

ea House at otanical ardens.

The rhododendrons, by the way, are in a specialized garden and they bloom in June, while the 100-plus species of begonias are gathered with the gesneriads in the tropical greenhouse.

A small but intriguing **Insectarium**, was opened in 1990 following the initiative of an enthusiastic collector named Georges Brossard. Part museum part zoo, the project was designed to educate children and adults about creatures that usually get the attention of humans only when they want to swat them dead. Inside this pavilion, which is itself shaped like an insect, kids and grown-ups can peer into display cases and absorb their minds in games and puzzles that shed a whole new light on the world of bugs.

An extraordinary variety of safely dead, perfectly preserved insects, from butterflies to golden scarab beetles, are mounted on the walls, while an assortment of living insects inhabit worlds behind glass walls. Some of these creatures seem to be a little shy of the spotlight, but they are easy enough to find with a little patience. All together, there are about 130,000 specimens here.

Île Ste-Hélène and Île Notre-Dame: Opposite Old Montreal, two islands in the St Lawrence River function as the city's fairgrounds. Until the 1960s, there was only one island here, **Île Ste-Hélène**, which was about half its present size. However, the earth excavated from the Métro tunnels was used to expand the island and to create a whole new one next door: **Île Notre-Dame**. This park became the site of Expo '67, the great exposition that drew 50-million visitors during the summer of Canada's centennial year, 1967.

More than any other single event in Montreal's history, Expo changed the way the city felt about itself, and awakened Montreal to its potential as a center for international gatherings of all kinds. Perhaps the notion that Montreal had at last entered "the big league" was what prompted the naming of Canada's first pro baseball team after Expo.

The Insectarium.

204

The original plans called only for temporary structures that would stand for just the summer of the exhibition, but many of the 83 pavilions were so sturdy and impressive that it made no sense to demolish them, so Expo survived for 14 years as *Terre Des Hommes* (Man and His World).

Today, the site has taken on a whole new persona. On Notre-Dame Island, the old French pavilion was converted in 1993 into the Casino de Montréal, and it has become a phenomenal success story. Currently the casino is expanding into a neighboring building, the Pavilion du Québec, connected by a futuristic walkway. Casino authorities claim it will be one of the world's largest gaming places.

On Île Ste-Hélène, the famous geodesic dome designed by Buckminster Fuller, has gone through a dramatic transformation. Despite a fire burning away its outer skin in 1978, the former American pavilion still stands 20 storeys high. With no internal supports, it encloses 7 million cubic feet (198,240 cubic meters) of air, and yet it weighs less than the weight of the materials that compose it. It is said that if the structure were a mile wide, it would float away.

However, in 1995 the pavilion became substantially more grounded, with the opening of Biosphere, as both an interpretive centre and a hub for the vast network of ecowatchers along the St Lawrence River and the Great Lakes' water systems. Through satellites and sophisticated computer technology, visitors exploring the four interactive exhibition halls receive a graphic lesson on the importance of water.

La Ronde, the amusement park built for Expo, is still going strong on Île Ste-Hélène. The original Mini-Rail and cable-car SkyRide still seem novel ways to get around the park. Montrealers with children make an annual pilgrimage to La Ronde to experience the thrills of rides such as Le Monstre, the world's second tallest roller coaster at 132 feet (46 meters), and a popular complex

called Aqua-Parc, with a water-slide for everyone from toddlers to daredevils.

During two weeks in the early summer, admission to La Ronde includes a ringside seat from which to view the annual International Fireworks Competition. Each night for two weeks a different national team attempts to put on the most spectacular pyrotechnics display over the river and the city skyline.

In mid-June the roar of Formula One racing cars of the Molson Grand Prix can be heard on the **Gilles Villeneuve Race Track** at Île Notre-Dame. A refuge from all this noisy excitement is not far away: a chunk of Île Ste-Hélène is still green, wooded and quiet, except for the traffic on the Jacques Cartier Bridge.

The past can be visited at the 1822 fort near the bridge, at the **Stewart Museum at the Fort**. As well as naval and other military paraphernalia, in the summer time visitors can see the Compagnie Franche de la Marine and the 78th Fraser Highlanders re-enact parades dressed in 18th-century costume.

Roller-coasting at La Ronde.

Chapelle
Saint
Bernard
1942

DAY TRIPS

Montreal is ideally situated for quick getaways to an astonishing variety of four-season adventures: river rafting on the Rouge; ice-fishing on Île Perrot; climbing frozen waterfalls in Estrie; hiking, skiing and mountain biking; crafts fairs and pleasure boat cruises; gondola rides and aqua slides; historic forts and ports, maple sugar feasting and sleigh rides at *cabanes à sucres* (sugar shacks); manors and museums; bushwhacking and moose tracking. Disappear with a tent into the wilds of a *réserve faunique* (wildlife reserve), rent a chalet, or sleep in a log castle with room service.

Points of the compass: To the north lie the deep silent woods, glacial lakes and alpine villages of the Laurentians, resting on the oldest rock formation on the planet – the Canadian Shield. To the south lie the rolling pastures, brightly painted barns and white-steepled towns of Estrie, a French version of New England. To the east are five of the Montérégian hills, carved by the ancient Champlain Sea, that arc across the St Lawrence plain, and the historic Richelieu Valley. This is the battleground of the Iroquois, French, English and Americans, and the scene of the 1837 Patriots Rebellion against the British regime. To the west lies the Outaouais, land of big logging lakes and rivers and the great fighting muskie.

The **Laurentians**, Quebec's *pays d'en haut,* and **Estrie** (the Eastern Townships) are the two main playgrounds for Montrealers. North America's first alpine ski rope-tows were erected at Prévost in 1930 and at St-Sauveur-des-Monts in 1934. Montrealers soon flocked to the Laurentians to try the newfangled sport, and the glamor of ski and après-ski began to saturate the region.

Today acrobatic skiing, torchlight parades, luging, and tobogganing are all popular on Quebec slopes. The Laurentians have the largest concentration of alpine ski centers and lighted runs in North America, and Estrie runs a close second. But summer brings another medley of pleasures – canoeing, sailing, horseback riding, camping, fishing, swimming, water-skiing, or cappucino-sipping on a well-situated café-terrace; antiquing, boutiquing, gallery browsing, summer theater and *bôites à chansons* which keep going till dawn.

Like the Laurentians, Estrie (from *est* for east and *patrie*) is ski and sailboat country, sprinkled with chic auberges and inns, artisan boutiques and impeccable restaurants. But the farm culture tempers the elegance of resort towns like Lac Brome, Eastman, North Hatley, Sutton and Magog with an earthy charm. The milder microclimate and proximity to the US border give the region an adventurous spirit.

The following day trip destinations are divided into four categories: Laurentians, Estrie, Montérégie, and Coeur-du-Québec. They provide a focus for day or weekend trips, but try taking the historic and scenic routes – #117 through the Laurentians, #138, known as the Chemin du Roy, #132, #342, #344 and #223. Exploring the back roads, called "rangs," will lead you to chance encounters, odd little museums, roadside curiosities and other unmapped treasures of Quebec.

● **Laurentians:** *Route: Laurentians Autoroute 15 North, exit 21 to 640 West, which leads to the park's eastern reception center; from Paul Sauvé Park, Route 344 West to **Oka**; ferry to **Hudson**; 342 west to **Rigaud**.*

Colorful sailboards float like confetti off the silvery 4½-mile (7-km) long beach of the **Parc d'Oka**, on the **Lac-des-Deux-Montagnes**. The lake's shallow waters are ideal for trying out the sport, and rental facilities are close by. But the most exotic recreation here is a canoe excursion through the marsh around Grand Bay. You'll paddle through a floating garden walled by rushes and cattails, carpeted with flowering lily pads and delicate duckweed, with marsh ducks, muskrats and Great Blue Herons in your wake, and possibly arouse the curiosity of beavers at work. For information on excursions led by park naturalists, tel: (450) 479-8337.

Parc de Récréation Paul-Sauvé's summer activities feature geological excursions, forest nature walks, bicycle trips to explore the dunes and effects of glaciation, and evening talks on Oka's native American legends. The park's flat wooded terrain is popular with cyclists and cross-country skiers.

Oka and **Hudson** are two charming lakeshore villages that are linked by an old ferry across Lac-des-Deux-Montagnes. French-Canadian Sunday-school songs describe pilgrimages to Oka to buy cheese made by monks at **l'Abbaye Cistercienne d'Oka**, one of the oldest monasteries in North America. Oka's Trappist monks came from the Bellefontaine Abbey in France, and you can see the humble miller's home where they first settled, stroll the gardens that

Taking a break.

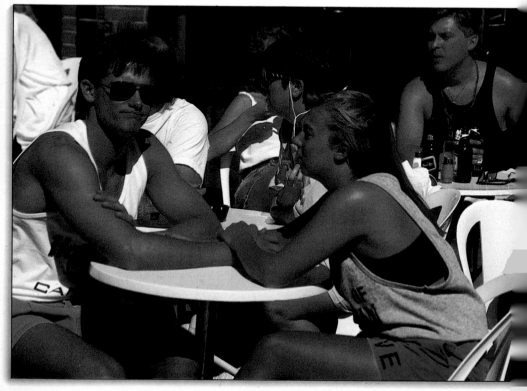

surround the monastery, and buy the world-famous Oka cheese that has been made here since 1893.

A climb to the top of the **Oka Calvary**, east of the village and across from Parc Paul-Sauvé, is loveliest in autumn. The stations of the cross up here were built between 1739 and 1742 to inspire the local Amerindians, and three of the seven original chapels have been preserved. Since 1870, Amerindians and pilgrims from all over Quebec have come to Oka to celebrate the Feast of the Holy Cross on September 14 and to enjoy the magnificent view of the Lac-des-Deux-Montagnes from the summit.

From Oka you can take the tiny car ferry across to **Hudson** to go antique hunting. The seasonal ferry leaves from the dock on Rue des Anges next to the Argenteuil Manor. From Hudson, you can drive on to **Rigaud**, a charming spot, and from mid-March to late April, gorge yourself on maple syrup dishes at the **Sucrerie de la Montagne**, 300 Rang St Georges, tel: (450) 451-5204 or 0831.

● **Rouge River rafting:** *Route: Hwy 15 North to 148 West; from April to September only.*

The Rouge River has some of the best whitewater rafting in North America on the 15-mile (25-km) course between Harrington and Calumet, Quebec.

"Steep Throat," a ledge drop of 12 feet (3.7 meters), has been called "the Everest of rafting in Canada," and other Rouge River rapids are known by such names as Confusion, Turbo in the Morning, Avalanche, Washing Machine, Slice 'n' Dice, and The Monster.

Don't be daunted. Experienced river guides will brief you on "body surfing," "hydraulic action" and "ledge drops" and be there to yank you back into the raft in less than 30 seconds should you inadvertently bail out. Most day packages provide 5–6 hours of rafting (about 11 miles/18 km) and include a lunch break, along with all equipment, one experienced river guide per raft, shuttle service from the base camp, and a post-dinner video show of the day's adventures.

ac des
ables, Ste-
gathe,
aurentines.

● **Ste-Adèle / Val David / Ste-Agathe-des-Monts:** *Route: Laurentians Autoroute 15 North to **Ste-Adèle**, or take the more scenic local 117 North. From Ste-Adèle, take 117 North to **Val David** and **Ste-Agathe-des-Monts**.*

Ste-Adèle is a lively ski resort and a thriving writers' and artisans' colony by the shores of Lac Rond and the slopes of Mont Ste-Adèle. At local studios artists make enamel plates and vases, jewelry and ornamental belt buckles, and do traditional wood sculpture and cabinetmaking. Visit the **Village de Séraphin**, an historical reconstruction of a mid-1800s Laurentian settlement, inspired by Québécois Claude-Henri Grignon's popular 1933 novel *Un homme et son péché* (A Man and His Sin). Each house in the village is based on a Grignon character or illustrates an episode in the life of Séraphin Poudrier, the novel's miser. The village of 20 buildings includes a post office, general store, doctor's office and school, with a miniature train running through the grounds.

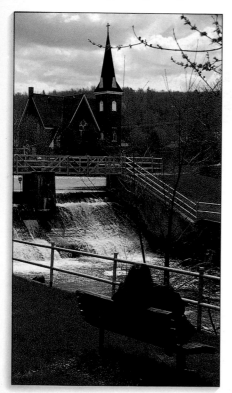

Val David is known for its abundance of traditional Québécois houses with mansard roofs, charming inns and fine cuisine and its talented painters and artisans – engravers, ceramicists, and basketweavers. Quebec's first *boite à chanson* (folksong club) was built here in 1959, and now the rustic structure houses the **Théâtre-de-la-Butte** café-theater featuring French-Canadian plays.

Rock climbers flock to Val David to scale **Mont Condor**, a devilish rock 125-ft (38 meters) high (halfway between Val-Morin and Val-David), and the awesome 75-ft (22-meter) high **Condor Needle**, one of the few rock needles in Eastern Canada.

Ste-Agathe-des-Monts is the metropolis of the Laurentians, and a hot spot for Québécois and international celebrities, especially during the Festival des arts Hiawatha, a dance festival held each July. With three public beaches and a gorgeous lake, the traffic of bikinis, sailboats and sailboarders is something fierce.

To get an idea of the Laurentians' old-guard wealth, take a quick cruise around **Lac des Sables** on the Bâteau Alouette. You'll see such baubles as the estate built by Twentieth Century Fox tycoon William B. Fox and the 42-room "summer cottage" built by a millionaire who kept his own orchestra to play for him day and night, and a greenhouse in which he cultivated only roses.

● **St-Faustin / Parc Récréational du Mont Tremblant:** *Route: Laurentians Autoroute 15 North, exit 83; to 117 North to Ste-Agathe-des-Monts; Chemin Tour du Lac to Chemin du Lac-Caribou to St-Faustin Educational Centers; from St-Faustin exit on 117, toward Lake Superior and Mont Tremblant park entrance.*

St-Faustin's Forest Education Centers of the Laurentians exhibit a fiery blaze in autumn. Two hiking trails and six interpretation trails wind around Lac du Cordon, over rustic boardwalks and footbridges. Quebec's eight Forest Education Centers are there to inform the **Village of Knowlton, Ville de Lac Brome.**

public on the anatomy and ecology of a forest, and this center has animations, videos, and free pamphlets on autumn coloration, conifers, and Quebec forests, richly illustrated and well written.

Naturalists will gladly show you the insides of a Jack Pine cone or let you whiff some oil extract of white pine, and the exhibits at the Interpretation Pavilion will tell you everything you always wanted to know about trees. Contact Chemin du Lac-Caribou, St Faustin, tel: (819) 326-1606.

Algonquin sorcerers called their mountain Manitonga Soutana (Devil's Mountain) because it roared and rumbled whenever the tranquility of its forested slopes was disturbed. To protect this wilderness, **Mont Tremblant**, the highest of the Laurentian peaks (3,150 ft/ 960 meters) was established as the first of Quebec's provincial parks in 1894. The mountain is thick with maple and pine forests, and it shelters black bears and Virginia stags, beavers, lynx, and hundreds of bird species. The park's 500 lakes and three major rivers – the Rivières Rouge, Matawin and du Diable – all provide great swimming, canoe camping, and fishing for trout or jumping landlocked salmon.

You can take a cruise on Lac Tremblant, go hiking and horseback riding, or take the chair lift up to the top of the mountain from the Station Mont Tremblant Lodge. You can camp here in winter as well as summer.

As for skiing, Mont Tremblant is the highest skiable peak in Eastern Canada, with a vertical drop of 2,132 ft (650 meters), and the longest trail in Quebec at 3.2 miles (5 km) long. *For park information, call (819) 688-2281, 424-2954.*

● **Estrie:** *Route: Eastern Townships Autoroute 10 (east) to exit 90, to 243 South to **Lac Brome**; 104 West to 215 South to **Sutton**; 139 North to **West Brome**; 139 North to Eastern Townships Autoroute (west).*

Lac Brome (Knowlton): A mill pond cuts through the heart of this Victorian

kwantshit oman from lingan.

village, and colorful boutiques in 19th-century homes give it a festive air. Lac Brome is a charming spot for lunch, brunch, coffee with wickedly rich desserts, antiquing and strolling beside the pond and lake. Flocks of wild ducks are omnipresent: they are Lac Brome's gastronomic specialty, and Lac Brome is surrounded by splendid (not necessarily flat) cycling country.

In stagecoach days Lac Brome (Knowlton) was a stop on the Boston-Montreal run, and this story is told in the **Pettes Memorial Library**, established in 1894 as the first free library in Quebec and in the **Brome County Historical Museum**, 130 Lakeside Road, tel: (514) 243-6782.

The museum's nine buildings house Abenaki artifacts, pioneer bric-a-brac (foot-warmers and pill-making machines), a local history archive (survey maps and old letters) a military collection, general store, blacksmith shop, fire tower and county courthouse. The white brick building was the original village school (1844) and contains a World War I Fokker biplane with the camouflage covering still intact. It was sent to Canada in 1919 as part of the war reparations act. For hiking and bicycling maps and news of local happenings, contact the Lac Brome Chamber of Commerce, tel: (450) 242-2870.

Sutton bustles with hikers and skiers bound for the long winding wooded trails of Mont Sutton, and shoppers bent on quilts and woven rugs, ceramics and pewter in the local artists' cooperatives. The main street of this ski resort at the base of Mont Sutton is flanked with graceful old houses, auberges, crafts shops, art galleries and tempting restaurants and outdoor cafés.

In summer the Saturday flea market on Curley Street is lively, and on Sunday the local tradition is brunch followed by a hike up Mont Sutton. Stargazing soirées are popular, as is summer mountain biking on skidoo trails. Local topographical and cycling maps give the best routes for excursions on 10-

Paddling in the Park d'Oka.

speed or *tout-terrain* mountain bikes. For information and maps on all the cycling routes in the area, contact Sutton's Chamber of Commerce, tel: (450) 538-8455 or 1-800-565-8455.

The **Sutton Heritage Museum** (at the corner of Rue Principale and Rue Montagne) tells the history of communications in a collection of antique switchboard and telephones, phonographs and radios housed in an early post office, telegraph office, printing shop, fire alarm center, telephone exchange and radio station. Open 1 May to 1 September, tel: (450) 538-2544.

F.G. Edwards Country Store, West Brome (just off Route 139) is worth a detour to visit, even if you don't buy a thing. A wheelbarrow and feed sacks deck the front porch, and locals hover around boxes of candy-colored seeds ready to sprout into Sugar Snap peas, pencil pod black wax beans and Kentucky Wonder green pole beans. F.G. Edwards & Co. Ltd is a hallowed institution founded in 1857 to serve the farmers of West Brome. As in horse and buggy days, it's still the place to swap yarns, post local news and buy everything from pitchforks, work socks and boots, horse bridles, yoyos and udder wash, to baby chicks, penny candy, ant traps and bird feeders. A browse through this aromatic shop will give you a feeling for rural life in Estrie.

● **Orford Arts Centre / Magog / Abbaye St-Benoît-du-Lac:** *Route: Eastern Townships Autoroute 10 to exit 115, to 141 North, to* **Parc Récréational du Mont-Orford**; *141 South to* **Magog**; *from Magog, follow signs to rural road to* **St-Benoît-du-Lac** *along the west side of* **Lac Memphrémagog**.

Mont-Orford: Classical music rings into the woodland air from studios scattered throughout Mont Orford **Arts Center**'s 222 sylvan acres (90 hectares). From early July to mid-August in this thriving arts center in the heart of Estrie's Appalachians is a festival of concerts and art exhibitions from Thursday to Sunday.

The Arts Center, in the **Parc de Récréation du Mont-Orford**, is popular in all seasons. In winter there is skiing, skating and snowshoeing. In summer there is swimming in the two lakes, hiking, golf, chairlifts to the summit, and hang-gliding over the Sutton Mountains and Lac Brome, the Monteregian hills, and St Lawrence plain.

Magog (Lac Memphrémagog): Magog isn't a spectacularly pretty resort town, but its location at the northern tip of Lac Memphrémagog, the 30-mile (48-km) long narrow lake linking Quebec with Vermont, makes it handy for boating.

Magog has a variety of restaurants, shops, art galleries, a public beach and federal quay. You can take a cruise, or rent a sailboat with a private skipper, fish for *ouananiche* (landlocked salmon), test your balance on a sailboard, and see Lac Memphrémagog from a snorkeling mask or while dangling from a parachute 150 feet (46 meters) in the air.

As an exhilarating, effortless and rather goofy way to see the lake, parasailing has caught on. Your harness is attached to a parachute, which is towed by a motor boat. For information on waterskiing and parasailing on Lac Memphrémagog, contact Les Activités Nautiques Tribord, Magog's Federal Wharf, tel: (819) 868-2222.

Abbaye St-Benoît-du-Lac: Gregorian chants echo over Lac Memphrémagog from the pink granite towers of the Benedictine abbey of St-Benoît-du-Lac. Commanding the lake like a fairy castle, the monastery's octagonal towers, triangular gables and narrow pointed windows were designed by Dom Paul Bellot (1876–1944), a French monk who settled here in 1937 to become one of Quebec's major ecclesiastical architects. Then, in dramatic contrast to the rest of the monastery, a starkly beautiful new church by Montreal architect Dan S. Hanganu was consecrated in 1994.

The monks of the Benedictine order of Solesmes, France, are the only people inhabiting this independent municipality. You can tour the abbey's rich mosaic

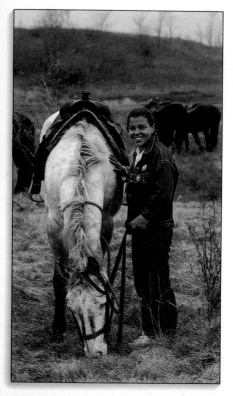

interior, participate in the vespers Gregorian chanting (Sunday mass; daily at 5pm except Thursday; 7pm Thursday only), pick apples in the abbey's orchard, and buy cider and delicious cheeses (St-Benoît, Ricotta and L'Ermite), made by the monks. You can even stay here as a guest and wake up to dawn over Mont Orford. The abbey reserves 40 rooms for men and 15 for women.

● **Stanstead Plain / Rock Island-Derby Line / Beebe Plain:** *Route: Eastern Townships Autoroute 10 to exit 121 to Highway 55 South to the **Stanstead Plain** Exit; from **Rock Island**, Route 247 West to **Beebe Plain**, and 247 North to Magog.*

Estrie's border towns, hotbeds of international gossip and smuggler's tales, give the region its spice. This pocket of townships, although it is run-down and neglected by North Hatley standards, is nevertheless intriguing.

Stanstead Plain has a number of buildings of architectural interest – Stanstead College (1872), the Ursuline School (1884), the Christ Church Anglican Church (1858) and Butter House (1866). The Colby Curtis Museum on Dufferin Street features antiquarian dolls, toys, military artifacts and mementos of 19th-century life.

Stanstead Plain's main street leads directly into **Rock Island** which straddles the Quebec–Vermont border. In some houses here a meal is cooked in Canada and eaten in the US; the bathtub is in Canada and the toilet is in the US – which makes for endless local jokes.

Dilapidated factories, mills and river buildings give Rock Island an air of decay, but there are architectural gems among them, notably the Romanesque revival **Haskell Free Library** and **Opera House**, built on the boundary line in 1904 (Route 143 and Rue Church). The ground floor is a feast of lustrous wood, marble and granite, gorgeously lit by stained-glass windows and chandeliers. The international boundary puts the circulation desk and stacks in Canada and the reading room in the United States.

Horse trekking has become a bi business.

Upstairs the 450-seat opera house is a delightful scale-model of the Boston Opera House. The performers sing on the stage in Quebec while the audience applauds in the US.

The white line down **Beebe Plain**'s main street, Canusa Avenue, divides the US from Canada. According to international law, Mrs Brown cannot cross the street to borrow a cup of sugar from Madame Blanche without first reporting the matter to customs. But in a spirit of community goodwill, local immigration officers ignore the small print.

● **Montérégie:** *Route: 132 West to Melocheville. Follow Hébert Blvd (Route 132) to the* **Beauharnois Hydro-Québec Generating Station** *and* **Emond Street**, *Melocheville.*

Enormous is the only way to describe the Beauharnois Generating Station, which is one of the world's largest hydroelectric facilities. Sitting between lakes St-François and St-Louis, the plant makes full use of the 79-ft (24-meter)

drop between the two lakes to power the water as it speeds through the adjacent lock at 2.1 million gallons (8 million litres) per second, producing an average of 11.7 billion kWh annually. In winter Quebec uses all the power produced, but come summer, its excess capacity is passed along to Ontario and the US via 735,000-volt power lines.

Guided tours of the generating station take in the Beauharnois information and interpretation centre, the vast alternator hall – where staff use either electric carts or tricycles to inspect the plant's 36 turbines (each weighing over 100 tons), the control room, and a sensational rooftop view of power lines extending in all directions, with Montreal and the St-Lawrence in the distance. Guided tours mid-May to early September, 80 Edgar-Hébert Street, Melocheville, tel: 1-800-365-5229.

Archaeologists at **Pointe-du-Buisson Archaeological Park** say it will take decades to interpret the tons of material unearthed on this 66-acre (27-hectare)

The black line on Haskell Free Library's door on Rock Island is the international border with the US.

woodland site by the St Lawrence River rapids. A remarkable Iroquois complex and 7,965 objects, four fireplaces and the traces of 42 poles of long house were found in the month of April 1967 alone.

Tomahawks, stone utensils, pipes and harpoons dating as far back as 5,000 years indicate that this site was once the hunting, fishing and burial grounds of several Amerindian peoples and a stopping point for explorers, missionaries, soldiers and merchants en route to the Great Lakes.

Hundred of artifacts are displayed in the two exposition centers. You can take a guided archaeological tour of five digging sites and on special days take part in activities related to Amerindian music and dance, Iroquois medicine, carving arrowheads, and making cornmasks and dolls. Pointe-du-Buisson Archaeological Park, 333 Rue Emond, Melocheville, tel: (450) 429-7857.

● **The Canadian Railway Museum / Côte Ste-Catherine Locks:** *Route*: *15 South to exit 42; 132 West to 209 South to St-Constant; from St-Constant, 209 North to 132 West to Côte Ste-Catherine-Locks*.

Depending on how enamoured you are with trains, you can spend a few hours or a day exploring the 118 pieces of rolling stock standing like old soldiers at the Canadian Railway Museum at St-Constant – the largest railway museum in Canada.

Assembled here are antique locomotives, trolleys and trams, sleepers and street sweepers, snowplows, boxcars and cabooses, parlor cars, diners and diesels, a one-car traveling schoolhouse and even some horse-drawn sleighs, spread over 15 acres (6 hectares) and housed in two giant hangars. An elaborate model electric train whistles through papier-mâché mountains and steams past tiny cows, using a variety of more than 200 locomotives and cars. It's the liveliest attraction in the Hayes Building, which houses Canadian Railway Historical Association archives, artifacts **All biked out.**

218

and memorabilia. At the authentic 19th-century railway station, you can board a diesel locomotive or a vintage Montreal street car for a short but dramatic mile.

Just down the road from St-Constant, another transport adventure takes place as deep-sea oil tankers, long lakers and grainers, make their way through the **Côte-Ste-Catherine-Locks** into the St Lawrence Seaway. The bridge lifts, the ship edges through the narrow canal; valves open and the water drains to lower the ship to seaway level, and a horn blast signals the ship to pass.

Cross the lifting-bridge to the far side of the lock for an eye-level view of the captain's deck and crew's quarters of ships from as far away as Panama and the former Soviet Union.

The bridge serves as the entrance to **Côte-Ste-Catherine Park**, which affords a stunning perspective of the thunderous Lachine Rapids, the Montreal cityscape and the Monteregian hills. The park has a swimming pond, camping area, and bicycle path along the whitewater's edge, and close by is an island colony of herons.

● **Fort Chambly / St-Jean-sur-Richelieu / Fort Lennox:** *Route: Autoroute 20 or highway 112 East to 223 South to* **Chambly**; *223 South to* **St-Jean-sur-Richelieu** *and* **St-Paul-de-l'Île-aux-Noix**.

Fort-Chambly's castle-like walls have been licked by the treacherous rapids of the "River of the Iroquois" for nearly three centuries, and Fort Chambly National Historic Park stands by the edge of the Richelieu Rapids, the names of the heroes of New France carved in stone at its gates. The first fort on this site was built of wood in 1665 by Captain Jacques Chambly and the soldiers of le Régiment de Carignan-Salières, to defend against Iroquois attack. And the first European settlement on the Richelieu grew up around its borders, becoming the town of Chambly. In 1709–11, the wooden fort was replaced by the massive structure with five-sided corner bastions that stands today.

It was occupied by the French until 1760, by the English until 1775, and by the Americans under General Montgomery until 1776. It later held American prisoners during the War of 1812 and Canadian patriots during the Patriot Rebellion of 1837–38.

After exploring Fort Chambly and its museum of weapons and artifacts, take a look at the **St Hubert House** (1760), **Maigneault House**, and the **Laureau House** (1775). You can see the operation of the Chambly canal's three locks, or go canoeing in the Chambly basin, just below the Richelieu Rapids. Open early March to early December, Fort Chambly, 2 Rue Richelieu, Chambly, tel: (450) 658-1585.

On the way to Fort Lennox, stop at **St-Jean-sur-Richelieu** to stroll through the old section of this historic military town, along Jacques-Cartier, St-Charles, Longueuil and St-Georges Streets and also on the promenade along the Chambly Canal. St-Jean has a lively public market on Wednesday and Sat-

c des
bles at
e-Agathe.

urday, and in August, during its 10-day Festival des Montgolfières, outrageously colorful hot-air balloons float over its rooftops and steeples. Cruises on the Richelieu leave from the wharf at the foot of St Georges Street.

At its northern end, **l'Île-aux-Noix** is an idyllic spot for picnicking and hikes along the marshy riverbank to observe painted turtles, muskrats, bullfrogs and diving kingfishers. And at the southern tip of this island, which is only 15 miles (24 km) from the US border, is the impressive star-shaped fort at **Fort Lennox National Historic Park**, with a moat 60 feet wide and 15 feet deep (18 by 4.5 meters).

The French built the fort in 1759 to defend against British advance, but they evacuated it the following year under British siege. In 1775, the Americans captured the l'Île-aux-Noix to use as a base to launch attacks on Montreal and Quebec City, but only a year later a smallpox epidemic forced them to abandon the fort.

Lively animated tours of Fort Lennox take you through the guardhouse (1824), gunpowder magazine, officer's quarters, guardhouse, prison, barracks and commissary, and a museum exhibiting military equipment and documents. On special days actors perform reenactments of 18th-century skirmishes, using replicas of period uniforms and weapons. Fort Lennox, open mid-May to end of September, is accessible by the Crosières Richelieu ferry from St-Paul-de-l'Île-aux-Noix, at the Reception Center on 61st Avenue, tel: (450) 291-3325.

● **Mont St-Hilaire / Vieux Beloeil:** *Route: Autoroute 20 East to exit 113; 133 South to **Mont St-Hilaire**; bridge over to **Beloeil**.*

When the wind is calm, and the air balmy, you can lie for hours on "Sugar Loaf," the flat rocky summit of **Mont St-Hilaire**, feasting on the contours of the land below. The Monteregian hill is only 1,350 ft (410 meters) above sea level, but it rises abruptly from the St Lawrence plain, affording a dreamy view of its sister peak, Mont Royal, in the heart of the metropolis, the Richelieu River and the sinewy St Lawrence, and Mont St-Bruno, St-Grégoire, Rougemont and Yamaska.

Mont St-Hilaire is an ecological marvel thriving only 22 miles (35 km) from Montreal – an environment so unspoiled that UNESCO designated it as the first Biosphere Reserve in Canada. This highest of the eight Monteregian hills shelters the last vestige of the dense woodland that once covered the St Lawrence Valley. In a lush hardwood forest with canopies of 100-ft (30-meter) red oaks and 250-year old white pines, there are hundreds of mosses and ferns, 600 species of flowering plants, 32 of flowering trees and 187 of birds.

Mont St-Hilaire's hiking trails wind through an aquatic zone, a wildflower meadow, lush ferny areas, along Lac Hertel, a lake once humming with seven mills, and up to an exposed windy summit with Arctic vegetation. The habitat

Orchards along the Richelieu.

is ideal for bird watching, cross-country skiing and snowshoeing.

Just across the Richelieu River from Mont St-Hilaire's apple orchards lies **Vieux Beloeil**, established in 1694. Its yacht harbor, boutiques, art galleries, artisan shops, restaurants and cultural center attract Montrealers in all seasons. Vieux Beloeil's magnificent old buildings include a presbytery built in 1772, the Près-Vert and Lanctôt houses, and the Rouville-Campbell Manor, now an art gallery.

The Quebec painter Ozias Leduc was born in the Correlieu House, and the local church contains one of his frescos.

● **Sorel / Ste-Anne-de-Sorel:** *Route: Eastern Townships Autoroute 10 to 30 North to Sorel; 132 East to Ste-Anne-de-Sorel*.

Canada's fourth oldest city, **Sorel**, is known for its busy shipyards and its lively marina – the focus of nautical tourism in Quebec. The **Place du Marché** at the end of Rue Roi near the port is a bustling marketplace, and the

Carré Royal is a magnificent 18th-century park curiously shaped like the Union Flag of the United Kingdom.

Sorel makes a really convenient base from which to explore the bewitching archipelago of islands off its shore.

Ste-Anne-de Sorel has come to be known as *Pays du Survenant* (Land of the Unexpected Visitor) because of Germaine Guèvremont's novel of that name. The islands' rich flora and faurna can be seen from the motorized canoes which will lead you through the marshes, to see the world's biggest heron breeding grounds. **Excursion dans le marais** is at 3755 Chemin Chenal-du-Moine, tel: (514) 742-3113. Open May 1 to September 30, but reserve ahead.

The Chemin Chenal-du-Moine leads across a steel bridge to **Île aux Fantômes**, whose dwellings are set up high on pilings as a protection against flooding. From a dead-end road you can cross over to the **Île d'Embarras** and its tiny fishing village strung with drying fish nets. Two old ice houses on the tip of the island are now restaurants featuring traditional regional cuisine – notably *gibelotte*, fish stew made from the locals' daily catches.

Croisières des Îles de Sorel Inc. operate cruises from mid-May to the end of the first week in September, from the quay at 1665 Chemin Chenal-du-Moine, tel: (450) 743-7227.

● **Village d'Antan / Odanak Abenaki Reserve:** *Route: Autoroute 20, exit 181 to* **Le Village Québécois d'Antan**; *from Drummondville, Route 143 to Route 132 northwest to* **Pierreville/Odanak**.

Le Village Québécois d'Antan (the Quebec Village of Yesteryear) in Drummondville is not as corny as it sounds. The 18th-century village that has been recreated on this pastoral site attracts serious historians, cultivated museum-goers, filmmakers, and Québécois looking for their roots, as well as those eager for nostalgia.

The village's 50 historic buildings and 30 historic reproductions constructed by regional artisans portray the days of colonization between 1810 and 1910. Guides in period costume animate 25 traditional houses in nine different architectural styles, and 18 artisan workshops, including a saddlery, tinsmith, shoemaker and broom-maker, and cabinet maker – *à la Québécois*.

The list goes on... an oddly stocked general store, apothecary, old post office, blacksmith forge, a sawmill, a telephone museum, an old style *caisse-populaire* (savings bank), a one-room schoolhouse, a *cabane à sucre*, a garage and gas station with antique cars, and even a covered bridge (*circa* 1878) transported from Stanbridge.

Farm animals have a cattle shed, henhouse, and pighouse, a safe distance from restaurant and picnic tables. Village Québécois d'Antan opens June 1 to the end of September, 1425 Rue Montplaisir, tel: (819) 478-1441.

Around the corner from Pierreville, the small town that is Canada's biggest producer of fire engines, is the **Odanak**

Competing b kayak.

Abenaki Reserve on the shores of the St Francis River. In the 17th century the Abenakis came from New England to settle in Odanak, and the Jesuits established a mission here to educate them.

In the heart of the reserve is a riverfront park graced with rustic gazebos, tepees, carved totem poles and contemporary Abenaki sculpture. The stone chapel built in 1828 is filled with Amerindian woodcarvings, and the red brick convent across the way from it has been transformed into a museum of Abenaki history and culture. On the rambling porch stand massive wooden sculptures of mythological figures, and inside are 14 rooms filled with Abenaki history, culture and crafts.

The **Musée des Abénaquis** contains displays on constructing birch-bark canoes, Abenaki cornhusk masks, ash-splint basket-weaving, and a model of a 17th-century Abenaki fort. Local shops sell sweetgrass baskets, buckskin jackets, native crafts, and smoked sturgeon, a local specialty. From Hwy 20 take exits 175–185; open daily 1 May to 31 October, otherwise closed weekends; 108 Rue Waban-Aki, Odanak, tel: (514) 568-2600.

● **Village du Bûcheron / Parc Nationale de la Mauricie:** *Route: 40 East to 55 North (at Trois Rivières); 55 North to 155 North to Grand-Piles; park entrance at St-Jean-des-Piles.*

On a cliff overlooking the St-Maurice River is the lovely village of **Grand-Piles**, once a transfer harbor for lumber boats, and the **Village du Bûcheron** (Lumberjack Village). The heyday of Mauricie's logging industry and lumberjack days (1850–1950) is celebrated in 25 log buildings containing hundreds of photos and over 5,000 artifacts. The Village has an art gallery and craft boutique, and on weekends you can see the sawmill in operation and have a typical lumberjack meal at the Cookerie. Open year round; 780 Fifth Avenue, Grand-Piles, tel: (819) 538-7895.

Mauricie National Park is a paradise for would-be Robinson Crusoes. This watery wilderness speckled with tree-covered islets has 34 lakes which are off-limits to motor boats. From the Île-aux-Pins lookout over **Lake Wapizagonke**, a peek through field glasses reveals a jaunty red canoe beside a camper dozing in blissful solitude on a white sandy islet beach.

The national park is a canoe-camping and trout fishing heaven. All the lakes are accessible by well-bridged portage trails, but the most popular route is the 7-mile (11-km) stretch up Lake Wapizagonke's shoreline of cliffs and densely forested hills.

The park is wild enough for moose, black bear and coyote, wolf and lynx, yet tame enough for picnicking, swimming, camping in summer and winter, cycling, hiking and birdwatching. More than 193 species of birds have been sighted here, and 116 of them nest in the region. Open mid-May to mid-October, tel: (819) 538-3232. Cross-country ski trails open from December to March, depending on snow conditions.

INSIGHT GUIDES

Travel Tips

Insight Guides portray destinations in depth, providing the complete picture and the top photography

Insight Pocket Guides focus on the best choices for places to see and things to do and include large fold-out maps

Insight Compact Guides' portability makes them the perfect books to carry with you for on-the-spot reference

Three types of guide for all types of travel

INSIGHT GUIDES Different people need different kinds of information. Some want *background information* to help them prepare for the trip. Others seek *personal recommendations* from someone who knows the destination well. And others look for *compactly presented data* for on-the-spot reference. With three carefully designed series, Insight Guides offer readers the perfect choice. Insight Guides will turn your visit into an experience.

The world's largest collection of visual travel guides

CONTENTS

Getting Acquainted

Climate 226
Economy 226
Government 226
Time Zones 226

Planning the Trip

What to Wear 226
Entry Regulations 226
Health 227
Money Matters 227
Maps 227
Public Holidays 227
Getting There 227
Traveling with Children 228
Disabled Visitors 228
Senior Citizens & Students 228
Tourist Information 228

Practical Tips

Security & Crime 229
Medical Services 229
Extension of Stay 229
Business Hours 229
Tipping 229
Media 229
Postal Services 229
Telecoms 230
Telegram & Telex 230
Consulates 230

Getting Around

On Arrival 230
Public Transport 230
Taxis 230
Car Rentals 230
On Foot 230
Bicycle Rental 231

Where to Stay

Hotels 231
Longer-Term Residences 233
Bed & Breakfasts 233
Residences/Student Housing . 233

Eating Out

Where to Eat 234
Drinking Notes 236

Attractions

Things to Do 237
Areas of Interest 237
Churches 237
Parks 238
Tours & Cruises 238

Culture

Museums 239
Art Galleries 240
Concerts & Opera 240
Ballet 240
Theaters & Movies 240
Nightlife 240
Jazz 240

Festivals

Calendar of Events 241

Shopping

General 242
Shopping Areas 243
Department Stores 243

Sports

Participant 243
Spectator 244

Language

General 245
On the Telephone 246
On the Road 246
Dining Out 247

Further Reading

General 250
Other Insight Guides 250

Art/Photo Credits 251
Index 252

Getting Acquainted

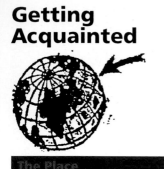

Unless otherwise stated, the area code for telephone numbers is 514 for Montreal and 450 for surrounds.

Located in the province of Quebec, at the confluence of the Ottawa River and the St Lawrence Seaway, Montreal is built on an island about 32 miles (40 km) long and 10 miles (16 km) wide. Prominent in the middle of the island is Mont-Royal. Montreal is the second-largest city in Canada after Toronto. Around two-thirds of the population is French, and it is claimed that Montreal is the largest French-speaking city after Paris.

Climate

Montreal has nearly five months of cold and snow. Montrealers, however, rarely hibernate. Skating, skiing and sledding are very popular. The Metro subway system is well heated, and the Underground City provides a haven from the cold. In summer, the city comes alive with the warm weather, and outdoor cafés and festivals bring people out on the streets. In July, the temperature can reach 90°F (32°C), yet average temperatures hover around 70°F (21°C) during the day. The average daily highs in Montreal are:

Month	(°C)	(°F)
January	−10	14
February	−10	15
March	−3	27
April	6	42
May	13	55
June	18	64
July	21	69
August	20	68
September	15	58
October	9	47
November	2	35
December	−7	20

Economy

Montreal is the headquarters for Canada's largest banks, railroad lines and insurance companies and an important center for shipping and industry.

Government

Montreal is governed by a mayor, a 56-member council elected for four years and a six-member executive committee selected by the council. As in all Canadian municipalities, the city government is controlled by the provincial legislature. In 1969, the Montreal Metropolitan Corporation replaced the Montreal Urban Community to administer the metropolitan area.

Time Zones

Montreal is in the Eastern Time Zone with New York City and Boston, one hour ahead of Chicago, and three hours ahead of San Francisco. On the last Sunday in April, the clock is moved ahead one hour for Daylight Savings Time. On the last Sunday in October, the clock is moved back one hour to return to Standard Time. This follows the mnemonic spring forward, fall back. At noon in Montreal it is:

11am in Chicago
9am in San Francisco
8am in Hawaii
5pm in London
2am (the next day) in Sydney.

Planning the Trip

In the cold winter months, travelers should bring warm clothing that can be worn in layers, hats, gloves and boots. In summer, bring a sweater for the cool evenings. Pack sportswear and a bathing suit since many Montreal hotels have health clubs and indoor pools.

VISAS & PASSPORTS

US citizens do not need a visa or a passport to enter Canada, just proof of citizenship (driver's license, birth certificate or passport). All other visitors need passports. People registered as aliens in the US should carry their US alien registration or green card. Visitors wishing to stay over three months may need a visa.

ANIMAL QUARANTINE

Dogs and cats coming into the country must be accompanied by proof of vaccination against rabies or they will be quarantined for 30 days before being admitted. Livestock, horses, and fowl must be accompanied by a permit, and they are subject to health inspection on arrival.

CUSTOMS

There are no restrictions on bringing in clothing or professional tools and equipment. Visitors from the US and UK aged 16 and over can bring in duty-free up to 200 cigarettes, 50 cigars, 2 lb (about 1 kg) of tobacco, personal cars (for up to six months), boats, canoes, rifles and shotguns (but no handguns or automatic weapons), 200 rounds of ammunition, cameras, recreational equipment and radios. If you are driving a rental car keep the contract with you. If you have questions before you leave, call Canadian Customs on (514) 283-9900, fax: 283-5757, web: www.vc.gc.ca.vco

Health

For a list of English-speaking physicians in Montreal contact:
Canada: 188 Nicklin Road, Guelph, Ontario, N1H 7L5.
Europe: Gotthardstrasse 17, 6300 Zug, Switzerland.
US: International Association for Medical Assistance to Travelers (IAMAT), 736 Rue Center, Lewiston, NY 14092.

If your health insurance does not cover medical problems while traveling, the following companies may be of assistance: **Health Care Abroad**, Wallach & Co, 107 West Federal Street, PO Box 480, Middleburg, VA 22117, tel: 1-800-237-6615 or (540) 687-3166; **Travel Guard International**, 1100 Centerpoint Drive, Stevens Point, WI 54481, tel: 1-800-782-5151, fax: 1-800-955-8785, web: www.noelgroup.com. Hospital and medical services are excellent. Rates for care vary, but adult in-patient care starts at around $2,000 a day for non-Canadians.

Money Matters

Traveler's checks and major credit cards are readily accepted in Montreal. Cash may be needed for small restaurants and stores, and many establishments accept US dollars. Buy Canadian dollars before you leave home to avoid long lines at the airports. Traveler's checks can be bought in Canadian dollars. At the current exchange rate, one Canadian dollar is worth 80–90¢ in US currency.

Banks in Montreal open 10am–3 or 4pm. For currency exchange try: **Bank of America Canada**, 1250 Rue René Lévesque W, tel: 938-9588, open daily 9.30am–5pm; **Thomas Cook**, Dorval Airport, tel: 636-3582, open daily

5.30am–8.30pm for all currencies, 5.30am–midnight for US dollars; **Currencies international,** 125 Rue Peel, tel: 392-9100, open Monday to Friday 8.30am–8pm.

A 6.5 percent provincial sales tax and a 7 percent federal goods and services tax apply to nearly all goods and services. Books and foods are taxed at only 7 percent, and ready-made meals are not taxed at all. For further information about the tax laws call Revenue Quebec, tel: 873-4692.

Maps

Excellent maps of the city are available at all tourist information offices. Street signs with a large question mark point to office locations around the city. The main office is at 1555 Rue Peel, tel: 873-2015, fax: 873-6050, web: www.tourisme.gouv.qc.ca, e-mail Infotourisme.gouv.qo.ca.

Getting There

BY AIR
Two airports serve Montreal: Dorval International is 14 miles (22 km) west of the city and has been handling domestic and most US flights; Mirabel International, 34 miles (55 km) northwest of the city, has been handling all flights from outside North America.

This is slowly changing. Dorval is handling more international flights, while Mirabel will concentrate more on charter flights and cargo.

BY RAIL
Amtrak has daily service from the US. To obtain information on fares, tel: 1-800-872-7245.

Montreal is connected to most major Canadian cities through VIA Rail, tel: 1-800-361-5390. The terminus for both companies is at 985 Rue de la Gauchetière Ouest, Bonaventure.

BY CAR
A number of highways lead into Montreal. At the Canadian border be prepared to show proof of citizenship and your vehicle's

Public Holidays

Government agencies and many banks, businesses and schools close on the following holidays:

New Year's Day: January 1
Good Friday
Easter Monday
Fête de Dollard/Victoria Day: May 21 (or closest Monday)
Fête Nationale (Saint Jean Baptiste Day, Quebec Holiday): June 24
Canada Day: July 1
Labor Day: 1st Monday in September
Thanksgiving: 2nd Monday in October
Christmas Day: December 25
Boxing Day: December 26

ownership papers. On holidays and weekends, traffic backs up and travelers can expect a wait of half an hour or more at the crossing. From New York, take I-87 (the New York State Throughway), which becomes Highway 15 at the border 30 miles (47 km) from the outskirts of Montreal. From New England, take Route I-89 to Route 133, which becomes a two-lane road at the border. From Vermont, take I-91, which becomes Highway 55 in Canada, and follow this route to Highway 10 to Montreal. From Toronto take Highway 401 directly to Montreal.

In Quebec, the road signs are in French but easy to decipher. The speed limit and distances are posted in kilometers. The official speed limit is 100 kph (62 mph) and the highways are well patrolled. Quebec has a seat-belt law.

BY BUS
Greyhound/Trailways connects Montreal with various cities in North America. Vermont Transit connects Boston, New York and other cities in New England with Montreal. Both lines use the Voyageur Terminal at 505 Maisonneuve Blvd Est, tel: 842-2281.

TRAVELING WITH CHILDREN

Montreal offers many entertaining possibilities for children, from zoos to theater productions. Most of the major sightseeing spots have special programs for children. Check the listings later in Travel Tips or the local newspapers for more ideas. Some of the city's most popular child-pleasers are listed below.

Park Safari: Located 43 miles (70 km) from the city in Hemmingford, tel: 1-800-465-8724, fax: (450) 247-3563. Drive-in wild animal park. Open in summer and early fall.

Angrignon Park and Farm: tel: 872-3816, fax: 872-4583.

Cirque du Soleil: tel: 722-2324, fax: 722-3692, web: www. cirquedusoleil.com. Inventive circus (no animals) that appeals to all ages.

Dow Planetarium: tel: (450) 872-4530, fax: Many special season events.

Granby Zoo: Granby, tel: (450) 372-9113. More than 1,000 animals.

Grands Ballets Canadiens: tel: 849-8681, fax: 849-0098. Performs *The Nutcracker Suite* every year around Christmas.

Kahnawake Indian Reservation: In Kahnawake, 11 miles (18 km) from Montreal, tel: (450) 632-6030, fax: (450) 632–6031. Native Canadian dances in summer and an ethnographic museum. Open year round.

La Ronde: Ile-Sainte-Hélène, tel: 872-4537. A 136-acre (55-hectare) amusement park with international shows and circus. Open seasonally.

Maison Théâtre: tel: 288-7211. Theater devoted exclusively to children and teenagers. Closed in summer.

Montreal Museum of Fine Arts: tel: (450) 285-1600, fax: 285-4070, web: www.mmfa.qc.ca. Has several programs designed for children and includes family activities on the weekends.

Musée d'Art Contemporain de Montréal, tel: 847-6226, fax: 847-6290. Children and family activities of all kinds involving current displays.

Saint Leonard Cave Exploration: tel: 328-8511 or 252-3323. Investigate 500-million-year-old rock formations.

Winter Fairyland – Angrignon Park: tel: 872-3816. Landscaped and lit up just for kids.

Infotouriste: The main office and the smaller branch in Old Montreal are designated by street signs with a '?'. The main Centre Infotouriste is at 1555 Rue Peel, tel: 873-2015.

Greater Convention and Tourist Bureau of Greater Montreal, 1010 Rue Ste-Catherine Ouest, Suite 410, tel: 844-4056, fax: 844-7141.

Tourisme Québec, CP 979, Montreal H3C 2W3, tel: 1-800-363-7777, fax: 864-3838, e-mail: info@tourisme.gouv.qc.ca

DISABLED

A brochure published by the Montreal Convention and Visitors Bureau, tel: 844-4056, fax: 844-7141, gives complete information about facilities accessible to disabled people. Other associations offering information include:

Association régionale pour le loisir des personnes handicapées de l'Ile de Montréal: 525 Dominion, Suite 340, tel: 933-2739, fax: 933-9384, e-mail: arlphim@videotron.net. Special information on recreational activities.

Canadian National Institute for the Blind: 2155 Rue Guy, Ste. 750, tel: 934-4622.

Raymond Dewar Institute: Library, viewing room and reference center available for use by the deaf and mute. 3600 Rue Berri, tel: 284-2581, fax: 284-5086. web: www.surdite.org.

Bell Canada: Offers a relay system for the deaf and mute. Special telephones may be obtained from the Raymond Dewar Institute, tel: 256-5757.

Keroul: Provides assistance to disabled persons. 4545 Avenue du Pierre de Coubertin, tel: 252-3104, fax: 254-0766, e-mail: keroul@craph.org.

SENIOR CITIZENS & STUDENTS

Discounts are available for seniors and students at most museums and interesting sites. For detailed information about special events or programs call the Tourist Office, tel: 873-2015.

Practical Tips

As a rule, it is safe to walk around downtown Montreal in the day and evening. Areas to avoid at night include the X-rated movie houses along Rue Ste-Catherine Est, Mont-Royal Park and Parc Lafontaine. Whenever possible, travel with another person while sightseeing or shopping, particularly at night. Do not walk in deserted or run-down areas alone. If driving, lock your car and never leave luggage, cameras or other valuables in view; put them in the glove compartment or trunk. Park under a street light.

Never leave your luggage unattended. While waiting for a room reservation, for example, keep your property in view. Never leave money or jewelry in your hotel room, even for a short time.

Carry only the cash you need. Use credit cards and traveler's checks whenever possible, and avoid displaying large amounts of cash.

Health care is excellent in Montreal, but it can be expensive, especially for non-residents. Most hospitals have emergency rooms with doctors on hand round the clock. For information on clinics and other health services consult the *Yellow Pages* of the telephone book.

HOSPITALS

Catherine Booth Hospital, 4375 Montclair, tel: 481-0431.
Centre Hospitalier Jacques Viger, 1051 St-Hubert, tel: 842-7181.
Jewish General Hospital, 3755 Chemin de la Côte, Ste-Catherine, tel: 340-8222.

Dialing **911** will connect you to the police or other emergency assistance. No coins are needed.

Maisonneuve-Rosemont Hospital, 5415 de l'Assomption, tel: 252-3400.
Montreal Children's Hospital, 2300 Tupper, tel: 934-4400.
Montreal General Hospital, 1650 Avenue du Cédar, tel: 937-6011.
Royal Victoria Hospital, 687 Pine West, tel: 842-1231.
Saint-Luc Hospital, 1058 St-Denis, tel: 281-2121.
Villa Medica Hospital, 225 Sherbrooke Est, tel: 288-8201.

PHARMACIES

There are many full-service pharmacies throughout the city. The Jean Coutu Drug Store, 1370 Avenue Mont-Royal Est, tel: 527-8827, provides a 24-hour service.

OTHER SERVICES

The **Dental Clinic**, 3546 Rue Van-Horne, tel: 342-4444, fax: 342-0611, offers 24-hour service.
Weather Information: tel: 283-4006.
Quebec Poison Control Center: tel: 1-800-463-5060, fax: 654-2747.
Travel Information: tel: 873-2015.

If you plan to extend your stay over the standard three-month limit, contact the Department of Employment and Immigration in Ottawa, Ontario.

Standard business hours are 9am–5pm. Banks are usually open weekdays 9am–5pm. Museums follow standard business hours, and shops are generally open Monday to Wednesday 10am–6pm, Thursday and Friday 10am–9pm, Saturday 10am–5pm. Most stores are closed on Sunday.

It is customary to tip waiters and taxi drivers 10–15 percent of the bill or fare. Some restaurants add the tip to the bill, but this will be identified on the check. For porters, $1 per suitcase is expected. For hotel doormen who hail a cab or give other assistance, $1 should be given. Checkrooms usually have a fixed rate of 75¢.

There are French and English language newspapers and radio and television stations in Montreal. For listing of television stations check the daily newspapers. Radio stations are listed in the *Yellow Pages* of the telephone book.

The two major daily newspapers in Montreal are *La Presse* (French) and *The Gazette* (English). Montreal also has three weekly newspapers with extensive arts and entertainment listings. *Mirror* and *Hour* (both English) and *Voir* (French) are available free of charge at various newsstands, restaurants and stores around the city. Many smaller newspapers, journals and special interest publications are also found in the city.

The main post office (general delivery) is at **1250 Rue University**, tel: 395-4539, fax: 395-0325, open Monday to Wednesday 8am–5.45pm, Thursday and Friday 8am–9pm, Saturday 9.30am–5pm.
1250 Rue Ste-Catherine Est, tel: 522-3220, fax: 522-5758. Monday to Friday 9am–5.30pm.

Stamps can also be bought at coin machines in airports, bus terminals, and hotel lobbies.

You can have mail addressed to you at **Poste Restante**, or general delivery at the post office at 1250 Rue University. The American Express office will also hold mail for its customers at 1141 Blvd de Maisonneuve Ouest.

Telecoms

Public pay phones require 25¢. Long-distance calls may be dialed directly to all points in North America and most European countries. Travelers can buy a La Puce phone pass from any Teleboutique. La Puce is a prepaid calling card in denominations of $10, $20, and $50.

There are teleboutiques at Place Alexis Nihon, 1500 Atwater, and Place Dupuis, 1475 St-Hubert. For more information, tel: 310-2355.

The area code for Montreal is 514, and 450 for surrounding areas.

Telegram & Telex

Telegrams and cablegrams are handled by CNCP Telecommunications at 740 Rue Notre-Dame Ouest, tel: 861-7311, fax: 395-5250. Open for inquiries by phone daily 8am–11.30pm or in person Monday to Friday 8am–4.30pm.

Consultates

South Africa: 1 Place Ville-Marie, tel: 878-9217.
UK: 1000 de la Gauchetière Ouest #4200, tel: 866-5863.
USA: 1155 St-Alexandre, tel: 398-9695.

Getting Around

On Arrival

Connaisseur Bus Service, tel: 934-1222, fax: 937-0288, is available from both Mirabel ($14.50) and Dorval ($9) airports. Several major **taxi companies** also provide service from the airports for roughly $25 from Dorval and $55 from Mirabel.

A **limousine service** is available from Dorval to downtown Montreal without a reservation for a flat rate of $40.50. From Mirabel, service can be arranged through **Montreal Limousine Inc.**, tel: 333-5466, fax: 333-1998. The trip from Mirabel to downtown will cost roughly $70. By cab or limousine, the trip from Mirabel takes 45–60 minutes, and from Dorval 20–30 minutes, depending on traffic conditions.

Public Transport

Public transport in Montreal is very efficient, clean and comfortable. The Société de Transport de la Communauté de Montréal (STCUM) administers both the bus and Metro, and the tickets and transfers are good on either service. Exact change is required on the buses.

The rubber-wheeled Metro trains operate from 5.30am–1am and run every three minutes on crowded lines. Routes of the Metro trains are indicated by the name of the last station on the line and by color.

The single fare for adults is $1.85, monthly passes cost $44.50, and a strip of six tickets costs $7.75. Free maps of the Metro and bus system are available at ticket booths. For more information, tel: 288-6287.

Taxis

The rate for all taxis in Montreal is $1 per kilometer with a $2.25 minimum. The orange or white plastic sign on a taxi roof is lit when the taxi is available. The major taxi companies include: Champlain, tel: 273-2435; Co-op, tel: 725-9885; La Salle, tel: 277-2552; Veterans, tel: 273-6351.

Car Rentals

Most car rental companies have branches at the airport, major hotels and their central offices. Rates vary by firm and by model and size of the car. Most companies offer unlimited mileage and special weekend rates as well as liability insurance. Gas and collision insurance are extra, and there is a 10 percent sales tax.
Avis, 1225 Rue Metcalf, tel: 866-7906 or 1-800-321-3652, fax: 866-5214. Open Monday to Friday 7am–10pm, Saturday 7am–8pm, Sunday 8am–10pm.
Budget, 1240 Rue Guy, tel: 937-9121 or 1-800-268-8900. Open Monday to Friday 7am–9.30pm, weekends 9am–5pm.
Thrifty/Viabec, 1600 Rue Berri, tel: 845-5954, fax: 845-9880. Open Monday to Friday 7.30am– 8.30pm, weekends 8am–5pm.
Hertz, 1475 Rue Aylmer, tel: 842-8537 or 1-800-263-0678. Open Monday to Friday 7am–9pm, weekends 8am–9pm.
Tilden, 1200 Rue Stanley, tel: 878-2771 or 1-800-387-4747, fax: 874-1601, web: www.nationalcar.com. Open daily 7am–11pm.
Via Route, 1255 Mackay, tel: 871-1166, fax: 871-1232. Open Monday to Friday 7am–9pm, Saturday 7.30am–5pm, Sunday 9am–9pm.

On Foot

Walking in Montreal is very enjoyable and finding your way around is quite easy. Street names and directions are in French. If you get lost or need directions ask a passerby. Montrealers will be more than willing to assist you.

Bicycle Rental

Riding a bike is popular in Montreal, especially in the scenic parks. Below are a few companies that rent bikes:

Bicycletterie J.R. Cyclery, 151 Rachel Est, tel: 843-6989. Open Monday to Wednesday 9am–6pm, Thursday to Friday 9am–9pm, Saturday 10am–5pm, Sunday 10am–3pm.

La Cordée Plain Air, 2159 Rue Ste-Catherine Est, tel: 524-1515. Open Monday to Wednesday 9.30am–6pm, Thursday to Friday 9.30am–9pm, Saturday 9am–5pm, Sunday 11am–5pm.

Velo Adventure, Promenade du Vieux Port de Montréal, tel: 847-0666. Open Monday to Friday 11am–6pm, weekends 9am–6pm.

Quadricycle International, St-Laurent, tel: 849-9953. Open September to October and April to May for weekends 10.30am–8pm, June to September daily 9.30am–midnight.

Where to Stay

Hotels

Most hotels in Montreal fall in the expensive to deluxe range, especially downtown. Large hotels often offer weekend or family discounts. Prices can range from $300 a night for a double room in a deluxe hotel to $55–$75 a night in a moderate hotel. For a free accommodation booking service, call 878-1000.

DELUXE

Ritz-Carlton
1228 Rue Sherbrooke Ouest
Montreal, Quebec H3G 1H6
Tel: 842-4212 or 1-800-363-0366
Fax: 842-3383
E-mail: ritz@citenet.net
Caters to an elite clientele.

Le Meridien
4 Complexe Desjardins
Montreal, Quebec H5B 1E5
Tel: 285-1450
Fax: 285-1243
E-mail:info@wyndham-mtl.com
Well situated in downtown Montreal, near Chinatown and Place des Arts.

Westin Mont-Royal
1050 Rue Sherbrooke Ouest
Montreal, Quebec H3A 2R6
Tel: 284-1110
Fax: 845-3025
Web: www.westin.com
Multilingual concierge, fitness center, good food and 24-hour room service in an excellent location.

La Reine Elizabeth
900 Blvd Réne-Lévesque Ouest
Montreal, Quebec H3B 4A5
Tel: 861-3511
Fax: 954-2256
Web: www.cphotels.ca
Dependable comfort in a good location.

EXPENSIVE

Best Western Ville-Marie
Hotel and Suites, 3407 Rue Peel
Montreal, Quebec H3A 1W7
Ttel: 288-4141 or 1-800-528-1234
E-mail: bestwest@generation.net
Good central location and a health club.

Le Pavillion
7700 Côte de Liesse
Rue St Laurent, Montreal
Quebec H4T 1E7
Tel: 731-7821 or 1-800-361-6243
Fax: 731-7267
Web: www.qualityinn.com
Minutes away from Dorval Airport. Meeting and banquet facilities for 250 people.

Hôtel La Barre
2019 Blvd Taschereau Est
Longueuil, Quebec J4K 2Y1
Tel: (450) 677-9101
Fax: (450) 677-5514
Concierge service, outdoor swimming pool and gardens.

Hôtel Ruby Foo's
7655 Blvd Decarie
Montreal, Quebec H4P 2H2
Tel: 731-7701 or 1-800-361-5419/
1-800-363-6535
Fax: 731-7158
Web: www.hotelruby.foos.com
Oriental decor, outdoor swimming pool, health club and spa, and a beauty salon.

Travelodge Montreal Centre
50 Blvd René-Lévesque Ouest
Montreal, Quebec H2Z 1A2
Tel: 874-9090 or 1-800-578-7878
Fax: 874-0907
European-style hotel in downtown Montreal. Offers voice-mail services.

Howard Johnson's
475 Rue Sherbrooke Ouest
Montreal, Quebec H3A 2L9
Tel: 842-3961 or 1-800-842-3961
Fax: 842-0945
Sauna and exercise room. Central location, walking distance to Metro and the Underground City.

Radisson Gouverneurs
777 Rue University
Montreal, Quebec H3C 3Z7
Tel: 879-1370 or 1-800-333-3333
Fax: 879-1760
Web: www.radisson-mtl.com
Revolving rooftop restaurant,

complete spa facilities, heated pool and aerobics classes.

Hôtel des Gouverneurs Place Dupuis
1415 Rue St-Hubert
Montreal, Quebec H2L 3Y9
Tel: 842-4881 or 1-888-910-1111
Fax: 842-1584
All rooms have views of Montreal, Mont-Royal or the St Lawrence river.

Hôtel La Citadelle
410 Rue Sherbrooke Ouest
Montreal, Quebec H3A 1B3
Tel: 844-8851 or 1-800-449-6654
Fax: 844-0912
Web: www.hilton.com
Piano bar, health spa, rooftop indoor pool and European-style atmosphere.

Montreal Bonaventure Hilton
1 Place Bonaventure
Montreal, Quebec H5A 1E4
Tel: 878-2332 or 1-800-445-8667
Fax: 878-1442
In more than 2 acres of gardens atop Montreal's Underground City. Two restaurants, exercise room and rooftop swimming pool, 24-hour room service.

Le Centre Sheraton
1201 Blvd René Lévesque Ouest
Montreal, Quebec H3B 2L7
Tel: 878-2000 or 1-800-325-3535
Fax: 878-3958
Gourmet restaurant, indoor pool, health club, shiatsu massage, and specialty boutiques all in a convenient location.

Holiday Inn Montreal Midtown
420 Rue Sherbrooke Ouest
Montreal, Quebec H3A
Tel: 842-6111 or 1-800-HOLIDAY
Web: www.holidayinn.com
Basic Holiday Inn style, two bars, café-restaurant, health club and indoor pool. Package rates available.

Days Inn
1005 Rue Guy
Montreal, Quebec H3H 2K4
Tel: 938-4611
Fax: 938-8718
Recently renovated. Two restaurants, bar and meeting facilities

Hôtel du Parc
3625 Avenue du Parc
Montreal, Quebec H2X 3P8
Tel: 288-6666

Fax: 288-2469
E-mail: rooms@duparc.com
In the Mont Royal district with squash and tennis courts, Nautilus equipment and an all-season indoor/outdoor pool.

MODERATE

L'Hôtel Montreal Crescent
1366 Blvd René-Lévesque Ouest
Montreal, Quebec H3G 1T4
Tel and fax: 938-9797
Small, and intimate in the heart of downtown.

Château De L'Argoat
524 Rue Sherbrooke Est
Montreal, Quebec H2L 1K1
Tel: 842-2046
Fax: 286-2791
E-mail: chateauargoat@videotron.ca
Small European-style hotel in the Latin Quarter. Complimentary continental breakfast.

Hôtel Manoir des Alpes
1245 Rue St-André
Montreal, Quebec H2L 3T1
Tel: 845-0373
Fax: 845-9886
E-mail: rnunes@po-box.mcgill.ca
Transformed Victorian building.

Auberge des Glycines Inc
819 Blvd de Maisonneuve Est
Montreal, Quebec H2L 1Y7
Tel: 526-5511 or 1-800-361-6896
Fax: 523-0143
Convenient location in heart of downtown.

Hôtel Le St-André
1285 Rue St-André
Montreal, Quebec H2L 3T1
Tel: 849-7070 or 1-800-265-7071
Fax: 849-8167
Complimentary in-room continental breakfast.

Hôtel de L'Institut
3535 Rue St-Denis
Montreal, Quebec H2X 3P1
Tel: 282-5120 or 1-800-361-5111
Fax: 873-9893
Web: www.ithq.qc.ca
Owned and operated by the Quebec Institute of Tourism and Hotels, this hotel is the training ground for future hotel and restaurant managers. Institutional exterior but the service is excellent.

Auberge de la Fontaine
1301 Rue Rachel Est
Montreal, Quebec H2J 2K1

Tel: 597-0166 or 1-800-597-0597
Fax: 597-0496
E-mail: info@aubergedelafontaine.com
Relaxed hotel overlooking Parc Lafontaine. Some rooms have terraces or balconies.

Hôtel de Paris
901 Rue Sherbrooke Est
Montreal, Quebec H2L 1L3
Tel: 522-6861
Fax: 522-1387
E-mail: hdeparis@microtec.net
Near the heart of the Latin Quarter. Reasonably priced.

Hôtel Maritime
1155 Rue Guy
Montreal, Quebec H3H 2K5
Tel: 932-1411 or 1-800-363-6255,
Fax: 932-0446
Web: www.hotelmaritime.com
Designed for the budget-conscious corporate traveler and private guests, this hotel also does special hockey packages.

Thrift Lodge
1600 Rue St-Hubert
Montreal, Quebec H2L 3Z3
Tel: 849-3214 or 1-800-613-3383
Fax: 849-9812
E-mail: tajmahal@videotron.net

Hôtel Atlantian du Parc
4544 Avenue du Parc
Montreal, Quebec H2V 4E3
Tel: 274-5000
Fax: 274-1414
Reasonable rates. All rooms have en-suite kitchenettes.

Days Inn Montreal Berri
1199 Rue Berri
Montreal, Quebec H2L 4C6
Tel: 845-9236 or 1-888-363-0363
Fax: 849-9855
E-mail: infolordberri.com
Center of the Latin Quarter.

Château Versailles Hotel and Tower
1659 and 1808 Rue Sherbrooke Ouest
Montreal, Quebec H3H 1E3
Tel: 933-3611 or 1-800-361-7199
Fax: 933-7102 or 933-8401
e-mail: versailles@montreal.net.ca
Converted from two Edwardian mansions in downtown. Special weekend rates October to May.

YWCA
1355 René-Lévesque Ouest
Montreal, Quebec H3G 1T3
Tel: 866-9941

Single and double rooms for women at reasonable rates. Longer-term residence (minimum eight weeks) also available. Convenient cafeteria, pool, sauna and whirlpool offered.

YMCA
1450 Rue Stanley
Montreal, Quebec H3A 2W6
Tel: 849-5331
Fax: 849-7821
Conveniently located and reasonably priced. Wide range of sports facilities and cafeteria for men, women and families.

Hôtel La Résidence du Voyageur
847 Rue Sherbrooke Est
Montreal, Quebec H2L 1K6
Tel: 527-9515
Fax: 526-1070
E-mail: twng@ican.net

Hôtel Viger Centre-Ville
1001 Rue St-Hubert
Montreal, Quebec H2L 3Y3
Tel: 845-6058 or 1-800-845-6058
Fax: 844-6068
Variety of low-rate rooms.

La Tour Belvedere
2175 Blvd de Maisonneuve Ouest
Montreal H3H 1L5
Tel: 935-9052
Fax: 935-9532
E-mail: tourbelvedere.com
Full facility parlor and one-bedroom suites available by the week or month.

Le Montford
1975 Blvd de Maisonneuve Ouest
Montreal H3 1K4
Tel: 934-0916
Fax: 939-2552
Web: www.lemontford.com
Studios, alcove suites, one- and two-bedroom suites in good location.

Manoir Le Moyne
2100 Blvd de Maisonneuve Ouest
Montreal H3 1K6
Tel: 931-8861 or 1-800-361-7191
Fax: 931-7726
E-mail: lemoyne@iber.com
Split-level rooms and suites with fully-equipped kitchens; whirlpool, restaurant and bar and summer garden terrace.

Bed and breakfast combines affordability with residential lodging.

A Bed and Breakfast – A Downtown Network
3458 Avenue Laval
Montreal, Quebec H2X 3C8
Tel: 289-9749 or 1-800-267-5180
Fax: 287-2386
E-mail: bbdtowncam.org
Discounts on tours, and family and extended rates are available. Multilingual hosts.

Bed and Breakfast Chez-Nous
3717 St-Famille
Montreal, Quebec H2X 2L7
Tel: 845-7711
Arranges overnight and longer-term accommodations.

Bed and Breakfast Network
422 Cherrier
Montreal, Quebec H2L 1G9
Tel: 738-9410 or 1-800-738-4338
E-mail: bbmtlnet@total.net
Accommodations in French- or English-speaking homes in downtown locations at reasonable prices. Also short-term apartment rentals.

Bienvenue Bed and Breakfast
3950 Laval
Montreal, Quebec H2W 2J2
Tel: 1-800-227-5897 or 844-5897
Fax: 844-5894
E-mail: bbvenue@mlink.net
Victorian house centrally located in Latin Quarter.

Hospitality Montreal Relay
3977 Rue Laval Street
Montreal, Quebec H2W 2H9
Tel: 287-9635
Fax: 287-1007
E-mail: pearson@videotron.ca
Arranges accommodations in private homes, complete breakfasts included.

Auberge Internationale de Montréal
1030 Mackay
Montreal, Quebec H3G 2H1
Tel: 843-3317
Fax: 934-3251
E-mail: info@ajmontreal.qc.ca
Rents rooms year-round.

Collège Français
5155 Rue De Gaspé
Montreal, Quebec H2T 2A1
Tel: 495-2581
Fax: 279-5131
Rents rooms year-round.

Concordia University Residences
7141 Rue Sherbrooke Ouest
Montreal, Quebec H4B 1R6
Tel: 848-4756
Rents rooms from mid-May to the end of August.

Résidence de L'Université de Montréal
2350 Rue Edouard Montpetit
Montreal, Quebec H3T 1J4
Tel: 343-6531
Fax: 343-2353
Rents rooms from mid-May to the end of August.

Résidence des étudiants de L'Université McGill
3935 Rue University
Montreal, Quebec H3A 2B4
Tel: 398-6367
Fax: 398-6770
Rents rooms from mid-May to mid-August.

Where to Eat

What To Eat

The French passion for fine cuisine means dining out is a pleasure. There is no shortage of restaurants (5,000) or varieties of cuisine. Although wine with the meal can be expensive, the food is often great value.

Where To Eat

EXPENSIVE
(Over $30 per person)

Auberge Le Vieux St-Gabriel
(Québécois), 420 Rue St-Gabriel
Tel: 878-3562
Fax: 878-4492

Beaver Club (French)
Hôtel Reine-Elizabeth
900 Blvd René-Lévesque Ouest
Tel: 861-3511
Fax: 954-2256

Café de Paris (French)
Hôtel Ritz-Carlton
1228 Rue Sherbrooke Ouest
Tel: 842-4212
Fax: 842-4907

Chez Delmo (seafood)
211 Notre-Dame Ouest
Tel: 849-4061

Chez La Mère Michel (French)
1209 Rue Guy
Tel: 934-0473 or 934-0709

Chez Pierre (French)
1263 Rue Labaelle
Tel: 843-5227
Fax: 849-8465

Gibby's (steaks and seafood)
298 Place d'Youville
Tel: 282-1837
Fax: 282-9771

Le Festin du Gouverneur (17th-century banquets)
Ile Ste-Héléne
Tel: 879-1141
Fax: 879-1315

Le Latini (Italian)
1130 Rue Jeanne-Mance
Tel: 861-3166
Fax: 861-8294

Le Saint-Amable (French)
410 Place Jacques-Cartier
Tel: 866-3471

Le Tour de Ville (French)
Radisson Gouverneurs
777 Rue University
Tel: 879-1370
Fax: 879-1761

Les Chenets (French)
2075 Rue Bishop
Tel: 844-1842
Fax: 844-0552

Les Halles (French)
1450 Rue Crescent
Tel: 844-2328
Fax: 849-1294

L'Habitant (French)
5010 Blvd Lalande
Pierrefonds
Tel: 684-4398.

Mediterraneo (Italian)
3500 St-Laurent
Tel: 844-0027
Fax: 844-9848

Milos (Greek)
5357 du Parc
Tel: 272-3522

Moishe's (steak house)
3961 Blvd St-Laurent
Tel: 845-3509
Fax: 845-9504

Rib 'n' Beef (steaks and seafood)
8105 Blvd Decarie
Tel: 735-1601
Fax: 735-1777

Toqué (French)
3842 St-Denis
Tel: 499-2084
Fax: 400-0292

Troika (Russian)
2171 Rue Crescent
Tel: 849-9333
Fax: 849-9334

MODERATELY EXPENSIVE
($20–$30 per person)

Alexandre (French)
1454 Rue Peel
Tel: 288-5105
Fax: 288-0932

Au Bain Marie (French)
1214 St-Andre
Tel: 286-9011
Fax: 385-1373

Bayou Brasil (Brazilian)
4552 St-Denis
Tel: 847-0088
Fax: 445-8764

Bazon (fusion)
2004 Hôtel de Ville
Tel: 526-4940

Biddle's Jazz & Ribs (ribs)
2060 Aylmer
Tel: 842-8656
Fax: 842-2665

Casa de Mateo (authentic Mexican)
440 St Francois Xavier
Tel: 844-7448
Fax: 844-4154

Casa Napoli (Italian)
6728 Rue St-Laurent
Tel: 274-4351
Fax: 274-3602

C'est La Vie (French)
Hôtel La Citadelle
410 Rue Sherbrooke Ouest
Tel: 844-8851
Fax: 844-0912

Chez Antoine Grill (coffee shop)
Radisson Gouverneurs
777 Rue University
Tel: 879-1370

Chez Bernard (French)
275 Rue Notre-Dame Ouest
Tel: 288-4288
Fax: 288-5403

Chez Desjardins (seafood)
1175 Rue Mackay
Tel: 866-9741

Chez Queux (French)
158 Rue St-Paul Est
Tel: 866-5194
Fax: 866-7758

Hélène de Champlain (French)
200 Tour de l'isle
île Ste-Hélén
Tel: 395-2424

Italasia (fusion)
4833 St-Laurent
Tel: 281-8008
Fax: 281-5556

Katsura (Japanese)
2170 Rue de la Montagne
Tel: 849-1172
Fax: 849-1705

La Bodega (Spanish)
3456 Avenue du Parc
Tel: 849-2030
Fax: 849-2946

La Boucherie (steak and seafood)
343 St-Paul Est
Tel: 866-1515
Fax: 866-5535

La Campagnola (Italian)
1229 de la Montagne
Tel: 866-3234
Fax: 876-4028
La Campannina (Italian)
2022 Rue Stanley
Tel: 845-1852
Fax: 845-3763
La Louisiane (Cajun)
5850 Sherbrooke Ouest
Tel: 369-3073
Fax: 369-3702
La Lutetia (French)
Hôtel de la Montagne
1430 Rue de la Montagne
Tel: 288-5656
Fax: 288-9658
La Main à la Pâte (speciality pasta)
1187 Van Horne
Tel: 271-1187
La Marée (French)
404 Place Jacques Cartier
Tel: 861-8126
Fax: 861-3944
Le Père St-Vincent (French)
429 Rue St-Vincent
Tel: 397-9610
Fax: 878-3627
La Piazzetta (Italian)
4097 St-Denis
Tel: 847-0184
Fax: 847-0129
La Rapière (French)
1155 Metcalf
Tel: 871-8920
Fax: 871-1923
La Sila (Italian)
2040 Rue St-Denis
Tel: 844-5083
Fax: 282-6519
LaVenture (French)
438 Place Jacques-Cartier
Tel: 866-9439
Fax: 866-3044
Le Caveau (French)
2063 Rue Victoria
Tel: 844-1624
Fax: 844-0854
Le Centaure (French)
Hippodrome Blue Bonnets
7440 Blvd Decaire
Tel: 739-2741
Fax: 340-2025
L'Express (Bistro)
3927 St-Denis
Tel: 845-5333
Fax: 845-7576
Le Fripon (French)
436 Place Jacques-Cartier

Tel: 861-1386
Fax: 861-7748
Le Mas des Oliviers (French)
1216 Rue Bishop
Tel: 861-6733
Fax: 861-7838
Le Relais Terrapin (continental)
295 Rue St-Charles Ouest
Longueil
Tel: (450) 677-6378
Fax: (450) 677-2881
Les Quatre Canards (continental)
Le Château Bronont
90 Rue Stanstead
Bromont
Tel: (450) 534-3433
Fax: (450) 534-0835
Les Trois Arches (French)
11131 Rue Meighen
Pierrefonds
Tel: 683-8200
Fax: 683-5028
Modigliani (Italian/French)
1251 Guilford
Tel: 522-0422
Fax: 527-0948
Porto Fino (Italian)
2040 Rue de la Montagne
Tel: 849-2225
Restaurant Rustic (steak and seafood)
47 Blvd St-Jean Baptiste
Tel: (450) 691-2444
Fax: (450) 691-6061
Restaurant Szechuan (Chinese)
400 Rue Notre-Dame Ouest
Tel: 844-4456
Fax: 844-7235
Resto-Bistro La Chronique (fusion)
99 Rue Laurier Ouest
Tel: 271-3095
Fax: 271-4770
Tonnerre de Brest (crêpes)
1134 Van Horne
Tel: 278-6061
Ty-Breiz Crêperie Bretonne (crêpes)
933 rue Rachel Ouest
Tel: 521-1444
Fax: 527-6434
Vaudeville (French)
361 Bernard Ouest
Tel: 495-8258

MODERATE
($10–$20 per person)

Alpenhaus (Swiss)
1279 Rue St-Marc
Tel: 935-2285
Fax: 935-7272
Asha (Indian)
3490 Rue Park
Tel: 844-3178
Brisket (deli)
1073 Côte du Beaver Hall
Tel: 878-3641
Fax: 878-3843
Brochetterie du Vieux-Port (steak and seafood)
39 Rue St-Paul Est
Tel: 866-3175
Fax: 866-6171
Café Ciné Lumière (bistro)
5163 St-Laurent
Tel: 495-1796
Café Sarejevo (Bosnian)
2080 Clark
Tel: 284-5629
Chez la mère Tucker/Mother Tucker's (steak and seafood)
1175 Place du Frère André
Tel: 866-5525
Fax: 871-1896
Chez Lévesque (French)
1030 Rue Laurier Ouest
Tel: 279-7355
Fax: 279-1337
El Coyte Restaurant-Bar (Mexican)
1202 Rue Bishop
Tel: 875-7082
Fax: 388-2222
El Toro (steak house)
1647 Rue Fleury Est
Tel: 388-8676
La Bourgade (French)
Hôtel Bonaventure Hilton
1 Place Bonaventure
Tel: 878-2332
Fax: 878-1442
La Cage aux Sports (BBQ and ribs)
395 Le Moyne
Tel: 288-1115
Fax: 288-1116
La Casa Grècque (Greek)
200 Prince-Arthur Est
Tel: 842-6098
Fax: 842-5888
La Maison VIP (Chinese)
1077 rue Clark
Tel: 861-1943
La Marguerite (French)
1472 Rue Crescent

Tel: 284-0307
Fax: 288-9764
Le Biftèque (steak house)
6705 Côte de Liesse
Tel: 739-6336
Fax: 739-1173
L'Etoile des Indes/Star of India
(Indian)
1806 Ste-Catherine Ouest
Tel: 932-8330
Le Keg (Canadian)
25 Rue St-Paul Est
Tel: 871-9093
Fax: 871-9818
Le Montréalais (Bistro)
Hôtel Reine-Elizabeth
900 Blvd René-Lévesque Ouest
Tel: 861-3511
Fax: 954-2873
Le Paris (French)
1812 Rue Ste-Catherine Ouest
Tel: 937-4898
Le Piemontais (Italian)
1145 Rue de Bullion
Tel: 861-8122
Fax: 861-6041
Naritha's Kitchen (Southeast Asian)
9 Duluth Est
Tel: 845-4717
Nil Bleu Restaurant (Ethiopian vegetarian dishes)
3706 St-Denis
Tel: 285-4628
Fax: 285-2304
Pierre du Calvet (French)
415 Rue Bonesecours
Tel: 849-3535
Fax: 282-0456
Pizza Mella (Italian)
107 Prince-Arthur Est
Tel: 849-4680
Fax: 849-6987
Publix Bar Resto Café (Bistro)
3554 St-Laurent
Tel: 284-9233
Fax: 284-3670
Restaurant Eduardo (Italian)
404 Duluth Est
Tel: 843-3330
Restaurant des Gouverneurs (international)
458 Place Jacques-Cartie
Tel: 861-0188
Restaurant Witloof (Belgian)
3619 St-Denis
Tel: 281-0100
Fax: 281-6789
Solmar (Portuguese)
111 Rue St-Paul Est

Drinking Notes

The legal drinking age in Quebec is 18. Some establishments (especially on Prince-Arthur Street) do not have a liquor license but allow customers to bring their own wine.

Microbrewery beers, produced by small, independent breweries, are very popular among Montrealers. Brands to try include: Boreale (Blond, Rousse, Noir and Fort); Brasal; La Maudite; La Fin du Monde; Blanche de Chablis; Cheval Blanc.

A wide selection of bars lines the St-Laurent strip between Sherbrooke and Mont-Royal. Also try out those along Rue St-Denis and Crescent Street.
Jello Bar

151 Ontario Est
Tel: 285-2621
Retro cocktail lounge specializing in martinis.
Shed Cafe
3515 St-Laurent
Tel: 842-0220
A fixture on the Main. Patio seating in summer.
La Cervoise
4457 St-Laurent
Tel: 843-6586
Beer brewed on the premises. Happy-hour specials.
Bar St-Sulpice
1680 Rue St-Denis
Tel: 844-9458
Old house in the Latin Quarter. Patio in summer.

Tel: 861-4562
Fax: 878-4764
Taj Mahal (Indian)
5026 Sherbrooke Ouest
Tel: 482-0076

Wrapps (Vegetarian)
5124A Sherbrooke Ouest
Tel: 482-8542

INEXPENSIVE
(under $10 per person)
Ben's Delicatessen
990 Blvd de Maisonneuve Ouest
Tel: 844-1000
Café Santropol (sandwiches, vegetarian dishes)
3990 St-Urbain
Tel: 842-3110.
Café Souvenir (breakfast café)
1261 Bernard Ouest
Tel: 948-5259
Euro-Deli (Italian)
3619 St-Laurent
Tel: 843-7853
Frites Alors (Belgian)
5235 Avenue du Parc
Tel: 948-2219
Just Noodles (Chinese/Thai)
2061 Ste-Catherine Ouest
Tel: 989-5826
Le Commensal (vegetarian)
1720 Rue St-Denis
Tel: 845-0248
Pizzelli Restaurant Bar (Italian)

4250 St-Denis
Tel: 849-2456
Schwartz's (Jewish deli)
3895 Rue St-Laurent
Tel: 842-4813

Food Facts

The city's tradition for find food dates from the 19th century, when Montrealers welcomed boats carrying tea from China, spices from India, and wines and spirits from Europe. But variety comes from France, famed for its food, and from immigrants, who began arriving in the early 1900s and are arriving still, woks and *paella* pans in hand. Added to this sophistication is the hearty country fare that dates from Quebec's early inhabitants and their need for "fuel food". Look for dishes like *tourtieres* (meat pies), *feves au lard* (pork and beans), *cretons* (coarse pork pate), and *tarte au sucre* (sugar pie). Don't forget, too, that Quebec supplies more than 90 percent of the maple syrup found on Canada's tables.

Attractions

Things To Do

Casino de Montréal: 1 Avenue de Casino, Ile Notre Dame, tel: 392-2746. The French Pavilion for Expo 67 now houses an enormous Las Vegas-style casino. The four floors contain over 2,500 slot machines and numerous electronic games, as well as blackjack, roulette and baccarat tables. Jeans and sneakers are banned. Many hotels offer special casino packages. Open daily 11am–3am.

Dow Planetarium: 1000 Rue Saint Jacques Ouest, tel: 872-4530; fax: 872-3102; web: www.planetarium. montreal.qc.ca. A Zeiss projector and 100 auxiliaries project the sky on a dome screen 20 meters in diameter. Shows are narrated in both French and English and change every few months. Open 12.30–8.30pm. Special reservations are needed for handicapped people.

Montréal Biodôme: 4777 Avenue Pierre de Coubertin, tel: 868-3000; fax: 868-3065; web: www. villemontreal.qc.ca/biodome. Open daily 9am–5pm. Features four eco-systems – a tropical rainforest, a Laurentian forest, the St Lawrence river, and the polar ecosystem.

Montreal Botanical Garden and Insectarium: 4101 Rue Sherbrooke Est, tel: 872-1400. This is the third most important botanical garden in the world after London and Berlin, and covers 180 acres (73 hectares). Included in this area are 62 acres (25 hectares) of Japanese gardens, which include 10 exhibition greenhouses and the largest bonsai and penjing collections outside of Asia. An Insectarium houses more than 350,000 insect specimens from around the world. There are special exhibitions at Christmas, Easter and Halloween. The garden is open 8am–sundown. The Greenhouses open 9am–5pm, the boutique is open 10am–5pm, and the Insectarium 10am–5pm.

Areas of Interest

Boulevard St-Laurent: International restaurants and specialty stores line this boulevard known as "The Main". Originally settled by Jewish merchants, The Main is home to Greeks, Slavs, Portuguese and Latin Americans. For smoked meat, *The Main* restaurant and *Schwartz's* are well-known.

Chinatown: This section of Montreal – bounded by Blvd René-Lévesque, Rue Viger, Blvd St-Laurent, and Rue Jeanne-Mance – is at its most active on the weekends.

Old Montreal: A 100-acre section of Montreal containing some of the greatest concentrations of 17th-, 18th- and 19th-century buildings in North America. In the 1960s efforts began to restore both the interior and exterior of Old Montreal's buildings. The area is always bustling with activity.

Old Port: On the waterfront, this important part of Old Montreal offers many summer and winter activities. River cruises depart from these shores.

Place Jacques Cartier: Formerly a marketplace, Place Jacques Cartier in Old Montreal is now a flower market and handicrafts center and is a favorite spot among artists and young people.

Prince-Arthur Street: This lively street is largely reserved for pedestrians. Greek, Vietnamese and Italian restaurants are found in abundance here. In the summer, street musicians and magicians entertain passersby.

Rue Crescent: On this lively street, the "older brother" of Rue St-Denis, are renowned art galleries, antique dealers, jewelry and gift shops, as well as exceptional restaurants.

Rue St-Denis (Latin Quarter): Victorian buildings abound on this street, where the French élite lived at the turn of the century. Make your way here for the densest concentration of restaurants, boutiques and night spots in Montreal.

Square St-Louis: On Avenue Laval, this square is lined with some of the most attractive architecture in Montreal. Generations of poets and artists have been attracted to the square, whose houses were restored in the 1960s.

Underground City

Nearly 14 miles (22 km) of passageways make up the weatherproof, climate-controlled Underground City, which lets you avoid the cold of winter or the heat of summer. The underground network has a railway station, two bus terminals, seven hotels, two department stores, 1,600 boutiques, 200 restaurants, 40 banks, 30 cinemas, two exhibition halls and 1,200 businesses.

Churches

Notre-Dame-de-Bonsecours Chapel: 400 St-Paul Est, tel: 845-9991. Open 1 November to 30 April 10am–3pm; 1 May to 31 October 9am–5pm. A Catholic chapel known as the Sailors' Church, it was built on the remains of the wooden chapel built for Marguerite Bourgeoys in 1657. The Marguerite Bourgeoys Museum is in the basement, open daily except Monday, 1 May to 31 October 9am–4.30pm, 1 November to 30 April 10am–3pm. The rooftop lookout gives a fine panoramic view of the waterfront.

Notre-Dame Basilica: Place d'Armes, tel: 849-1070. Montreal's oldest parish is well-known for works of art and its neo-Gothic architecture. Concerts are held here throughout the year. The church is open October to July Monday–Saturday 8.30am–6pm, Sunday 1.30–6pm; July to October Monday–Saturday 8.30am–8pm, Sunday 1.30–8pm. There are guided tours July to October.

St Joseph's Oratory: 3800 Rue Queen Mary, tel: 733-8211, open daily 6am–9.30pm, admission free. Museum open daily 10am–5pm, donations suggested. Built in 1924, this mountainside basilica is the world's largest pilgrimage center devoted to St Joseph, the patron saint of Canada. The interior is rather uninteresting, but the dome of the basilica, one of the largest in the world, is remarkable. Behind the basilica is the sanctuary, tomb and votive chapel of Brother André, the monk who constructed the first small chapel to St Joseph in 1904.

Parks

Angrignon Park and Farm: A large farm with over 100 animals, offering guided tours and special programs for children. The farm is open daily June to Labour Day 9am–5pm, admission free. The park is open year round and popular winter activities include ice skating and cross-country skiing. For more details, tel: 872-4689 or 872-3816.
Ile-Sainte-Hélène: This park offers swimming pools and a summer amusement park and is also the site for the International Festival of Fireworks each May. Admission to the island is free but there are fees for the various activities offered. To check on specific events, tel: 872-6093. For information on La Ronde (the summer amusement park), tel: 872-4537.
Mont Royal Park: Reached from either Camillien Houde Parkway or Remembrance Road. This park of 495 acres (200 hectares), one of Montreal's favorite places to relax, overlooks the city and the region. A variety of recreational activities, from cross-country skiing to birdwatching, are offered. To find out more about special sporting or recreation events, tel: 872-6559.
Olympic Park: This site of the 1976 Olympic Games includes the world's tallest inclined tower, a stadium that houses both the Expos, baseball games and rock concerts, and a public swimming center. For more information, tel: 252-8687; web: www.vio.gouv. qc.ca.

Cruises

Amphi Tour: An amphibious bus tours the land and water of Old Montreal and the Old Port. Open 1 May to 31 October 10am–midnight, tel: 849-5181.
Croisières Bellevue: Open May to end-September, these cruises leave from Ste-Anne Locks daily except Mondays at 1.30pm, 3.30pm and 7.30pm, tel: (450) 457-5245.
Croisières de Port de Montréal: Guided cruises in the afternoon and dinner/dance cruises in the evening from May to October. Departures are from the Clock Tower Pier and the Jacques Cartier Pier. For reservations and information , tel: 842-3871 or 1-800-667-3131.
Lachine Rapid Tours: 105 Rue de la Commune. A 90-minute jet-boat trip down the Lachine rapids. Open summer 10am–6pm. Costs $48 per person; group rates are also available. For reservations, tel: 284-9607.
Le Bateau-Mouche: 90 St-Paul West, tel: 849-9952. Glass-topped boats offer a distinctive perspective of the city, from early May to early October. Daytime cruises last an hour, evening dinner cruises last 3 hours.

Tours

There are many sightseeing companies in Montreal. Some focus on standard tourist attractions, others on architecture and urban restoration.

FLIGHTSEEING
Delco Aviation: Flights over Montreal in a sea plane. The views are spectacular. The company also offers destinations outside of Montreal. The fee is $200 for the flight (one to five people), which is available daily 8am–8pm, tel: 663-4311.

BUS TOURS
Several companies offer narrated tours in buses, vans or limousines. Many offer walking tours as well. The length of tours varies, and many options are available. Check with the companies below for more information.
Gray Line, 1001 Rue du Square Dorchester at Infotouriste Office, tel: 934-1222.
Hertz Tourist Guides, tel: 739-7454.
Visites de Montréal, tel: 933-6674
Guidatour, tel: 844-4021.
Taxi Lasalle, tel: 277-2552.

CARRIAGE RIDES
Calèches Boisvert Inc.: Departures from Notre-Dame Street, Square Dorchester, Mont Royal Park, Place d'Armes, and Place Jacques Cartier. The fee is around $50 an hour, tel: 653-0751.

WALKS
Heritage Montreal: Tours of Montreal architecture, tel: 286-2662.
Step on Guides: 1302 St-Antoine. City tours lasting 3 hours; tours of Old Montreal and the Underground City, tel: 935-5131

Culture

In addition to their permanent collections, many of the museums listed below have changing exhibits. Call for details of special exhibits and events, or check the arts section in the newspapers.

Biosphere: Parc-des-Îles, Île Ste Hélène, tel: 283-5000 or 496-8300; fax: 283-5021; e-mail: biosphere.ec.gc.ca. open 10am–5pm Tuesday to Sunday. Free to children under six. An interactive museum about the St-Lawrence river and the Great Lakes.

Canadian Center for Architecture: 1920 Rue Baile, tel: 939-7000; fax: 939-7020; web: www.cca.qc.ca. The only collection of its kind, it includes 20,000 prints and drawings, 45,000 photographs and architectural archives. Open Wednesday to Friday 11am–6pm, Thursday 11am–8pm, Saturday and Sunday 11am–5pm.

Canadian Railway Museum: 122A Rue St-Pierre, St Constant, tel: (450) 632-2410. Open daily 5 May to 2 September 9am–5pm; weekends and holidays 2 September to 20 October. Significant collection of railway, tramway and steam locomotive equipment. Has daily tram rides and Sunday train rides.

Château Ramezay Museum: 280 Rue Notre-Dame Est, tel: 861-3708, fax: 861-8317, e-mail: mcr1@globetrotter.ca. Housed in an impressive residence built in 1705, this ethnographic museum has exhibitions of artefacts, paintings and costumes. Open daily 1 June to 30 September 10am–6pm, daily except Monday 1 October to 1 June 10am–4.30pm.

Lachine Museum: 110 Chemin de Lasalle, Lachine, tel: 634-3471 ext 346 or 332, fax: 637-6784. As well as furniture and artifacts dating from the early colonial period, this museum also features the story of the early commerce and industrial history of Lachine in the 19th century. Open Wednesday to Sunday 11.30am– 4.30pm, Admission free.

Marc-Aurèle Fortin Museum: 118 St-Pierre St, tel: 845-6108, fax 845-6100. The main collection is devoted entirely to the world of Canadian artist Marc-Aurèle Fortin but there are also exhibitions on other Quebec painters. Open Tuesday to Sunday 11am–5pm.

McCord Museum of Canadian History: 690 Rue Sherbrooke Ouest, tel: 398-7100, fax 398-5045, web: www.musée-mccord.ca. One of the most important history museums in Canada, the McCord owns Impressive collections of paintings, prints, drawings, textiles, decorative arts, and photographic archives dating from the 18th century to the present day.

Montreal History Center: 335 Place d'Youville, tel: 872-3207, web: www.ville.montreal.qc.ca/chm/htm. Offers interpretations of Montreal's history.

Montreal Museum of Decorative Arts – Le Château Dufresne: 2200 Crescent, tel: 284-1252, fax: 284-0123, web: www.madm.org. Houses the Liliane and David M. Stewart collection of international design dating from 1940. There are also regular exhibitions on furniture, glassware, textiles and ceramics. Open Wednesday to Sunday 11am–5pm. Closed Monday and Tuesday. Children under 12 are admitted free.

Montreal Museum of Fine Arts: 1379 Rue Sherbrooke Ouest, tel: 285-1600, fax: 285-4018, web: www.mbam.qc.ca. Founded in 1860, this museum is the oldest in Canada. Canadian and Quebec art are featured and the museum owns important collections of engravings, sculptures, paintings, furniture and silverware. Traveling exhibitions of masterworks are featured regularly.

Lectures, films, workshops and concerts are held in the auditorium. Special children's activities and guided tours are also offered.

Musée d'Art Contemporain de Montréal: 185 Ste-Catherine Ouest, tel: 847-6226. Features works of art created after 1940. A specialized reference center is available for consultation. Open Tuesday to Sunday 10am–6pm. The reference center closes at 5pm and for the weekend. Tel: 847-6906. Open 11am–6pm, Wednesday until 9pm. Closed Monday.

Musée des Soeurs Grises: 1185 St-Mathieu St, tel: 932-7724, fax 937-0533. Features the tomb, religious objects and death chamber of Mother d'Youville. Open Wednesday to Sunday 1.30–4pm. Admission free.

Redpath Museum: 859 Rue Sherbrooke Ouest, tel: 398-4086, fax: 398-3185, www.mcgill.ca/redpath. Houses a fossil exhibition with dinosaur bones and an anthropological collection including two Egyptian mummies. Open Monday to Friday 9am–5pm, Sunday 1–5pm, closed Friday from Fête National to Labor Day. Admission free.

Saint-Laurent Art Museum: 615 Blvd Ste-Croix, tel: 747-7367, fax: 747-8892, e-mail: mas101@globetrotter.qc.ca . In the former chapel of Collège Saint-Laurent. Features a permanent collection of Quebec art and handicrafts from wood sculpture to textiles and Amerindian art. Concerts are frequently held on Sunday. Open Thursday to Sunday 1–5pm, Wednesday 1–9pm. Closed Monday and Tuesday.

Stewart Museum at the Fort: 20 Chemin Tour de l'Ile, tel: 861-6701, fax 284-0123, web: www.mlink.net/stewart. This museum of Canadian history has a unique collection of firearms, ancient maps, scientific and navigation instruments and articles illustrating the daily lives of Canadian settlers. Open daily 10am–5pm. Closed Tuesday September to April.

Art Galleries

Articule: 4001 Berri, tel: 842-9686. Canadian contemporary art and media installations.
Canadian Guild of Crafts Quebec: 2025 Rue Peel, tel: 849-6091. Inuit art and Canadian crafts such as blown glass, porcelain and ceramics.
Galerie Dominion: 1438 Rue Sherbrooke Ouest, tel: 845-7471. Canadian and international painting and sculpture from the 19th and 20th centuries.
Galerie Simon Blais: 4521 Clark, tel: 849-1165. Canadian contemporary art.

Concerts & Operas

Montreal offers music from classical to various ethnic music groups. For events on a particular day, consult the arts sections of the city's newspapers. The list below includes Montreal's permanent companies.
McGill Chamber Orchestra is one of Montreal's oldest chamber groups, and it plays in the Place des Arts and the Eglise Saint-Jean-Baptiste.
Metropolitan Orchestra of Montreal, young musicians perform at the Theatre Maisonneuve, tel: 598-0870.
Montreal Symphony Orchestra has an international reputation, and performs at Place des Arts and in the city's parks during summertime, tel: 842-3402.
Opéra de Montréal was founded in 1980 and stages four or five operas a year. Considered one of the 10 best companies in North America.

Ballet

The **Grand Ballets Canadiens** has been performing for more than 30 years. Their repertoire includes classical and modern pieces and work by new Canadian composers and choreographers. Tel: 790-2787, web: www.infoarts. net (for listings of all current arts events, spectacles and performances.)

Theaters

Montreal offers at least 10 major French theater companies and many smaller theaters (see *Yellow Pages* of telephone book for full listing).

English Theaters
Centaur Theater, 453 Rue St-François Xavier, tel: 288-3161.
Saidye Bronfman Center, 5170 Chemin de la Côte Ste-Catherine, tel: 739-2301.

French Theaters
Théâtre Saint-Denis, 1594 Rue St-Denis, tel: 849-4211.
Théâtre D'Aujourd'hui, 3888 St-Denis, tel: 282-3900.
Théâtre de la Chappelle, 3700 St-Dominique, tel: 843-7738, fax: 987-9754, e-mail: tlc@cam.org.
Théâtre du Nouveau Monde, 84 Rue Ste-Catherine Ouest, tel: 866-8667.
Théâtre du Rideau Vert, 4664 Rue St-Denis, tel: 845-0267.
Théâtre Quat-Sous, 100 des Pins Est, tel: 845-7277.

Movies

As the host of major film festivals, Montreal's selection of films is noteworthy. There are close to 100 movie theaters in the city, so check the newspapers for showings and locations. Some of the specialized cinemas include:

Cinéma du Parc, 3575 Park, tel: 287-7272.
Cinémathèque Québécoise, 335 Blvd de Maisonneuve Est, tel: 842-9763, fax: 842-1816, web: www.cinematheque.qc.ca.
IMAX Theater, Vieux Port de Montréal, Corner St-Laurent and de la Commune, tel: 496-IMAX (4629).

Public Libraries

There are a number of public libraries in Montreal. The Montreal Central Library is located at 1210 Rue Sherbrooke Est, tel: 872-5923. Other resource libraries include:

Nightlife

It is worth strolling round Montreal at night as the streets are a buzz of activity. Clubs and bars provide varied avenues for entertainment. Check listings in the newspapers for up-to-date happenings. Cocktail lounges are open until 2am, bars and cabarets until 3am. Major hotels have nightclubs with discos, comic shows and other entertainment.
    Dance clubs come and go in Montreal. The weekly arts and entertainment newspapers give up-to-date listings and descriptions of the clubs.
Balattou, 4372 St-Laurent, tel: 845-5447. Tropical mix of soca, salsa, rai, reggae and dancehall.
Bar Minuit, 115 Laurier W., tel: 271-2110.
Le Belmont, 4423 St-Laurent, tel: 845-8443.
Salsatheque, 1220 Peel, tel: 845-0016. Latin dance.
Sky, 1474 Ste Catherine E (a gay dance club), tel: 529-6969.

Bibliothèque Nationale du Québec in three locations (tel: 873-1100):
• Saint-Sulpice Building, 1700 Rue St-Denis.
• Conservation et Siège Social, 2275 Holt.
• Aegidius Fauteux Building, 4499 Avenue de L'Esplanade.
Collections spéciales et Archives privées, 125 Sherbrooke Ouest, tel: 873-1100 (for all buildings).

Jazz

L'Air du Temps, 191 Rue St-Paul Ouest, tel: 842-2003. Local and international talent. Opens at 5pm.
Biddle's, 2060 Rue Aylmer, tel: 842-8656.
Café Sarajevo 2080 Clark, tel: 284-5629.
Café Thélème 311 Ontario E, tel: 845-7932.
Upstairs, 1254 Mackay, tel: 931-6808.

Festivals

Calendar of Events

Festivals of all kind abound in Montreal – including art, music, film, theater, sports, and folk dancing – demonstrating the city's truly international character. The main season for celebration is May to September. The Calender of Events, available at information centers in the city, is a detailed list of all festivals and celebrations. The main information office is located at 1010 Ste-Catherine Ouest, tel: 844-4056. The Société de Fêtes et Festivals de Québec also publishes an extensive list of festivals in the Montreal area, tel: 252-3037, web: www.festivals.qc.ca.

January–February
La Fête des Neiges, mid-January to early February: snow sculptures, cross-country skiing competitions, barrel-jumping, dog-sled races, ice-canoe races, folk dancing, strolling makeup artists and clowns.

April
Théâtre du Monde

May
International Children's Theater Festival of Quebec
International Festival of Young Cinema.
La Super Enfant-Fête
La Tour des Enfants
Montreal Air Show
Montreal International Chinese Film Festival
Montreal International Mime Festival (held at Complexe Desjardins and along Rue St-Denis)
Museum Day (Open House at 16 of the city's museums)
Sun Carnival

Super Motorcross Laurentide
Theater Festival of the Americas

June
Antiques Bonaventure: the dealers descend
Beer Mundial: taste over 250 brands of beer from 25 countries
Benson & Hedges International Fireworks Competition
Carifête: festival of dance and music from the Caribbean
Festival du Nouveau Cinéma de Montréal: film buff's heaven
Fringe Festival: theatre festival presenting new works by young artists from around the world
Jour de St-Jean-Baptiste: Quebec's national holiday on 24 June
Lachine International Folk Dancing Festival
La Classique Cycliste de Montréal.
Le Tour de L'Ile de Montréal.
Molson Grand Prix: part of the Formula One world circuit
Montréal International Music Competition
Worldwide Kite Rendez-vous

July
Drummondville World Folklore Festival
Festival Juste Pour Rire/Just for Laughs Festival
Lachine Music Festival
Lanaudière International Festival: lots of classical music
Montreal International Jazz Festival: big names in concert halls plus free outdoor concerts and carnival atmosphere in the streets

August
Du Maurier Open: an international tennis competition
Haut-Richelieu Hot Air Balloon Festival and North American Championship
Lasalle Car Festival
Les Fêtes Gourmandes Internationales de Montréal
Les Francofolies de Montréal: a celebration of francophone songs
Montreal World Film Festival
Rock Sans Frontières
St-Jean-sur-Richelieu Hot Air Balloons Festival
World Footbag Championship: the "Hacky sack" competition

September
Black and Blue Weekend
Festival Internationale de Nouvelle Dance: in odd-numbered years only
Marathon de L'Ile de Montréal
Montreal International Marathon: 42-km run for both professionals and amateurs
Montreal International Rock Festival
Montreal International Music Festival: classical music gets its turn

October
Autumn Moon Festival: in Chinatown near the beginning of month
Canadiens ice hockey games resume at the Molson Centre
International Festival of New Cinema and Video.
International Scientific Film Festival
Montreal New Music Festival

November/December
As the cold weather sets in, social activities grow fewer, except for a brief flurry of festivities around Christmastime.

Just for Laughs

For 10 days from mid-July to early August, Montreal hosts the Festival Juste Pour Rire, or, the Just for Laughs Festival. At least 500 performers from more than a dozen countries stage around 300 shows, both indoors and out, making this the world's largest bilingual comedy show. These shows are sometimes filmed and shown around the world. There are also acrobats, street comedians, mime artists, clowns and other comedic characters, all primed and guaranteed to make you laugh. Many people make it an entire month in Montreal, having stayed on for the laughs after going to the International Jazz Festival, which runs from early to mid-July.

Shopping

General

Montreal, Canada's fashion capital, offers an astounding number of boutiques and department stores. Gourmet food, handicraft objects and fashionable clothes are in abundance.

Montrealers are such avid shoppers that they have coined a word of their own: *le magasinage* warrants a separate entry in the French Robert dictionary. No wonder the Montreal economists worry whenever the consumer spending rate drops a few points!

Shopping can take a variety of forms. Everyday shopping is on local streets, some reflecting the bygone charm of a small-town main street, others renovated and revitalized. Busy weekend shopping is in a string of trendy regional shopping malls around Montreal, the teenagers' favorite haunts. These shopping centers showcase local clothing manufacturers turned retailers such as Le Château or San Francisco – small concerns turned big by going public through a government-sponsored stock savings plan. This is just one of many business success stories in Montreal of late.

There is also **window shopping**, and Montrealers go for it with their characteristic verve, especially on downtown **Rue Ste-Catherine**, where musing and browsing extends way past store hours and into the wee hours of the night.

For the well-to-do, Montreal, with its weekly auctions, antique dealers and fur salons, is a bargain when shopping for **furs** (furriers the world over flock to Montreal every year for the international fair), **Inuit art**, **antiques** and collectibles. Furriers

concentrate in the rundown fur district along **Boulevard de Maisonneuve**, east of Rue Union.

There are scores of **art galleries** in the Victorian row houses of **Rue Sherbrooke**, in what used to be called the Golden Square Mile, an exclusive area on the south slope of Mont Royal where the business tycoons of the Victorian era built expansive villas, many of which still stand.

Handicrafts by Quebec artisans are for sale in the **Rue St-Paul** boutiques of Old Montreal, in Le Rouet stores or at the Canadian Guild of Crafts on Rue Peel. **Rue Notre-Dame**, east of Rue Atwater, boasts antique dealers specializing in wondrous Victorian furniture and European goods.

For followers of **fashion**, Montreal is a treasure-trove. Textile and clothing represents 60 percent of manufacturing jobs in the city. Montrealers follow fashion with passion, and they love to parade the latest European trends on downtown streets. Watch for the up-and-coming in the dramatic store windows of Rue Ste-Catherine, the trendy boutiques of downtown **Place Ville-Marie** and **Place Montreal Trust**, and the lavish designer stores of Ogilvy's on Rue Ste-Catherine, Holt Renfrew on Rue Sherbrooke, and in Westmount Square and Rockland Shopping Center in the posh anglophone districts of Westmount and Town of Mount Royal.

If it's **bargains** you're looking for, shop right off the factory rack in the Chabanel Fashion District on **Rue Chabanel** west of Rue St-Laurent. This may seem a bit overwhelming at first. Rue Chabanel sports six-story buildings packed with everything you can imagine: jeans, bathing suits, lingerie, sweaters, and more! On Saturday morning, regulars (often the women who work in these modern-day sweat shops) go through these floors like nobody's business. Newcomers just gawk and zigzag through this unique shopping experience.

On Sunday in Old Montreal, while others recovers from Saturday

night, bargain hunters flock to the clothes discounters along **Rue Notre-Dame** east of Rue McGill.

Shopping in Montreal can take you into some of the more colorful neighborhoods in the city. On **Rue Laurier** in Outremont, a posh French district on the northern slope of Mont Royal, the merchants have a reputation for delivering the very latest European trends in clothes, **food** (world renowned pâtissier Lenôtre of France opened its first North American store on Rue Laurier) or home fashions.

Rue St-Denis, its cafés and restaurant terraces spilling on to the sidewalk, is known as the Quartier Latin for its student population. Rue St-Denis has gone from late granola to early avant-garde, and is now venturing into **design** and **decoration**, offering shoppers beautiful things for the home. Not to be missed is Arthur Quentin and, for coffee lovers, La Brûlerie. Also of interest is **Plaza St-Hubert**, a favorite with neighboring Greek, Italian and Middle-Eastern families. It comes alive in the spring, when preparations are under way for the famous weddings these communities celebrate.

Last but not least is Rue St-Laurent – **The Main** – a kind of no-man's-land between the mostly French districts of Eastern Montreal and the anglophone sectors of the westend. Successive flows of immigrants have left distinctive traces of their passage here. From Rue Viger northward, Chinese, Eastern Europeans, Greeks, Portuguese and Italians have carved niches.

The Chinese community, for example, has congregated around **Rue de la Gauchetière** and placarded bright red and yellow signs on the Victorian grey stones of the area. It is a pleasure to see whole families buying their weekly groceries on Sunday after the traditional Cantonese Dim Sum buffet in one of the local eateries.

Past Rue Sherbrooke, Hungarians and Polish Jews are still very present with their aromatic delis and sausages. Not to be missed are institutions like the

Montreal Pool Room with its steamés, and Schwartz's smoked meat sandwiches. Only a few Greek signs remain on Rue St-Laurent, the Greek community having since made its way to Avenue du Parc and Rue Jean-Talon. The Greeks are replaced by Portuguese immigrants with their clothing and ceramics stores.

Further north around Rue Jean-Talon is **Little Italy** with its espresso cafés, *gelateria* (Ice cream parlors) and *pasticeria* (pastry shops). Little Italy huddles round Marché Jean-Talon, one of the lesser known attractions of Montreal, where saris, tchadors and Mao shirts form a delightful tapestry. Wherever you hail from, you will have compatriots in Montreal.

Shopping Areas

Faubourg Ste-Catherine: 1616 Rue Ste-Catherine Ouest, tel: 939-3663. Reminiscent of New York's Fulton Market and Boston's Quincy Market, this shopping spot hosts fruit, vegetable and import stands and an array of restaurants and snack bars.

Atwater Market: 138 Rue Atwater, tel: 937-7754. Very lively on weekends, this market features specialty foods. Over 60 farm producers sell fresh fruit and vegetables.

Jean-Talon Market: 7075 Rue Casgrain, tel: 937-7754. In "Little Italy" and bordered by cheese counters, fishmongers and butchers shops. Has 100-plus farm producers.

Maisonneuve Market: 4375 Rue Ontario Est, tel: 937-7754. Outdoor market open May to October.

St-Jacques Market: Amherst and Ontario, tel: 937-7754. Open year-round, it offers fruit and vegetable stands in spring and summer and flowers and plants in the fall and winter.

Complexe Desjardins: 2 Complexe Desjardins, tel: 281-1870. Offering a huge number of boutiques, bars, and cinemas, this underground shopping center is decorated with fountains, trees and waterfalls.

Place Bonaventure, tel: 397-2205. Includes 135 shops with merchandise from all over the world. Restaurants, cinemas, banks, a post office and a supermarket are all located within this downtown shopping concourse.

Place Montreal Trust: McGill College/Ste-Catherine, tel: 843-8000. Five levels of boutiques and services. Direct access to the Metro.

Other shopping areas include Rue St-Denis, Boulevard St-Laurent, Avenue du Laurier, Rue Ste-Catherine, Rue Crescent and Rue Sherbrooke.

Department Stores

Eaton's: 677 Rue Ste-Catherine Ouest, tel: 284-8411. Quality and value are the trademarks of this department store, founded in 1869. The dining room in the downtown store has a unique art-deco decor.

Holt Renfrew: 1300 Rue Sherbrooke Ouest, tel: 842-5111. Fine fashion for men and women and designer clothes from Europe, Canada and the US.

Ogilvy: 1307 Rue Ste-Catherine Ouest, tel: 842-7711. Elite merchandise ranging from home fashions to high fashion.

Sport

Participant

Outdoor sports are very popular in every season. Information about all local facilities on offer can be obtained from Access Montreal, tel: 872-1111 or 872-2237 (24 hours).

BICYCLING

A network of cycle paths covers 140 miles (225 km) of Montreal – you can buy maps from sporting goods stores. Favorite routes include: Lachine Canal, the Seaway, Christophe Colomb and Berri Streets, Rachel Street, Angrignon Park and Mont Royal Park.

Vélo Québec, La Maison des Cyclistes, 1251 Rachel Est, tel: 521-8356, is an organization devoted to cycling. It provides brochures, guidebooks and information on paths.

Cycles can be rented from:

Bicycletterie J.R. Cyclery, 151 Rachel Est, tel: 843-6989. Monday to Wednesday 9am–6pm, Thursday to Friday 9am–9pm, Saturday 10am–5pm, Sunday 10am–3pm.

La Cordée Plain Air, 2159 Rue Ste-Catherine Est, tel: 524-1515.

Quadricycle International, Rue St-Laurent, tel: 849-9953. September, October, April and May open weekends 10.30am–8pm; June to September open daily 9.30am–midnight.

Velo Adventure, Promenade du Vieux Port de Montreal, tel: 847-0666. Monday to Friday 11am–6pm, weekends 9am–6pm.

BOATING

Sailing is possible May to September.

École de Voile de Lachine, 2105 Blvd St-Joseph, Lachine, tel: 634-4326. Private or group lessons, approved by the Quebec Sailing Federation. It also rents light sail boats and windsurfers.

RAFTING

Two companies run excursions: **Lachine Rapid Tours Inc.**, 511 Succursale Champlain, Lasalle, H8P 3J4, tel: 767-2230. **New World River Expeditions**, 100 Rouge River, Calumet (90 minutes northwest of Montreal), tel: 1-800-361-5033.

FISHING

There are numerous lakes and rivers around Montreal that provide great fishing spots. For specific suggestions, call the Ministère de l'Environnement et Faune for day-trip ideas, tel: 24–48 hours ahead at 873-3636.

GOLF

There are many golf courses in Montreal and the surrounding region. The following courses are close and open to non-members: **Fresh Meadows Golf Club**, 505 Elm Avenue, Beaconsfield, tel: 695-2661. Nine holes. **Golf Dorval**, 2000 Rue Reverchon, Dorval and 1455 Cardinal Avenue, tel: 631-4711 (both). Reservations needed on weekends; 36 holes. **Golf Municipal de Montréal**, Entrance at Viau, north of Sherbrooke, tel: 872-4653. Accessible by Metro. Reservations necessary 24 hours in advance. **Brossard Municipal Golf Course**, 4705 Rue Lapinière. Brossard, autoroute 10 Est, Exit 9, tel: (450) 923-7035.

HORSEBACK RIDING

For information, contact Québec à Cheval, tel: 252-3002, or the Fédération Equestre du Québec, tel: 252 3053.

JOGGING

Joggers can run in any of the city's parks; Mont Royal Park for its view over the city.

SKATING

Outdoor skating rinks are abundant in Montreal, and there are at least 21 indoor rinks. Ile-Notre-Dame has one of the largest rinks – it is a mile long. Other favorite spots include Lafontaine Park, Angrignon Park, and Mont Royal Park.

SKIING

Cross-country skiing is popular in many parks. The Botanical Garden has a winter trail that is very scenic. Downhill skiing is also available around Montreal. Beginners flock to Mont Royal, Hirondelles and Ignace-Bourget parks. Experts have unlimited opportunities less than an hour away in the Laurentians or in Estrie. For more details, tel: 872-1111.

SWIMMING

There are many indoor and outdoor pools open to the public. Listed below are a few of the possibilities: **Cégep du Vieux-Montréal** (indoor), 255 Rue Ontario Est, tel: 872-1178. **Centre Claude Robillard** (indoor), 1000 Rue Emile-Journault, tel: 872-6900. **Université de Montréal** (indoor), 2100 Blvd Edouard-Montpetit, tel: 343-6150. **John Abbott College** (indoor), 21275 Lakeshore Rd, St-Anne de Bellevue, tel: 457-6610, ext. 325. **Olympic Park** (indoor), 4141 Avenue du Pierre de Coubertin, tel: 252-4622. **Ile-Sainte-Hélène** (outdoor), tel: 872-6093. For more locations call: 872-1111.

TENNIS

Public tennis courts are available for hire in Somerled, Lafontaine, Jeanne-Mance and Kent parks. For information and more locations, tel: 872-1111.

Spectator

Check the Festivals section of this guide's Travel Tips and the events listing in the local newspapers.

AUTO RACING

The Grand Prix Molson du Canada is part of the world circuit of Formula One racing. The event is held in June at Gilles Villeneuve Track, Ile-Notre-Dame, tel: 350-4731.

BASEBALL

The Montreal Expos play at Olympic Park, 4141 Avenue Pierre de Coubertin, tel: 253-3434 for information, 790-1245 for tickets. From outside Montreal, tel: 1-800-361-4595; web: www.reseauadmission.com. Admission for adults is $7–28, for children $5–26.

FOOTBALL

The Alouettes play in the Olympic Park stadium from July to November. For more information, tel: 252-4141.

HARNESS RACING

The Hippodrome de Montréal Racetrack at 7440 Blvd Decarie hosts major trotting events. The Prix de l'Avenir and the Blue Bonnets Amble are two of the more important. Open Monday, Wednesday, Friday and Saturday at 7.30pm; Sunday from 1.30pm; closed Tuesday and Thursday. Admission for the clubhouse and the stands is $4. For more details, tel: 739-2741.

HOCKEY

The legendary Montreal Canadiens have moved from the old Forum to the new Molson Centre. For tours of the new arena, tel: 932-2582; for tickets, tel: 790-1245, web: www.reseauadmission. com.

SOCCER

The Montreal Impact Soccer Club formed in 1993. Games are held on Wednesday and Friday at the Claude Robillard Centre, 100 Rue Emile-Journault. The season runs from mid-May to early October. Admission is $8 for adults, $4 for children under 12. Season tickets are $107–205. For information, tel: 328-3668.

TENNIS

The Du Maurier Open at Jarry Park attracts the world's best players. Usually held in August. For tickets and information, tel: 273-1515.

Language

General

Even if you speak no French at all it is worth trying to master a few simple phrases. The fact that you have made an effort is likely to get you a better response. Pronunciation is key; they really will not understand if you get it very wrong. Remember to emphasise each syllable; not to pronounce the last consonant of a word as a rule (this includes the plural "s") and always to drop your "h"s. Whether to use "vous" or "tu" is a vexed question; increasingly the familiar form of "tu" is used by many people. However, it is better to be too formal, and use "vous" if in doubt. It is very important to be polite; always address people as Madame or Monsieur, and address them by their surnames until you are confident first names are acceptable.

Learning the pronunciation of the French alphabet is a good idea and, in particular, learn how to spell out your name in the French alphabet.

Montréal claims to be the second-largest French-speaking city in the world, after Paris. Some 65 percent of the city's residents and 70 percent of those in the metropolitan area are French-speakers (francophones), with 12 percent and 15 percent English-speakers (anglophones), respectively. Despite nationalistic insistence, the province's French has never been pure. After 300 years of separation from the motherland, how could it be? Québecois and French visitors struggle to find words in common. Over the past decades, as Montréalers acknowledge

differences and gain confidence, this is amusing rather than disconcerting.

Unique to Montreal is joual, a patois whose name is garbled French for horse: cheval. The earthy dialect flourishes among the city's working class and in the work of playwright Michel Tremblay.

Pronunciation of mainstream French also differs. Accents distinguish French in Québec from French in Paris or Marseilles. Québec's francophones form sounds deep in the throat, lisp slightly, voice toward diphthongs, and bend single vowels into exotic shapes. It has also incorporated some English words, such as "chum", as in mon chum, or ma chumme, and blonde, for girlfriend, while le fun is a good time.

Even if you don't speak much French, starting a conversation with 'Bonjour,' is likely to evoke a positive response. Indeed, some shopkeepers hedge, with an all-purpose: 'Hi-bonjour.'

French words and phrases

How much is it? *C'est combien?*
What is your name? *Comment vous appelez-vous?*
My name is... *Je m'appelle...*
Do you speak English? *Parlez-vous anglais?*
I am English/American *Je suis anglais/américain*
I don't understand *Je ne comprends pas*
Please speak more slowly? *Parlez plus lentement, s'il vous plaît?*
Can you help me? *Pouvez-vous m'aider?*
I'm looking for... *Je cherche*
Where is...? *Où est...?*
I'm sorry *Excusez-moi/Pardon*
I don't know *Je ne sais pas*
No problem *Pas de problème*
Have a good day! *Bonne journée!*
That's it *C'est ça*
Here it is *Voici*
There it is *Voilà*
Let's go *On y va. Allons-y*
See you tomorrow *A demain*
See you soon *A bientôt*
Show me the word in the book

Montrez-moi le mot dans le livre
At what time? *A quelle heure?*
When? *Quand?*
What time is it? *Quelle heure est-il?*
● *Note. The French generally use the 24-hour clock.*

yes	*oui*
no	*non*
please	*s'il vous plaît*
thank you	*merci*
(very much)	*(beaucoup)*
you're welcome	*de rien*
excuse me	*excusez-moi*
hello	*bonjour*
OK	*d'accord*
goodbye	*au revoir*
good evening	*bonsoir*
here	*ici*
there	*là*
today	*aujourd'hui*
yesterday	*hier*
tomorrow	*demain*
now	*maintenant*
later	*plus tard*
right away	*tout de suite*
this morning	*ce matin*
this afternoon	*cet après-midi*
this evening	*ce soir*

On Arrival

I want to get off at... *Je voudrais descendre à...*
Is there a bus to the Louvre? *Est-ce qui'il ya un bus pour le Louvre?*
What street is this? *A quelle rue sommes-nous?*
Which line do I take for...? *Quelle ligne dois-je prendre pour...?*
How far is...? *A quelle distance se trouve...?*
Validate your ticket *Compostez votre billet*

airport	*l'aéroport*
train station	*la gare*
bus station	*la gare routière*
Métro stop	*la station de Métro*
bus	*l'autobus, le car*
bus stop	*l'arrêt*
platform	*le quai*
ticket	*le billet*
return ticket	*aller-retour*
hitchhiking	*l'autostop*
toilets	*les toilettes*

This is the hotel address *C'est l'adresse de l'hôtel*
I'd like a (single/double) room... *Je*

voudrais une chambre (pour une/deux personnes) ...
...with shower *avec douche*
...with bath *avec salle de bain*
...with a view *avec vue*
Does that include breakfast? *Le prix comprend-il le petit déjeuner?*
May I see the room? *Je peux voir la chambre?*

washbasin	*le lavabo*
bed	*le lit*
key	*la clé*
elevator	*l'ascenseur*
air conditioned	*climatisé*

On the road

Where is the spare wheel? *Où est la roue de secours?*
Where is the nearest garage? *Où est le garage le plus proche?*
Our car has broken down *Notre voiture est en panne*
I want to have my car repaired *Je veux faire réparer ma voiture*
It's not your right of way *Vous n'avez pas la priorité*
I think I must have put diesel in the car by mistake *Je crois que*

On the telephone

How do I make an outside call?	*Comment est-ce que je peux téléphoner à l'exterieur?*
I want to make an international call	*Je voudrais une com-munication pour l'étranger*
local call	*une com-munication locale*
dialling code	*l'indicatif*
I'd like an alarm call for 8 tomorrow morning	*Je voudrais être réveillé a 8 heures demain matin*
Who's calling?	*C'est qui à l'appareil?*
Hold on, please	*Ne quittez pas s'il vous plaît*
The line is busy	*La ligne est occupée*
I must have dialled the wrong number	*J'ai dû faire un faux numéro*

j'ai mis le gazole dans la voiture par erreur

the road to...	*la route pour...*
left	*gauche*
right	*droite*
straight on	*tout droit*
far	*loin*
near	*près d'ici*
opposite	*en face*
beside	*à côté de*
car park	*le parking*
over there	*là-bas*
at the end	*au bout*
on foot	*à pied*
by car	*en voiture*
town map	*le plan*
road map	*la carte*
street	*la rue*
square	*la place*
give way	*céder le passage*
dead end	*impasse*
no parking	*stationnement interdit*
motorway	*l'autoroute*
toll	*le péage*
speed limit	*la limitation de vitesse*
petrol	*l'essence*
unleaded	*sans plomb*
diesel	*le gazole*
water/oil	*l'eau/l'huile*
puncture	*un pneu crevé*
bulb	*l'ampoule*
wipers	*les essuies-glace*

Shopping

Where is the nearest bank (post office)? *Où est la banque/Poste/PTT la plus proche?*
I'd like to buy *Je voudrais acheter*
How much is it? *C'est combien?*
Do you take credit cards? *Est-ce que vous acceptez les cartes de crédit?*
I'm just looking *Je regarde seulement*
Have you got? *Avez-vous...?*
I'll take it *Je le prends*
I'll take this one/that one *Je prends celui-ci/celui-là*
What size is it? *C'est de quelle taille?*
Anything else? *Avec ça?*

size (clothes)	*la taille*
size (shoes)	*la pointure*
cheap	*bon marché*
expensive	*cher*
enough	*assez*

too much	*trop*
a piece	*un morceau de*
each	*la pièce (eg ananas, 15F la pièce)*
bill	*la note*
chemist	*la pharmacie*
bakery	*la boulangerie*
bookshop	*la librairie*
library	*la bibliothèque*
department store	*le grand magasin*
delicatessen	*la charcuterie/ le traiteur*
fishmonger's	*la poissonerie*
grocery	*l'alimentation/ l'épicerie*
tobacconist	*tabac (also sells stamps and newspapers)*
markets	*le marché*
supermarket	*le supermarché*
junk shop	*la brocante*

Sightseeing

town	*la ville*
old town	*la vieille ville*
cathedral	*la cathédrale*
church	*l'église*
mansion	*l'hôtel*
hospital	*l'hôpital*
town hall	*l'hôtel de ville/ la mairie*
nave	*la nef*
stained glass	*le vitrail*
staircase	*l'escalier*
tower	*la tour*
walk	*le tour*
museum	*le musée*
art gallery	*la galerie*
exhibition	*l'exposition*
swimming pool	*la piscine*
to book	*réserver*
tourist information office	*l'office du tourisme*
free	*gratuit*
open	*ouvert*
closed	*fermé*
every day	*tous les jours*
all year	*toute l'année*
all day	*toute la journée*

Dining out

Note: *Garçon* is the word for waiter but never used directly; say *Monsieur* or *Madame* to attract their attention.

Table d'hôte (the "host's table") is one set menu served at a set price. **Prix fixe** is a fixed price menu. **A la carte** means dishes from the menu are charged separately.

breakfast	*le petit déjeuner*
lunch	*le déjeuner*
dinner	*le dîner*
meal	*le repas*
first course	*l'entrée/les hors d'oeuvre*
main course	*le plat principal*
made to order	*sur commande*
drink included	*boisson compris*
wine list	*la carte des vins*
the bill	*l'addition*
fork	*la fourchette*
knife	*le couteau*
spoon	*la cuillère*
plate	*l'assiette*
glass	*le verre*
napkin	*la serviette*
ashtray	*le cendrier*

BREAKFAST AND SNACKS

baguette	long thin loaf
pain	bread
petits pains	rolls
beurre	butter
poivre	pepper
sel	salt
sucre	sugar
confiture	jam
miel	honey
oeufs	eggs
...à la coque	boiled eggs
...au bacon	bacon and eggs
...au jambon	ham and eggs
...sur le plat	fried eggs
...brouillés	scrambled eggs
tartine	bread with butter
yaourt	yoghurt
crêpe	pancake
croque-monsieur	ham and cheese toasted sandwich
croque-madame	...with a fried egg on top
galette	type of pancake
pan bagna	bread roll stuffed with salade Niçoise

FIRST COURSE

An *amuse-bouche, amuse-gueule* or appetizer is something to "amuse the mouth", served before the first course

anchoiade	sauce of olive oil, anchovies and garlic, served with raw vegetables
assiette anglaise	cold meats
potage	soup
rillettes	rich fatty paste of shredded duck, rabbit or pork
tapenade	spread of olives and anchovies
pissaladière	Provençal pizza with onions, olives and anchovies

MAIN COURSE

La Viande	**Meat**
bleu	rare
à point	medium
bien cuit	well done
grillé	grilled
agneau	lamb
andouille/ andouillette	tripe sausage
bifteck	steak
boudin	sausage
boudin noir	black pudding
boudin blanc	white pudding (chicken or veal)
blanquette	stew of veal, lamb or chicken with creamy egg sauce
boeuf à la mode	beef in red wine with carrots, onions and mushroom
à la bordelaise	beef with red wine and shallots
à la Bourguignonne	cooked in red wine, onions and mushrooms
brochette	kebab
caille	quail
canard	duck
carbonnade	casserole of beef, beer and onions

Emergencies

Help!	*Au secours!*
Stop!	*Arrêtez!*
Call a doctor	*Appelez un médecin*
Call an ambulance	*Appelez une ambulance*
Call the police	*Appelez la police*
Call the fire brigade	*Appelez les pompiers*
Where is the nearest telephone	*Où est le téléphone le plus proche?*
Where is the nearest hospital?	*Où est l'hôpital le plus proche?*
I am sick	*Je suis malade*
I have lost my passport/ purse	*j'ai perdu mon passeport/ porte-monnaie*

carré d'agneau	rack of lamb
cassoulet	stew of beans, sausages, pork and duck, from southwest France
cervelle	brains (food)
chateaubriand	thick steak
choucroute	Alsace dish of sauerkraut, bacon and sausages
confit	duck or goose preserved in its own fat
contre-filet	cut of sirloin steak
coq au vin	chicken in red wine
côte d'agneau	lamb chop
daube	beef stew with red wine, onions and tomatoes
dinde	turkey
entrecôte	beef rib steak
escargot	snail
faisan	pheasant
farci	stuffed
faux-filet	sirloin
feuilleté	puff pastry
foie	liver
foie de veau	calf's liver
foie gras	goose or duck liver pâté

gardiane	rich beef stew with olives and garlic, from the Camargue
cuisses de grenouille	frog's legs
grillade	grilled meat
hachis	minced meat
jambon	ham
langue	tongue
lapin	rabbit
lardon	small pieces of bacon, often added to salads
magret de canard	breast of duck
médaillon	round piece of meat
moelle	beef bone marrow
navarin d'agneau	stew of lamb with onions, carrots and turnips
oie	goose
perdrix	partridge
petit-gris	small snail
pieds de cochon	pig's trotters
pintade	guinea fowl
pipérade	Basque dish of eggs, ham, peppers, onion
porc	pork
pot-au-feu	casserole of beef and vegetables
poulet	chicken
poussin	young chicken
rognons	kidneys
rôti	roast
sanglier	wild boar
saucisse	fresh sausage
saucisson	salami
veau	veal

Poissons	**Fish**
Amoricaine	made with white wine, tomatoes, butter and cognac
anchois	anchovies
anguille	eel
bar (or loup)	sea bass
barbue	brill
belon	Brittany oyster
bigorneau	sea snail
Bercy	sauce of fish stock, butter, white wine and shallots
bouillabaisse	fish soup, served with grated cheese, garlic croutons and rouille, a spicy sauce
brandade	salt cod purée
cabillaud	cod
calmars	squid
colin	hake
coquillage	shellfish
coquilles Saint-Jacques	scallops
crevette	shrimp
daurade	sea bream
flétan	halibut
fruits de mer	seafood
hareng	herring
homard	lobster
huître	oyster
langoustine	large prawn
limande	lemon sole
lotte	monkfish
morue	salt cod
moule	mussel
moules marinières	mussels in white wine and onions
oursin	sea urchin
raie	skate
saumon	salmon
thon	tuna
truite	trout

Légumes	**Vegetables**
ail	garlic
artichaut	artichoke
asperge	asparagus
aubergine	eggplant
avocat	avocado
bolets	boletus mushrooms
céleri	grated celery
rémoulade	with mayonnaise
champignon	mushroom
cèpes	boletus mushroom
chanterelle	wild mushroom
cornichon	gherkin
courgette	zucchini
chips	potato crisps
chou	cabbage
chou-fleur	cauliflower
concombre	cucumber
cru	raw
crudités	raw vegetables
épinard	spinach

frites	chips, French fries
gratin dauphinois	sliced potatoes baked with cream
haricot	dried bean
haricots verts	green beans
lentilles	lentils
maïs	corn
mange-tout	snow pea
mesclun	mixed leaf salad
navet	turnip
noix	nut, walnut
noisette	hazelnut
oignon	onion
panais	parsnip
persil	parsley
pignon	pine nut
poireau	leek
pois	pea
poivron	bell pepper
pomme de terre	potato
pommes frites	chips, French fries
primeurs	early fruit and vegetables
radis	radis
roquette	arugula, rocket
ratatouille	Provençal vegetable stew of aubergines, courgettes, tomatoes and peppers
riz	rice
salade Niçoise	egg, tuna, olives, onions and tomato salad
salade verte	green salad
truffe	truffle

Fruit	**Fruit**
ananas	pineapple
cerise	cherry
citron	lemon
citron vert	lime
figue	fig
fraise	strawberry
framboise	raspberry
groseille	redcurrant
mangue	mango
mirabelle	yellow plum
pamplemousse	grapefruit
pêche	peach
poire	pear
pomme	apple
raisin	grape
prune	plum

reine claude   greengage

Sauces   **Sauces**
aioli   garlic mayonnaise
bearnaise   sauce of egg,
                butter, wine and
                herbs
forestière   with mushrooms
                and bacon
hollandaise   egg, butter and
lemon sauce
lyonnaise   with onions
meunière   fried fish with
                butter, lemon
                and parsley
                sauce
meurette   red wine sauce
Mornay   sauce of cream,
                egg and cheese
Parmentier   served with
                potatoes
paysan   rustic style;
                ingredients
                depend on the
                region
pistou   Provençal sauce
                of basil, garlic
                and olive oil;
                vegetable soup
with the sauce.
provençale   sauce of
                tomatoes, garlic
                and olive oil.
papillotte   cooked in paper

Pudding   **Dessert**
Belle Hélène fruit with ice
                cream and
                chocolate sauce
clafoutis   baked pudding of
                batter and
                cherries
coulis   purée of fruit or
vegetables
gâteau   cake
Ile flottante whisked eggs
                whites in custard
sauce
crème anglaise custard
pêche melba   peaches with ice
                cream and
                raspberry sauce
tarte tatin   upside down tart
                of caramelised
                apples
crème caramel caramelised egg
                custard
crème Chantilly whipped cream
fromage   cheese

Drinks

drinks   *les boissons*
coffee   *café*
...with milk/cream
                au lait/crème
...decaffeinated *déca/décaféiné*
...black espresso *express/noir*
...American filtered coffee *filtre*
tea   *thé*
...herb infusion *tisane*
...camomile *verveine*
hot chocolate *chocolat chaud*
milk   *lait*
mineral water *eau minérale*
fizzy   *gazeux*
non-fizzy   *non-gazeux*
fizzy lemonade *limonade*
fresh lemon juice served with
sugar   *citron pressé*
fresh squeezed orange juice
                orange pressée
full (eg full cream milk) *entier*
fresh or cold *frais, fraîche*
beer   *bière*
...bottled *en bouteille*
...on tap   *à la pression*
pre-dinner drink *apéritif*
white wine *kir*
with cassis
(black-currant
liqueur)
kir **with** *kir royal*
champagne
with ice   *avec des glaçons*
neat/dry   *sec*
red   *rouge*
white   *blanc*
rose   *rosé*
dry   *brut*
sweet   *doux*
sparkling wine *crémant*
house wine *vin de maison*
local wine *vin de pays* **Where**
is this wine from? *De quelle région*
vient ce vin?
pitcher   *carafe/pichet*
...of water/wine *d'eau/de vin*
half litre *demi-carafe*
quarter litre *quart*
mixed   *panaché*
after dinner drink *digestif*
brandy from Armagnac region of
France   *Armagnac*
Normandy apple brandy
                calvados
cheers!   *santé!*
hangover   *gueule de bois*

Days of the week

Days of the week and months are not capitalised in French.

Monday   *lundi*
Tuesday   *mardi*
Wednesday   *mercredi*
Thursday   *jeudi*
Friday   *vendredi*
Saturday   *samedi*
Sunday   *dimanche*

spring   *le printemps*
summer   *l'été*
autumn   *l'automne*
winter   *l'hiver*

Numbers

0	*zéro*
1	*un, une*
2	*deux*
3	*trois*
4	*quatre*
5	*cinq*
6	*six*
7	*sept*
8	*huit*
9	*neuf*
10	*dix*
11	*onze*
12	*douze*
13	*treize*
14	*quatorze*
15	*quinze*
16	*seize*
17	*dix-sept*
18	*dix-huit*
19	*dix-neuf*
20	*vingt*
21	*vingt-et-un*
30	*trente*
40	*quarante*
50	*cinquante*
60	*soixante*
70	*soixante-dix*
80	*quatre-vingt*
90	*quatre-vingt-dix*
100	*cent*
1000	*mille*
1,000,000	*un million*

Note: The number 1 is often written like an upside down V, and the number 7 is crossed.

Further Reading

General

W.H. Atherton, *Montreal 1535–1914*
Miriam Chapin, *Quebec Now*
Marcel Chaput, *Why I Am a Separatist*
John Irwin Cooper, *Montreal: The Story of 300 Years*
Donald Creighton, *Canada – The Heroic Beginnings*
Aline Gubbay, *The Mountain and the River*
Hugh MacLennan, *The Two Solitudes*
Kenneth McNaught, *The Penguin History of Canada*
Brian Moore, *Black Robe* (novel)
Francis Parkman, *The Jesuits in North America*
Mordecai Richler, *Oh Canada, Oh Quebec*

Other Insight Guides

Other Insight Guides which highlight destinations in this region include *Insight Guide: Canada* and *Insight Guide: Vancouver*, which combine background essays, a comprehensive places section, detailed travel tips and lavish color photography.

Also available are Insight Pocket Guides which provide tailor-made itineraries devised by local hosts and including their personal recommendations on where to stay, eat out and stay up late. These are accompanied by a handy pull-out map.

Titles include *Insight Pocket Guide Montreal*, *Insight Pocket Guide Quebec* and Insight Pocket Guides to Toronto and British Columbia.

ART & PHOTO CREDITS

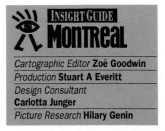

Cartographic Editor **Zoë Goodwin**
Production **Stuart A Everitt**
Design Consultant
Carlotta Junger
Picture Research **Hilary Genin**

Index

a

Abbaye St-Benoît-du-Lac 216
Abenaki tribe 225
Académie Querbes 189
Agouhanna 37
Algonquin tribe 36
American Revolution 51
Amerindians 129, 217
Amherst, Lord Jeffrey 50
apartment living 82
Aquarium de Montréal 205
architecture 71
  British legacy 25
  château-style 154
Avenue du Musée 155
Avenue Greene, Westmount 187
Avenue McGill College 161
Avenue Van Horne, Outremont 188

b

Bank of Commerce 140, 158
Bank of Montreal 138, 160
  founding of 161
Banque Royale Tower 160
Baxter Block 168
Beaver Club 54
beaver 37
Beebe Plain 217
beer garden 174
Bibliothèque Nationale du Québec 175
Bill 101 75, 98
Bill 178 99
Biodôme 202
birth rate 24, 25
Bloc Québécois 75
Boer War monument 157, 158
boîtes à chanson 135, 212
Botanical Gardens 202–204
Bouchard, Lucien 75
Boulevard St-Laurent 167, 168
  ethnic areas 71
Bourassa, Robert 33
Bourgeau, Victor 138, 158
Bourgeois, Marguerite 32, 133
  canonization 33, 41, 45
  founder of church 131
  origins of 44
British North America Act 65
British
  defeat of Montcalm 50
  ousting Americans 54

Brome County Historical Museum 214
Brother André 194, 195
Brother Marie-Victorin 202
building boom (1950s) 151
Burns, Robert (statue) 157

c

calèches 136
Callières, Hector de 42
Calvet, Pierre de 129
Canadian Pacific Railway 33
Canadian Railway Museum (St-Constant) 218
Canadiens (hockey team)
  cultural pride 112
  fans 26
  founding of 109
  legendary players 111
  reputation 110
  rivalry with Maple Leafs 112
Cartier (shop) 153
Cartier, Jacques
  arrival of 36
  origins of 36
Cassons, François Dollier de 42, 45
  views on fur trade 49
Catholicism
  first Mass 38
  influence of 44
  waning power 45, 76
Centaur Theater 145
Centre d'Histoire de Montréal 144
Centre Molson, Le 110
Chambly, Jacques 219
Champlain, Samuel de 32, 38, 142
Charest, Jean 75
Charter of Rights and Freedoms 98
Château Apartments 154
Château Champlain Hotel 158
Château Ramezay 42, 128, 129
Chateauguay, battle of 60
Chinatown 164–167
Chinese 28
  immigration 164
Chinese Catholic Church 166
cholera epidemics 62
Chrétien, Jean 75, 101
Christ Church Cathedral 161, 162
Christianity
  first baptism 40
  first religious order 41
  introduction 38
Church of St Andrew and St Paul 154, 155
church, influence of 76
Cinéma Parallèle 168

Cinémathèque Québécois 173
Cirque du Soleil 147
Cohen, Leonard 81
Collège Ste-Marie 165
Colonial House 71
Company of One Hundred Associates 39
Concordia Salus 61
confederation 96
costume parades 205
Côte St-Antoine 183
Côte-Ste-Catherine-Locks 219
Crystal Palace 33
cultural life 29

d

Dali, Salvador 154, 155
Dawson College 188
de Gaulle, Charles 128
de Ramezay, Claude 128
department stores
  Eatons 161
  Ogilvy's 155, 160
  Simpsons 160
Dickens, Charles 130
Dimakopoulos, Dimitri 173
Dollard, Adam 44
Dominion Square 157
Dominion Square Building 159
Dorchester Square 157
Drapeau, Jean 33, 74, 151, 199
driving habits 29
Ducharme, Réjean 29, 81
Duplessis, Maurice 72, 76
Durham, Lord 64
d'Youville, Maria 144

e

Eatons store 161
Ecole Nationale de Cirque 147
Ecurie d'Youville 144
Edward VII statue 162
Eglise du Gésu 165
Eglise St-Germain 190
Eglise St-Viateur 189
Equality Party 100
Erskine and American United Church 154
Estrie 209, 214
Expo '67 33, 133

f

Fenians 60
Ferguson, Maynard 179
Festival International de Nouvelle Danse 177

festivals 147,176
  range of 28
Fête des Neiges 126
Fête Nationale 176
filles du roi 45, 52
Fort-Chambly 219
Fort Lennox 220
Fortin, Marc-Aurèle 145
Fowke, Edith 57
francophone influence 26
Franklin, Benjamin 53, 128
French settlers 35
Front de Libération de Québec 33, 73
Fuller, Buckminster 133, 204
fur trade 37, 49

g

Gagnon, André-Philippe 147
Gazette du Commerce et Littéraire, La 53
gentry 157
Gilles Villeneuve Race Track 205
Golden Square Mile 153
Granche, Pierre 164
Great Fire 32, 64
Greeks 28
Griffintown 71
Gubbay, Aline 35

h

habitants 42, 49, 52, 56, 57
Habitat 133
Harbor Commission Building 133
Haskell Free Library 216
hockey *see* ice hockey
Holocaust Memorial Center 91
Hôpital des Soeurs Grises 144
Hosmer, Charles 156
Hôtel de Ville 127
House of Wing 166
Hudson 210
Huron tribe 36

i

ice hockey 107–113
  invention of 108
  quality of play 110
  rules codified 109
Ile Notre-Dame 204
Ile-Ste-Hélène 38, 204
immigrants 71, 168
Insectarium 204
International Film Festival 147
International Fireworks Festival
  147, 205

International Jazz Festival 147,
  176, 177, 179
International Mime Festival 176
Inuit carvings 154
Iroquois tribe 36, 40, 219
  peace treaty with 42
  raid on Lachine 42
Italians 27

j

Jacques Cartier Bridge 33
Jardin Botanique 202–204
jazz 147, 176–177, 179
Jesuits 44
Jews 27
  first synagogue 87
  Hassidim 89
  influence of 27
  Jewish areas 87
  Sephardic Jews 90
Just For Laughs 132, 147
Juste pour rire 132, 147

k & l

Keeley, Patrick 165
Krieghoff, Cornelius 49, 50
La Presse 142
La Ronde 205
Lac Brome 213
Lac des Sables 212
Lac Memphrémagog 215
Lac-des-Deux-Montagnes 210
Lachine (origins of name) 42
Lachine Canal 61
lacrosse 184
language 23, 26, 132
  and identity 99, 101
  Bill 101 effects 98
  disputes 75
  linguistics 132
  lurid signs 176
Laporte, Pierre, murder of 73
Laurendeau, André 77
Laval, Bishop 44
Le Devoir 142
Lévesque, René 25
  beliefs 101
  in government 97
  Parti Québécois 74

m

Macdonald John A. 65
Magog 215
Main, The 71, 167, 168
Maison des Coopérants 162
Maison du Calvet 129

Maison Hurtubise 185
Maison Papineau 129
Maisonneuve, Sieur de
  fight with Iroquois 41
  Mount Royal cross 186
  origins of 39
  statue 135–136
Man and His World exhibit 204
Mance, Jeanne 41
Maple Leaf flag 77
maple syrup 49
Marché Bonsecours 130, 131
Mary Queen of the World Cathedral
  158
Mauricie National Park 223
McDonald's restaurant 135
McGee, Thomas d'Arcy 60
McGill University
  first classes 32
  founding of 54
  view of 161
McGill, James 54
McLennan, Hugh 26
Meech Lake Accord 33, 74, 98
Mesplet, Fleury de 53
Métro 153
Moishe's Steakhouse 168
Molson brewery 55
Molson Grand Prix 205
Molson's Bank 140
Molson, John 55
Morgan, Henry 71
Mont Condor 212
Mont Orford 215
Mont Royal
  cross 33, 40, 186
  geology of 35
  park 186
Mont St-Hilaire 220
Mont Tremblant 213
Montagnais tribe 36
Montcalm, Marquis of 50
Montreal Contemporary Arts
  Museum 163
Montreal Gazette 142
Montreal Jazz Festival 147
Montreal Symphony Orchestra
  147, 163
Montreal
  city motto 61
  first hotel 55
  first theater 55
  geology of 35
  incorporation of 61
  origins 23
Monument National 167
Moroccans 28
Mulroney, Brian 98, 101
Museum of Fine Arts 154

n

National Theater School 167
Nelson's Monument 126
newspaper industry 141
nightlife 26
North-West Company 54
Notre-Dame Cathedral 42, 137
Notre-Dame-de-Bonsecours 41,
  131, 132
Notre-Dame-des-Neiges 186
Nouveau Palais de Justice 127
numismatic display 140

o

O'Donnell, James 138
Ogilvy's Department Store 155,
  160
Oka 210
Olier, Jean-Jacques 39
Olmstead, Frank Law 186
Olympic Games 33
Olympic Stadium 199–202
Ostell, John 138
Outremont 188–191
  cafés 191
  cinema 189
  City Hall 189
  origins 183
  population breakdown 26

p

Palais de Justice 127
Papineau, Louis Joseph 61, 129,
  175
Parc Joyce 190
Parc Mont-Royal 186
Parc Paul-Sauvé 210
Parc Pratt 190
Parchemin, Le 162
Paris, comparisons with 23
Parizeau, Jacques 75, 100, 101
parlor games 67
Parti Québécois 74–75, 97–100,
  101,
Patriotes, Les 61–64
Pei, I.M. 159
Peterson, Oscar 179
Philips Square 161
Pilote (dog) 40
Place d'Armes 127, 133, 141
Place des Arts 163
Place Desjardins 164
Place d'Youville 142
Place Jacques Cartier 125, 126
Place Montreal Trust 161
Place Royale 142, 143

Place Vauquelin 127
Place Victoria 140
Place Ville-Marie 159, 161
Pointe-à-Callière 142, 144
Pointe-du-Buisson Archaeological
  Park 217
political debate 95–101
population growth 71
Price, Bruce 158

q

Quebec Act (1774) 51
Quebec
  independence, call for 97
  political structure 24
Quiet Revolution 25, 45, 73, 76,
  77, 97

r

racial groups 23
railways, coming of 65
Ramezay family 49
Rasco's Hotel 130
reading habits 29
Récollet Order 38
Relations 39
Richelieu Rapids 219
Richelieu, Cardinal 39
Richler, Mordecai 81
  and Ritz-Carlton 156
  on ice hockey 108
Rigaud 210
Ritz-Carlton Hotel 153, 156
Ritz, Charles 156
Rochon, Gilbert 147
Rock Island 216
Roman Catholicism 42
Ronde, La 205
Rouge River 211
Royal Bank 140
Rue Bonsecours 129
Rue de la Commune 133
Rue de la Gauchetière 158,
  164–166
Rue McGill 144
Rue Notre-Dame 126
Rue Prince-Arthur 177, 178
Rue St-Denis 173
Rue St-Jacques 139–140
Rue St-Laurent 28, 167–168
Rue St-Paul 129, 134
Rue St-Pierre 134
Rue St-Vincent 134
Rue Ste-Catherine 160

s

St George's Anglican Church 159
St James United Church 163
St Joseph's Oratory 194–195
St Lawrence River 151
St Lawrence Seaway
  opening of 33
  route 219
St Patrick's Basilica 165
St Patrick's Day 27
St-Faustin 212, 213
St-Jean-sur-Richelieu 219, 220
Ste-Adèle 212
Ste-Agathe-des-Monts 212
Salle Wilfrid-Pelletier 163, 173
Santropol 168
Schwartz's Delicatessen 168
Scottish merchants 25, 51, 54,
  55, 183
seigneurs 42, 56
separatism 74
Seven Years' War 49
She Stoops to Conquer 55
Shopping 249–251
Shubert Baths 168
Simpsons department store 160
Sisters of Charity 144
skiing 213
slavery 51
slums 71
Sorel 221
Southam Building 165
Stanstead Plain 216
Stewart Museum at the Fort 205
Stowe, Harriet Beecher 42
style 28
Sulpicians Order 42, 139, 183,
  184
Summer Olympics (1976) 74
Sun Life Building 158
Sutton 214
Sutton Heritage Museum 215
Swinging in Paradise 179

t

Taillibert, Roger 199
theater 147
Théâtre du Rideau Vert 173
Théâtre La Butte 212
Théâtre St-Denis 173
Ticonderoga, battle of 50
Toronto Maple Leafs 109, 112
tour buses 137
Trafalgar Girls' School 155
Tremblay, Maurice 67, 190
Trudeau, Margaret 102, 103

Trudeau, Pierre 102, 103
  and October Crisis 74
  beliefs 101
  on French Canadians 97,101
  vision of Canada 98
  where he lives 81
Twain, Mark 42
typhus epidemic 64

U

Underground City 151–153
Union Nationale 76
Unity Building 165
Université de Québec à Montréal
  173, 176
Université Laval 175

V

Vélodrome 202
Vieux Beloeil 221
Vieux-Port 126, 131, 135
Vieux Séminaire 139, 140
Viger, Denis-Benjamin 175
Viger, Jacques 61
Village de Séraphin 212
Village du Bûcheron 223
Village Québécois d'Antan 222
Ville-Marie, founding of 32
Voltaire 50

w & y

Wells, John 139
Westmount 55, 183–188
  City Hall 185
  origins 183
  population breakdown 26
Westmount Lookout 187
Westmount Park 185
Wills, Frank 161
Windsor Hotel 158
Windsor Station 158, 159
Wolfe, (General) James 32, 50
women, role of 52
World Film Festival 176
world wars, impact of 72
Young, John 143

The Insight Approach

guide to bali

The book you are holding is part of the world's largest range of guidebooks. Its purpose is to help you have the most valuable travel experience possible, and we try to achieve this by providing not only information about countries, regions and cities but also genuine insight into their history, culture, institutions and people.

Since the first Insight Guide – to Bali – was published in 1970, the series has been dedicated to the proposition that, with insight into a country's people and culture, visitors can both enhance their own experience and be accepted more easily by their hosts. Now, in a world where ethnic hostilities and nationalist conflicts are all too common, such attempts to increase understanding between peoples are more important than ever.

Insight Guides:
Essentials for understanding

Because a nation's past holds the key to its present, each Insight Guide kicks off with lively history chapters. These are followed by magazine-style essays on culture and daily life. This essential background information gives readers the necessary context for using the main Places section, with its comprehensive run-down on things worth seeing and doing.

Finally, a listings section contains all the information you'll need on travel, hotels, restaurants and opening times.

As far as possible, we rely on local writers and specialists to ensure that information is authoritative. The pictures, for which Insight Guides have become so celebrated, are just as important. Our photojournalistic approach aims not only to illustrate a destination but also to communicate visually and directly to readers life as it is lived by the locals. The series has grown to almost 200 titles.

Compact Guides:
The "great little guides"

As invaluable as such background information is, it isn't always fun to carry an Insight Guide through a crowded souk or up a church tower. Could we, readers asked, distil the key reference material into a slim volume for on-the-spot use?

Our response was to design Compact Guides as an entirely new series, with original text carefully cross-referenced to detailed maps and more than 200 photographs. In essence, they're miniature encyclopedias, concise and comprehensive, displaying reliable and up-to-date information in an accessible way. There are almost 100 titles.

Pocket Guides:
A local host in book form

However wide-ranging the information in a book, human beings still value the personal touch. Our editors are often asked the same questions. Where do *you* go to eat? What do *you* think is the best beach? What would *you* recommend if I have only three days? We invited our local correspondents to act as "substitute hosts" by revealing their preferred walks and trips, listing the restaurants they go to and structuring a visit into a series of timed itineraries.

The result: our Pocket Guides, complete with full-size fold-out maps. These 100-plus titles help readers plan a trip precisely, particularly if their time is short.

Exploring with Insight:
A valuable travel experience

In conjunction with co-publishers all over the world, we print in up to 10 languages, from German to Chinese, from Danish to Russian. But our aim remains simple: to enhance your travel experience by combining our expertise in guidebook publishing with the on-the-spot knowledge of our correspondents.

The World of Insight Guides

400 books in three complementary series cover every major destination in every continent.